PUBLIC HISTORY AND
THE FOOD MOVEMENT

Public History and the Food Movement argues that today's broad interest in making food systems fairer, healthier, and more sustainable offers a compelling opportunity for the public history field.

Moon and Stanton show how linking heritage institutions' unique skills and resources with contemporary food issues can offer accessible points of entry for the public into broad questions about human and environmental resilience. They argue that this approach can also benefit institutions themselves, by offering potential new audiences, partners, and sources of support at a time when many are struggling to remain relevant and viable. Interviews with innovative practitioners in both the food and history fields offer additional insights.

Drawing on both scholarship and practice, *Public History and the Food Movement* presents a practical toolkit for engagement. Demonstrating how public historians can take on a vital contemporary issue while remaining true to the guiding principles of historical research and interpretation, the book challenges public historians to claim an expanded role in today's food politics. The fresh thinking will also be of interest to public historians looking to engage with other timely issues.

Michelle Moon is Director of Interpretation and Program Evaluation at the Newark Museum in Newark, New Jersey, USA. She is the author of *Interpreting Food at Museums and Historic Sites* (2015) and maintains an active practice in museums, food, and community resilience.

Cathy Stanton is a Senior Lecturer in Anthropology at Tufts University, USA. She is both a scholar and a practitioner of public history, with a particular focus on the uses of history and culture within both urban and rural redevelopment projects.

PUBLIC HISTORY AND THE FOOD MOVEMENT

Adding the Missing Ingredient

Michelle Moon and Cathy Stanton

Routledge
Taylor & Francis Group

NEW YORK AND LONDON

First published 2018
by Routledge
711 Third Avenue, New York, NY 10017

and by Routledge
2 Park Square, Milton Park, Abingdon, Oxon, OX14 4RN

Routledge is an imprint of the Taylor & Francis Group, an informa business

Library of Congress Cataloging-in-Publication Data
A catalog record for this book has been requested

ISBN: 978-1-62958-114-9 (hbk)
ISBN: 978-1-62958-115-6 (pbk)
ISBN: 978-1-31511-434-7 (ebk)

Typeset in Bembo
by codeMantra

CONTENTS

List of Boxes   *vii*
Acknowledgments   *viii*

Introduction: History as the Missing Ingredient   1

SECTION I
A Role for Public History   **17**

  1 Stories Without Endings: Food History's Roots and Legacies   19

  2 Slow Food, Fast Learning: Navigating the "Food Movement"   41

SECTION II
Research Foundations   **61**

  3 The Triple Top Line: A Different Way to Think About
      Food and Farm History   63

  4 A Primer on Policy   86

  5 A Primer on Primary Sources   100

SECTION III
Moving into Action   **121**

  6 A Fresh Approach to Food and Farm Interpretation   123

  7 Growing Relationships   147

  8 Leaping the Barriers   167

    Epilogue: How Do We Measure Success?   178

Appendix: "Triple Top Line" Timeline of U.S. Food
        and Farming History   *183*
Bibliography   *197*
Index   *203*

LIST OF BOXES

Our Pathways to Engaging with Food — 13

Work in Progress—An Interview with Darwin Kelsey: From
    "What" to "Why" — 34

Work in Progress—An Interview with Severine von Tscharner
    Fleming: Giving Ourselves Some Ballast — 55

Work in Progress—An Interview with Brian Donahue: Rethinking
    the Backstory — 79

Work in Progress—An Interview with Anne Effland: Policy Is about
    Social Choices — 94

Work in Progress—An Interview with Valerie Segrest: Food,
    History, and Healing — 113

Work in Progress—An Interview with Lisa Junkin Lopez: Valuing
    What Museums Do Best — 141

Work in Progress—An Interview with Niaz Dorry: The Slow Work
    of Building Trust — 159

Work in Progress—An Interview with Rolf Diamant: Keeping Food
    on the Institutional Agenda — 173

ACKNOWLEDGMENTS

As the twenty-first century matures, bringing with it hindsight on recent times, we recognize how fortunate we have been to witness revolutionary changes in the way we think about food—as citizens, as consumers, and as agents of change. This book is both a reflection of, and we hope a contribution to, that continuing transformation. The ideas we offer here have emerged from many conversations and collaborations over the past several years. Our thinking has benefited from the perspectives and responses of the scores of colleagues who participated in workshops and sessions we led at the American Association for State and Local History, National Council on Public History, and other conferences. We are also indebted to food professionals, from growers and migrant farmers to food processors, distributors, and activists, for the education they have provided us, directly and indirectly. Editorial guidance from Jennifer Collier and Jack Meinhardt at Left Coast Press as well as Dominic Shryane and Marc Stratton at Routledge and suggestions from peer reviewers have helped to make the book stronger. The interviewees whose ideas are included here have enriched our understandings of food history in ways that go far beyond the page.

Michelle would particularly like to acknowledge her colleagues at Strawbery Banke Museum in Portsmouth, NH, and Mystic, CT, both of which provided fertile test beds for the rich possibilities of a connected, contemporary food interpretation, and also her peers in the global Slow Food network, whose insistence that critical issues in food cannot be separated from one another brought an entirely new frame to her interpretation practice. Faculty and advisers in the Museum Studies program at the Harvard Extension School, particularly Kathy Jones, Laura Roberts, Mary Molloy, and thesis reader Linda Norris, challenged and improved her thinking on museums' role in society and interpretive planning for civically engaged practice. The supportive and collegial community at the American Association for State and Local History has also provided continuing inspiration for pushing interpretive ideals forward.

Cathy owes a particular debt of gratitude to those who were involved in the Ethnographic Landscape Study for the Martin Van Buren National Historic Site, which provided an invaluable platform and a fascinating research site for thinking through many of these issues. Closer to home, members of North Quabbin Energy and colleagues and students at Tufts University and the University of Massachusetts Amherst have been important interlocutors and collaborators. Those involved in the 2015 "Farm Values: Civic Agriculture at the Crossroads" project, particularly at Mount Grace Land Conservation Trust, have also helped immeasurably in figuring out how some of the ideas in this book might look in practice. It has been a true pleasure to have such engaged and committed partners over the years.

Michelle Moon and Cathy Stanton

INTRODUCTION

History as the Missing Ingredient

Practicing history helps to cultivate a long perspective. It can be a counterbalance to claims that things have never been this bad before, that a given situation is unprecedented, that the entire future is at stake—for a culture, a nation, humanity, or the planet itself—if some particular course of action is not taken immediately. Explorers of history tend to gain a sense of the human past and present as a long series of adaptations, course-corrections, unintended consequences, complex encounters and equally complex compromises, in which occasional outright disasters and dramatic shifts are the exception rather than the rule and in which predictions of doom have a cyclical history of their own. These are habits of mind that favor slowness, careful reflection, and a reluctance to jump onto bandwagons, qualities that can be extremely valuable in thinking through any pressing challenge.

We are true believers in those values, so we are aware of the irony of starting this book by talking about the unique urgency of the present moment. Our hope is that we can create a framework for bringing together these seemingly incompatible things—the long, slow perspective of history and the pressing need to act—and to show why food is an exceptional vehicle for bridging the gap between them.

First, the sense of urgency. In a nutshell, we are motivated by the rapidly changing climate and humans' role in accelerating those changes. We share the increasingly widespread sense that the window of opportunity for addressing some of the most obvious contributing causes—primarily our still-expanding fossil fuel dependency and related issues like greenhouse gas emissions and the vulnerabilities inherent in the extremely large-scale systems and supply chains enabled by petroleum—is already closing or perhaps has closed, leaving human societies with a set of challenges that will require adaptability and collective wisdom in the coming decades. There is beginning to be a good deal of discussion in the museum and public history fields about these issues, in some cases as part of the projects that will be mentioned in the chapters and interviews in this book.

But we believe that in general, these fields have not fully settled into a set of roles that can channel their distinctive and valuable contributions into the work being done to understand and respond to climate change and all that connects to it. To use the food metaphor that inspires our title, a nuanced sense of history has too often been the "missing ingredient" in the richly bubbling stew of climate change discussion and action.

This book works to show what that reconfigured role might look like. It offers tools for reshaping food interpretation, bringing it into dialogue with other contemporary efforts to rethink and reshape food systems—and, by extension, systems that provide other kinds of vital resources to our communities. This introductory chapter sets out a rationale for seeing this kind of work not as a distraction or an add-on to what museums and public history already do, but as squarely within the mandate to serve as a mode of public service and education in a democratic society. Before exploring those questions of mission and values, however, we need to clarify why we have chosen food—out of all the possible arenas where problems of resource use and community resilience are being tackled—as our starting point.

Why Start with Food?

When we think about the cluster of issues linked with climate change and the extraction of finite planetary resources—energy use, wealth disparities, environmental degradation, and more—it doesn't take long to become daunted and discouraged. There are dedicated people around the world working directly on those issues, but the majority of us are not full-time activists or policy-makers. Individuals who want to connect their everyday lives and work with these big projects need points of entry, where they can envision and create change without becoming instantly overwhelmed by the scope and complexity of the interlinked problems. For the authors of this book (see sidebars), as for many other people, food provides that entry point.

Food is accessible. It is immediate and familiar. It is universal, in the sense that all humans must eat to stay alive; yet at the same time, it's richly specific in its cultural, regional, and personal variations. With its intimate ties to sense of place, memory, and identity, it forges links between culture and biology, past and present, small and large scales, the personal and the political. These links are often deeply felt, helping to work against the distances and abstractions created by enormous systems and problems. Because food is tied so closely to our everyday choices and our very survival, people feel empowered to act on food issues. Those actions are often expressed on an individual level: a change in shopping or cooking habits, starting a home garden, seeking out more information about what's in our food and where it came from. But concern about food just as often manifests in unexpected convergences between the personal and the collective. Such flashpoints have a long history. Parisian women who marched on Versailles in 1789 in response to the high price of bread are part of the same lineage as those involved in the food protests around the Middle East that were a key component of the "Arab Spring" movement in 2011. And the public outcry that followed Upton Sinclair's 1906 exposé of the Chicago meatpacking industry in *The Jungle* prefigured later controversies over pesticide use and pollution from agricultural waste.[1]

Many factors have contributed to the popularity of locally produced food in the U.S. over the past decade: the search for novel culinary experiences, the marketing of both rural and urban places as destinations for travel and consumption, and a cyclical return of anti-modern sentiments, all of which also have their own long histories. But we believe that at bottom, the contemporary local food movement is driven by widespread and growing concern about how to live in ways that rely less on large-scale and fossil-fuel dependent systems. We see this not as a momentary trend, but as a sign of increasing public willingness to confront the costs and consequences of our modern industrial food system—and, by extension, our modern industrial society as a whole. The attempt to eat more locally is by no means a blanket solution to anything. But there *are* no blanket solutions to this cluster of problems; there are only points of engagement and—at best—a slow movement toward clearer shared understandings and more intentional collective actions. Sourcing more of our food at a local farmers market does not change the world, but it reflects an openness to grappling with some of the realities of making changes in both our individual lives and the larger systems that support us and can create meaningful local impact. Just as food provides many people with an accessible starting point for trying to live in less energy-dense, more just, and more locally oriented ways, we see the contemporary focus on food as an opportunity for the history field to connect directly with vital public processes and discussions in ways that are fully in keeping with the core purposes we seek to serve.

Arguing that food should take a more central role in historical presentation may seem strange to some who see it as already there. After all, don't most living history sites and villages have a hearth fire going somewhere, with a costumed interpreter browning corn cakes on a griddle? What about the oral history projects that explore the role of food and farming in ethnic and rural communities? Don't most house-museum installations feature a tea service, a dough trencher, or some other object representing the presence of food in daily life? It's true that food has long been a component of historic interpretation, particularly at living history sites, historic houses, and farm museums, where visitors expect to see a rich and full depiction of the activities of daily life in a setting representing the past. As we discuss in Chapter 1, food history interpretation has antecedents in the earliest historic preservation projects; over the ensuing decades, museums and historic sites have continued to develop depth and breadth in food topics. Today, many public history organizations present one or more common modes of food interpretation: cooking demonstrations, gardening or farming demonstrations, tastings, talks, or classes and workshops. Through years of cumulative research and practice, foodways interpreters in museum settings have developed forms of knowledge newly valuable to contemporary Americans.

But interpreting food *in* history is not quite the same thing as interpreting the history *of* food. History organizations, broadly speaking, have been slow to connect their carefully developed content knowledge to the current groundswell of interest in contemporary food politics, generally being content to tweak existing programs to highlight overlaps with the local food movement. Standard presentations of food in most museums and historic sites are still narrowly confined within an illustrative mode of period interpretation that we think of as the "butter churn" approach—"This is how people used to make butter— here, take a turn and try it yourself." Such demonstrations are engaging, often memorable, and certainly not irrelevant in terms of helping audiences gain a clearer awareness of food production labor or of the convenience and variety they experience within modern industrial food systems. But such narrow presentations stop short of offering a space for people to formulate larger questions about those systems. It's easy for a museumgoer to walk away from such demonstrations having only confirmed the nostalgic impressions circulating in media and pop culture, or having projected incomplete understandings onto a complicated past, instead of engaging in the reflective inquiry that good interpretation aims to present. In this simple, demonstrative approach, visitors may not perceive that the past included many of the same complex dimensions of food discussions we're familiar with in the present-day world—questions about economics and inequality, public health, quality and safety, supply chains and trade networks. The perennial complexity of food-related issues is too often squashed or omitted, creating a puzzling gap between an apparently simple past and a contemporary world of seemingly unprecedented difficulty.

Where food interpretation *is* connected to contemporary or political questions, it is often presented as a "hook" designed to redirect audience members' attention to interpretive messages deemed more significant and weighty.[2] There is a tendency to think of food as inherently lightweight—isn't that part of its friendly appeal and the reason it's useful in easing into more difficult topics? We are advocating a trickier balance: making use of that appeal but refusing to change the subject. We see food as a starting point, but not just to transition into more serious matters or "real" history. It is a starting point for unpacking the rich, complex, confusing, daunting, and ultimately empowering stories inherent in food itself. Food is not merely a topic along the way to interpreting more consequential questions; food itself *contains* those questions while offering an exceptionally accessible point of entry into them. We need to start with food and then *stay* there long enough to do that difficult work of unpacking its import.

This is work that requires the tools of the community organizer as well as the archival researcher and public educator. Expanding that toolkit is one of the biggest challenges for museums and history organizations that aim for a deeper interpretation of food topics. But the potential results are exciting and important, fitting squarely within contemporary ideas about expanded civic roles for museums and historic sites. Reframing food interpretation within broader questions and knotty problems at the personal, regional, and national levels, past and present, we can convene a conversation of variety and sophistication, helping to position historical institutions and projects as centers of learning and discourse on issues central to the lives of our audiences and communities.

Food, Mission, and Values

There are good reasons that people involved in interpreting history have been reluctant to enter the realm of contemporary debate too directly. In intensely politicized arenas like the discussion of climate change, historians—like scientists—are rightly leery of having their careful, provisional knowledge distorted by partisan maneuvering or oversimplified by audiences unfamiliar with the deeper debate. Institutional missions and contexts may not seem to support attention to climate-, environmental-, and social justice-related issues, while interpreters' and historians' specific skills and expertise may not always seem directly applicable either. Audiences may well prefer familiar and comforting food interpretation that emphasizes old-fashioned skills like hearth cooking and nostalgic agrarian landscapes rather than the often-grittier realities of day-to-day food production and everything to which it connects. Both interpreters and audiences may see food issues as a low priority, compared with interpreting other pressing histories of social justice, such as racism, violence, or access to education. And in a scenario where radical changes in climate prompt mass upheavals and disruptive weather events unprecedented in known human experience, is the record of the past even relevant at all?

But there are as many good reasons we should overcome our professional and institutional reluctance to act. We know that history is not a direct guide to the future, but it is a crucial tool for understanding how we arrived at the problems of the present—a key task as people grope toward some kind of shared analysis and attempt to address those problems. And despite the continued appeal of nostalgic and aesthetically pleasing food presentations and landscapes, people in our audiences and communities are increasingly aware of the ferment of policy and ethical questions surrounding food at present. They are reading the work of writers like Michael Pollan, watching food-related documentaries like "Supersize Me" and "Food, Inc.," and thinking about food safety and the implications of labeling (or not labeling) genetically engineered food or countries of origin. They are recognizing profound racial and economic inequalities in food distribution, food quality, and food labor and are working toward solutions. Members of the Millennial generation, in particular, care deeply about food. They opt for organic and ethically produced food more often, more regularly cook from fresh ingredients instead of using packaged foods, and favor small, independent providers when possible.[3] As the existing and impending effects of the changing climate loom larger, more people are connecting the dots among food, climate issues, and questions about sharing and using resources in general. There are fewer things that seem truly separate from this big cluster of questions and more and more reasons to become actively engaged in them as interpreters, educators, stewards, citizens, and members of our own communities.

Those who practice history in public, whether in museums, historical organizations, government agencies, or other settings are generally motivated by a sense that historical knowledge is an essential foundation for good critical thinking and civic decision-making. This motivation makes itself felt in the ongoing shift of museum and public history work toward civic engagement and participation around a wide range of issues. Yet many historical institutions and organizations are also struggling to stay afloat financially and to articulate a strong rationale for why this work should be supported in a crowded and competitive cultural marketplace and a time of shrinking budgets. Another answer to the question "Why start with food?" is that a new approach to food interpretation can help us to make that strong case for our own relevance.

Museums, and history museums in particular, openly acknowledge that over the past two decades they have found themselves facing a set of related and intensifying crises: of finances, of attendance, and most painfully, of relevance. Where the bicentennial fever of the 1970s made history museums hip, in more recent years a stagnation of strategies and lack of audience cultivation has threatened to render history museums a cultural sidelight. Outdoor museums seem appropriate perhaps for families with young children and school groups, while historic house museums have become the haunt of older heritage tourists. In both cases, the majority of museum participants are white, educated, and relatively affluent.[4] Museum leaders, analyzing the trajectory of demographic change, caution that continuing to serve only the audiences who have traditionally visited is a recipe for shrinking attendance and revenue, as those narrow segments of the population become proportionally smaller within the larger trajectory of demographic change, as well as a prescription for social irrelevance. At conferences and in boardrooms, museum professionals agonize over this public disaffection, searching for underlying reasons in factors ranging from the lower cost of travel to competition from online entertainment, implicit biases and unacknowledged cultural barriers, poor-quality history teaching, or a cutthroat funding environment that favors STEM (Science, Technology, Engineering, and Mathematics) and health-related charitable efforts above the humanities.

Some observers posit that the 20-year juggernaut of attendance decline reflects a cultural break in which younger generations are simply bored by the passive formats of the past, demanding instead high theatricality and the chance to be at the center of the action, personalizing events and influencing outcomes. But an equally powerful demand of contemporary audiences is a stronger sense of connection to a meaningful narrative larger than themselves—a moving and creative response to the distraction and alienation that comes with immersion in a 24/7 beeping, pinging, image-driven, and status-conscious digital and social environment. Food, which brings pleasure, facilitates family and cultural memory, connects people through exchange, and anchors celebrations, can provide one such grounding narrative. Rarely has that narrative been sufficiently highlighted in museums to capture the potential audience's attention, yet indicators are that a ready audience awaits.[5] People are already seeking links between food's past and its present. Museums willing to address themselves directly to these wide audiences, creating meaningful places to inhabit both massively scaled and intimate personal narratives, can reach new participants and draw them into closer, more sustaining relationships with institutions they find authentically valuable.

Food Interpretation as Work in Progress

This book is intended to address both "how to" and "why to" reshape food interpretation in dialogue with civic questions and processes. But food is extremely dynamic as both a topic for exploration and an arena of action. And that means that between the "why" and the "how" there is a good deal of territory whose outlines are only just beginning to come into focus. Between the time we submitted the proposal for this book and the time we finished writing, a lot of things in the "eat local" movement had changed, and they will change again by the time the book reaches your hands. This moving-target quality can be difficult for practitioners who are used to more stable kinds of content or outcomes. We know that our understandings of the past are continually in motion, but at least the materials we work with tend to stay still long enough for us to contemplate them in order to create some kind of settled interpretive product. The same is not necessarily true with the kind of food interpretation we are advocating here. This is both its great strength—it offers opportunities to engage directly with vital public and civic processes—and its biggest challenge, suggesting the need for a deep cultural shift in the way historic site interpretation tends to work. Embracing that challenge requires thinking about this work as a long, ongoing, uneven, sometimes unruly process that takes place on many levels—in our local communities and societies writ large, in our institutional and organizational settings, and also within ourselves.

At present, the network of public historians engaged in new forms of food and farming interpretation is improvisational, decentralized, and inquisitive, working in hybridized ways that draw on vocabularies well outside of museum-like institutions, iterating and redesigning with each new initiative. There are few fixed models here, and a good deal of experimentation and speculation, tacking back and forth between tried-and-true techniques and a sense of exploring in areas not yet fully defined. Many organizations, perhaps unsure whether interest in food is another passing fad, are stuck in a form of analysis paralysis, wanting to study the phenomenon from every angle before carving out a narrow spot in the interpretive program for a workshop here or an update to the daily program there. But a few institutions have adopted a bold experimental mode, embracing food communities with an admirable nimbleness and energy. In this book, we have tried to reflect their work, particularly in the interviews featured under the heading "Work in Progress." Those segments, as well as the author sidebars included in this chapter, give some sense of how this work looks and feels to practitioners in a variety of settings where the interpretation of food history intersects with public engagement around present-day food issues. Their pilot projects and experimental strategies may yet become the basis for solid long-range commitments to embed historical explorations of food issues in core offerings, rather than tacking on one-off projects in a concession to the zeitgeist.

The "process" quality of this mode of food interpretation extends into the language we use, and it is worth adding a note about terminology here. One thing that quickly becomes clear when we begin to explore the history of food is that even the most basic terms are freighted with particular perceptions, tastes, and associations, often conflicting, confusing, and shot through with differences and inequalities of many kinds. One person's "junk food" is another person's "affordable meal"; a "culturally appropriate" food for some may violate definitions of what is healthful or "sustainable" for others. Terminology around farming seems particularly unstable: what constitutes a "conventional" farm, an "industrial" one, a "family farm," an "organic" or "sustainable" one, or indeed a "farm" at all? Who is the "farmer" on a farm where most of the actual work of growing food is done by machines and migrant laborers?

In fact, the very words "farm" and "farmer" tend to stand in for a bevy of specialized food producers who don't all work with foods that grow directly out of the ground.[6] At times in this book, we will also use the same convenient shorthand, allowing "farm" and "farming" to take in the full range of providers that fill our plates, including orchardists, foragers, ranchers, sugarmakers, beekeepers, fishermen, aquaculturists, and others, and primary processors like vintners, cheesemakers, brewers, bakers, and butchers.[7] Official and certified definitions are often at odds with vernacular ones or with actual practices and methods (for example, many small farms choose to use organic methods but do not adopt organic certification because of the additional costs and work involved). "Localness," as discussed in Chapter 3, also proves surprisingly difficult to pin down, appearing more as an open question than a distinct characteristic. Nor do the boundaries stop at "food" itself. One of the ideas being shared around the food movement at present is that we need to think much more broadly about our food sources and the systems that support them, not only to encompass non-agricultural modes like fishing, permaculture, and foraging, but also to consider land and resource use more generally as integral parts of our food systems. Water is perhaps the most crucial element of this kind of expansive view of our resource base, one that is assuming greater and greater prominence in public thinking as aquifers shrink, rivers flood, fertile regions become arid and vice versa, and oceans rise in erratic ways all around the globe. Water issues obviously overlap with—but also go far beyond—food issues *per se*. Where, then, does "food" begin and end? Or does it?

The slipperiness of these terms makes itself felt throughout the chapters that follow. Anyone moving into a more engaged food interpretation will need to contend with that slipperiness to at least some extent. Our discussions throughout this book shift between talking about *farming* and talking about *food* writ large; sometimes it is simpler to do so than to stop and dig into the question (admittedly a historically important one) of why we tend to be so fixated on agriculture to the exclusion of other kinds of subsistence and sustenance. The good news is that this instability in language actually opens avenues for investigation and interpretation. (Why does one state define a family farm differently from how a neighboring state does? Where and when did the family farm become such an iconic and taken-for-granted feature of the agricultural landscape?) The better news is that we are not alone in wrestling with these old and new definitions. This is a core task for most people within the food movement, and our willingness to do so alongside them—with the historical insights that we can bring to the endeavor—can create immediate openings for conversation and engagement. The chapters that follow are intended both to expand the rationale for a more civically engaged food interpretation and to provide some tools for putting these ideas into practice.

Ways to Use this Book

The complexities of food mean that every reader of this book is likely to come to it with a unique set of goals, questions, and experiences. We have designed the book to be useful in a number of ways to public historians and museum interpretation teams as well as, potentially, to food producers and their supporters. We have tried to envision a complete toolkit for practitioners working on a truly engaged interpretation of food, and we realize that some readers will already be well on their way to building that toolkit.

We suggest strongly that you spend time with the Chapter 1 discussion about the importance of reflexive practice, as well as the core interpretive framework—what we're calling the "triple top line"—outlined in Chapter 3. Beyond that, different readers will find different paths through the book. Some may want to read it from beginning to end, but others may want to dip into particular sections and just skim others or note them for later. Some of the chapters may serve as "think pieces" for those who are still in the process of reflecting on the role that food interpretation plays at their institutions or their own relationship to food history and the present-day food movement. Specific segments of the book might be useful as readings to share as part of discussions in planning and training or as an introduction for allies and partners who are approaching food-related projects from quite different perspectives. Brief bibliographical essays at the end of chapters point to the key sources that have informed our arguments, as well as offering suggestions for further reading on key topics.

We've also included a timeline that weaves together the various histories we trace in the book—environmental and technological change, energy use, food interpretation, policy, food production and consumption themselves—as a framework for building the kind of triple top line narrative we're advocating. We hope readers will find ways to plug their own key events into this timeline and that it may help illuminate some of the moments of change—and the potential for asking new questions—within local and regional stories. All of these pieces fit together, but not every reader will need all of them or need them at present.

Our hope is that the book will offer a range of ideas and materials and that it may serve as a reference, an inspiration, and a challenge. The fact that there is no one-size-fits-all approach is part of our point: productive modes of engaged food interpretation will emerge from unique places and relationships. This book aims to support individual efforts to develop those unique practices.

The first of the three sections takes a step back from the actual materials of food history and makes a case for a more reflexive practice of interpreting food. As we have already noted, there is no shortage of food interpretation in the museum and public history world. What is in short supply is a willingness to take a really hard look at our own positions as public historians working within our social, political, economic, organizational, and cultural settings. The concept of reflexive practice has gained more currency as these fields have matured and developed a clearer sense of their own lineages. But it is still a difficult idea to put into practice, especially when approaching the line that separates educational, preservationist, and usually not-for-profit work from "real world" food systems and economies. In order to approach that line thoughtfully and effectively, practitioners need to be aware of where it is and where they stand in relation to it.

To that end, Section I explores two key contexts for food interpretation. The first, in Chapter 1, is a brief genealogy of food interpretation itself. We examine some of the different origin points and modes of presenting food as they emerged over the course of the nineteenth and twentieth centuries: the historic preservation movement, industrial exhibitions, domestic science, model farms, and food tourism. In Chapter 2, we shift to the contemporary landscape with an overview of the varied and dynamic "food movement"—a term that incorporates an enormous range of people and projects all the way from boutique gastronomy to radical social-justice advocacy. Taken together, the two chapters are designed to broaden interpreters' sense of themselves as inheritors of a particular set of conventions as well as potential participants in a lively and complex present-day field of action. "Work in Progress" interviews with Darwin Kelsey, a pioneer of the living history museum movement of the 1960s and 1970s, and Severine von Tscharner Fleming, advocate and organizer for today's young and beginning farmers, help to deepen a sense of how people in different locations in both the history realm and the food movement are continuing to build on the surprisingly long lineage of experimenting with food history for civic purposes.

Section II delves into some areas of content expertise that may be useful in reshaping food interpretation. Chapter 3, "The Triple Top Line: A Different Way to Think about Food and Farm History," argues that most of what we think we know about food history is not wrong, but it *is* distorted by a "winner's version" of how our present-day food systems came to be. Playing on the idea, current in social enterprise, of the "triple bottom line" that values the ecological and social impacts of business as well as financial ones, we suggest a more critical way to approach food histories. Our triple top line narrative begins with big questions about particular kinds of environmental relationships, economic imperatives, and energy sources, particularly, "What happens when a finite set of environmental resources meets an economic system based on endless growth and an energy source that seems to promise that growth?" Chapter 3 also foregrounds the issue of scale and discusses some of its complexities—where *are* the boundaries around "local," anyway?—and its importance in strengthening public conversations about rescaling our food systems. Chapter 4 offers a basic introduction to U.S. food and farm policy. Two "Work in Progress" interviews in this section—with Brian Donahue of Brandeis University and Anne Effland of the U.S. Department of Agriculture—draw on the deep expertise of historians who bridge the worlds of farming and policy-making, pointing to ways that interpreters can address this gap in their own work. Chapter 5 discusses the use of some specialized primary sources relating to food production and consumption. Much of Chapter 5 focuses on government data, reflecting the important role that government at all levels has gradually come to play in monitoring and regulating food in the U.S., but it also discusses sources at what seems to be the opposite end of the spectrum—everyday and often intimate materials like cookbooks and restaurant menus—and shows some of the ways that official and "vernacular" sources and projects have been intertwined over time. A "Work in Progress" interview with Native educator and nutritionist Valerie Segrest, coordinator of the Muckleshoot Food Sovereignty Project, discusses the use of living sources, community knowledge, and oral history to trace links among food, place, identity, and health and to build food sovereignty.

Section III presents practical methodologies for beginning this work. Chapter 6, "A Fresh Approach to Food and Farm Interpretation," considers the on-again, off-again relationship between cultural organizations and civic initiatives. The chapter makes a case that direct engagement in civic life is fully within the ethical parameters of our fields and the implicit and often explicit missions of our institutions. Focusing primarily on museum settings, this discussion explores core structural and strategic methods for refocusing food interpretation around contemporary dialogue and action. Chapter 7, "Growing Relationships," sets out questions and ideas about existing and potential partnerships, especially those that cross—or aspire to cross—lines of cultural, economic, and political difference. Returning to the notion of reflexivity, the chapter urges practitioners to build a sense of their own positions and privileges and to challenge the structures that have historically created distances and inequalities among potential collaborators. Chapter 8 examines some of the most common barriers that practitioners undertaking this kind of work encounter, including negotiating regulatory environments, retraining personnel, and finding new funding sources, offering suggestions for overcoming or dismantling the obstacles. "Work in Progress" interviews in this section present examples of savvy practitioners sidestepping roadblocks and envisioning new ways to integrate knowledge about the past with principled action in the present. Lisa Junkin Lopez discusses her work at the Jane Addams Hull-House Museum in Chicago, articulating a vision of museums as dialogic, living entities in service to their communities. Niaz Dorry, coordinating director of the Northwest

Atlantic Marine Alliance, speaks to the challenges of shifting the terms of the relationship between environmentalists and those who fish for a living so that new solidarities can emerge. Finally, Rolf Diamant, founding superintendent of Marsh-Billings-Rockefeller National Historical Park, offers advice for spanning the public-private divide and developing a shared ethos of resource stewardship and management.

A brief epilogue tackles the question of how we know we're succeeding when we undertake this kind of engaged work around food systems. Is it enough just to participate in civic discussions about the past, present, and future of food? Or should we look for more consequential outcomes of our participation? Although the former is a crucial step, we make an argument for the latter and suggest some ways of developing metrics for evaluating our impact.

Two final notes about terminology and geography. First, we have addressed this book primarily to an audience of professionals working in the areas of museum interpretation and public history, and as with *food* and *farming*, we have used *museum* and *public history* somewhat interchangeably throughout. But just as food and farming clearly overlap without being precisely the same, there are both wide areas of commonality and distinct differences between museum work and public history practice. For those who identify as public historians, history provides the connecting tissue within a highly variegated set of interlocking locations that may include archives, governmental and non-governmental agencies and institutions, historical consulting firms, history museums, and other public-facing projects. For those who think of themselves primarily as museum professionals, museums are the point of connection, with methods and theory that often span the museum field more generally, including art, natural history, and science museums. The distinction makes itself felt in different routes through training—museum studies versus public history programs, for example—and different professional organizations, conferences, and networks.

At the same time, all of these edges are productively blurry, and we see their borderlands as fruitful sites for working toward more engaged and critical interpretations of food. We have leaned toward the term "public history" in our title and in much of the discussion that follows, in large part because we hope that these ideas will resonate with practitioners across that wider range of locations. At some points in the chapters, we do focus more specifically on issues relating to museums—for example, in the Chapter 6 delineation of what a robust interpretive planning process for food history might look like. But in general we have tried not to be bogged down in defining the niceties of the distinctions between museum work and public history work. It has felt more useful to speak to what we see as the broader shared interests of this entire cluster of fields in contributing to civic knowledge and deliberation about food and all that connects to it.

Second, we want to acknowledge the somewhat regional character of many of the examples in the chapters and interviews that follow. Both of us are based in the northeastern U.S., and it shows. We do see the American northeast as a particularly vibrant node within the food movement at present, in part because large-scale food production has never become as entrenched here as elsewhere in the country and so the opportunities for rescaling are perhaps more immediate. But we are not merely being chauvinistic about our own region. Though we're aware that there is important work being done all around the country and beyond, it was not our aim in this book to survey or represent all of it. Rather, we hope to reinforce a sense of what an *emplaced* approach to a new food interpretation looks like, because we believe this kind of work must be undertaken in specific places and through active relationship with other people in those places. If we are going to reshape the large systems that put so much distance between us and our food sources, turning food and people alike into commodities and abstractions, we need to locate our efforts firmly within the actual places we already occupy.

So we have not tried to counterbalance the northeastern focus of much of our discussion in the book, but have let it stand as a reflection of the questions about scale that we see as inherent in this approach to food interpretation. Even where local food industries arose in connection with the expansion of large-scale food distribution networks, history museums can explore the ramifications of these massive changes on the local and regional realms. And even where the core interpretive stories and audiences may in fact be national ones, our institutions and communities are still "in place," in ways that can and should shape not just the stories we tell but the relationships we build as we do this work. We look forward to seeing strong regional food interpretation developing alongside strong regional food cultures and systems in the decades to come.

OUR PATHWAYS TO ENGAGING WITH FOOD

Michelle Moon

My family history includes grandmothers who cooked with love, creativity, and respect for food; a grandfather who raised figs, peaches, peppers and okra, fished and crabbed in the Gulf of Mexico, and foraged wild berries; a mother who made sure I was at home in the kitchen; a father who bakes a mean Texas pecan pie; and a brother who is a heck of a baker. I worked my way through college and the early years of my museum career as a restaurant server, hanging around the pass-through to learn all I could from chefs, prep cooks, food vendors, and experienced servers.

But the catalyst for me to become more deeply involved in food issues came through museum work. While serving as Director of Education at Strawbery Banke Museum in Portsmouth, NH, in 2006, I coordinated the revival of a long-defunct hearth-cooking program, creating fresh links to culinary and

(Continued)

garden interpretation across the site. Though focused on the past, this newly unified food history program sang in harmony with a region then developing a sense of itself as a hub of neo-agrarianism. A 30-year-old farmers market was booming with renewed energy, a locavore networking group coalesced, and restaurateurs started advertising locally produced menu items. It dawned on our staff that this familiar old vehicle, the outdoor history museum, had a lot to offer a cutting-edge food scene: historical perspectives, connections with the region's past, heirloom plant varieties harbored for decades, and traditional know-how about eating seasonally and stewarding resources. Together with staff and community members, I co-founded a Slow Food chapter that hosted regular events at the museum. While I valued the food learning and policy progress that the movement brought, I was most awed to witness its singular power to unite individuals to tackle difficult issues.

Food fit into a personal mission that underlies all of my public history work: building community resilience. An idea initially borrowed from the field of ecology, "community resilience" refers to the ability of a given community to withstand the shocks of disruption, to restabilize and thrive. In our lifetimes, we have already endured many such shocks and can expect many more: violent attacks, climate disasters, megastorms, flooding, droughts, supply chain disruptions, food safety crises, disease epidemics, shortages. The qualities that enable communities to rebound and regroup—often termed "resilience factors"—come mainly from bonds between people. A rich web of relationships, strong mutual trust, a diversity of skills—these are the things we, as a society, need in order to contend with the forces of change. Food, with its universality, broad appeal, and connection to story and memory, is one of the most effective ways to bring disparate people together, forging the ties that transform us from millions of isolated points into a connected, resilient social fabric.

Cathy Stanton

I arrived at food interpretation as a platform for engagement and action via war, oil, and cars, in that order. Like many other people, I was deeply troubled by the rush to war in Iraq after the September 11, 2001, attacks, and I felt the need to stand up in some way against the questionable rationales that were being offered for military action. I joined a peace vigil that met in a local park for seven years and stood in silence for an hour a couple of Saturdays every month, which gave me lots of time and opportunity for thinking about root causes and larger connections relating to the Iraq war.

The politics of petroleum, of course, were hard to ignore. Several of us from the vigil formed another group to educate ourselves and others in our community about issues relating to energy use, a project that has formed the nucleus of several energy committees and projects in our area. As a scholar casting around for my next project—I had finished my PhD shortly after joining the vigil—I settled on cars and heritage, curious about how the rise of the automobile had helped to erase the physical and social patterns of the past while paradoxically giving people access to it via car-oriented heritage tourism. But two things intervened: first, the necessity to make a living, which involved a number of jobs and a good deal of commuting, and second, what felt like the utter intractability of car culture. I could (and did) buy a car that ran on vegetable oil, I could (and did) try to drive fewer miles every year. But I couldn't make as much change as I wanted to in my car habits, and it was easy to feel overwhelmed by the immensity of the set of problems around transportation and oil-dependency.

And so I got to food. I was already a scholar of historic sites and historical memory, and I'd done some work exploring the ways in which nostalgic agrarian impulses intersect with both historic sites and contemporary place-making and place-marketing efforts. Connecting that work with deeper concerns about economic and environmental viability has felt like a way to bring together my intellectual and political concerns and to link them with an arena where I can continue to make more consequential—and rewarding—changes in my own habits of living.

Notes

1 Many observers saw the Middle Eastern uprisings of 2010 and 2011 as directly related to the effects of a globally changing climate and its effects on water and food supply in this arid region. A 2013 report from the Center for American Progress, the Center for Climate and Security and the Stimson Center noted, "The Arab Spring would likely have come one way or another, but the context in which it did is not inconsequential. Global warming may not have caused the Arab Spring, but it may have made it come earlier" (Ines Perez and ClimateWire, "Climate Change and Rising Food Prices Heightened Arab Spring," *Scientific American*, March 4, 2013, accessed online).

2 Articles in a 2012 food-themed issue of *The Public Historian* journal reflect this approach; Adam Steinberg's discussion of food interpretation at New York's Lower East Side Tenement Museum is tellingly titled "What We Talk about When We Talk about Food: Using Food to Teach History at the [Lower East Side] Tenement Museum," while Andrew Haley's illuminating exploration of the emergence of "taste" in American culture similarly treats food and history as somehow distinct. "Food is familiar," Haley notes, "and history often is not" (Adam Steinberg, "What We Talk about When We Talk about Food: Using Food to Teach History at the Tenement Museum," *The Public Historian* 34:2 (May 2012), 79–89; Andrew F. Haley, "The Nation Before Taste: The Challenges of American Culinary History," *The Public Historian* 34:2 (May 2012), 53–78).

3 The strong orientation of Millennials toward food and their high level of awareness regarding food issues have fascinated pollsters and marketing analysts. As early as 2012, a joint study found that Millennials were much less likely to favor the "one-stop" convenience traditional grocery stores and more likely to seek out "farm-to-fork," fresh, local, natural, and organic options (Scott Mushkin *et al.*, "Trouble in Aisle 5," Jeffries and Co., Inc., 2012. *AlixPartners.com*, June 27, 2012). Eve Turow tackled the topic in depth in her e-book *A Taste of Generation Yum: How the Millennial*

Generation's Love for Organic Fare, Celebrity Chefs, and Microbrews Will Make or Break the Future of Food (Eve Turow, 2015. *EveTurowPaul.com*).

4 These and other trends in museum participation are discussed at length in a report generated by the American Alliance of Museums' Center for the Future of Museums. See Betty Farrell and Maria Medvedeva, "Demographic Transformation and the Future of Museums," Washington, DC: American Alliance of Museums Press, 2010.

5 A Reach Advisers survey found that "just over half of regular museumgoers have an explicit interest in food" and "would love for museums to engage them via food." Susie Wilkenning, "Do Museums Need to Care About Foodies?" *Center for the Future of Museums* blog, Washington, DC: American Alliance of Museums, September 22, 2011.

6 The more encompassing term "producers" is favored in the Slow Food movement, while "co-producers" is the equally expansive term for allies, supporters, and others whose role may go well beyond the purely economic relationship suggested by the word "consumers."

7 In many circles, the gender-neutral "fishers" is used in place of "fishermen." In using the more traditional term here, we are following the practice and preference of most female fishermen of our acquaintance in New England.

SECTION I
A Role for Public History

1

STORIES WITHOUT ENDINGS

Food History's Roots and Legacies

If it's true that public history representations of food production and consumption have been too simple and too narrow, how did that come to be? Food and farming, of course, aren't new topics for public history. They've been embedded in museum presentations since Mount Vernon opened its orchards and outbuildings to patriotic pilgrims in 1858 and in cultural documentation efforts at least since 1935, when the Works Progress Administration sent dozens of writers around the U.S. to document food traditions for a project called *America Eats.* But closer examination of the history of the public interpretation of food reveals that while food topics have often been *presented* in public educational settings, they have rarely been *problematized.* Food has usually featured in interpretive and historical projects without having been subject to the critical inquiry and planning that strengthen historical investigations and give import to interpretive messages. Past food systems are experienced as closed questions, stories whose beginnings, middles, and ends are all packed away neatly in the long ago.

Before articulating a new vision for food and farming interpretations, it's essential to ask a series of reflective questions. Who has led the invention of public presentations of food, especially as historically themed experiences? What messages did they aim to promote? What ideas did they overlook? How did changing understandings of food and society affect those presentations, and how did those presentations affect the way audiences thought about food and society? Digging into these questions about our own professional past can help today's practitioners gain a clearer sense of how we are also actors within the histories we present, rather than interpreting the past from a more removed position. Reflexivity, or an ability to see ourselves as part of the world we are presenting, is an essential tool for situating food interpretation so that it is in closer dialogue with contemporary questions about food.

The Roots of Food Interpretation

Over the past two centuries, the nation revolutionized its food production—and also its methods of commemorating and communicating about the past. Museum and public history practice developed, expanded, professionalized, and adopted an ever-wider range of sources and methodologies. Attitudes and ideas about the food system intersected at key points with evolving ideologies of historical interpretation, influencing the food experiences offered to public history audiences and constraining the messages and ideas about food made available to them. The way the public encountered and considered food's history—as well as its present and future—has been mediated through interpretive experiences structured to achieve goals both stated and unstated, goals often linked to larger social and political ideologies and preferred outcomes.

We've identified four key strands of activity that have informed today's vocabulary of methods for presenting the public history of food. Unfolding over the course of the nineteenth and early twentieth centuries, these strands are rooted in intellectual movements, many of them linked to governmental, industrial, social, and political efforts to implement practical improvements in social and material life. These efforts were often-ambivalent reactions to larger processes set in motion by industrialization: the expanding influence of applied scientific research, the transition from an agrarian to a manufacturing economy, urbanization, changing demographics, gender and family roles, and sweeping changes in landscapes and built environments.

Until recently, these strands of activity were seen as unconnected, understood as roughly contemporaneous but independent genres of public educational experience. Their combined influence and relationships to one another, to the over-arching story of industrialization, and to their influence on the presentation of food and farming history have gone almost unnoticed. But they are the roots that yielded present-day assumptions about appropriate topics and methodologies for food and farming in public history.

The four key strands, discussed in detail in the following sections, are as follows:

1. The Historic Preservation Movement
2. Industrial Exhibitions
3. Domestic Science and the Home Economics Movement
4. Farm Displays, Model Farms, and Farm Vacations

The Historic Preservation Movement

Today's historic houses trace their origins to the pre-Civil War eastern U.S., where preservation associations formed to set aside places related to famous figures from the nation's founding era. Largely native-born, affluent, educated, white, and female, the preservationists who led these groups belonged to the social elite. Influenced by the ideology of female domesticity, they saw themselves as nurturing, morally instructive guardians extending their responsibilities to the civic sphere, where they asserted a role cultivating public virtue. In response to their concerns about an industrial-era decline in the American character, they recast Revolutionary-era political and military leaders as godlike heroes, worshipfully idealized, and used the objects and architecture associated with those figures to promote patriotic virtues of loyalty, respect for leaders, and strength of character.

Working through formalized, independent associations—groups like the Daughters of the American Revolution, the Mount Vernon Ladies' Association, and the Colonial Dames—preservationists networked with one another through speaking engagements and the dissemination of reports and meeting proceedings. Collectively, they established a model that was copied by hundreds of historic houses by the early twentieth century. The precedents they set for the selection of interpretive messages can still be discerned today. Positioning the nation's founders as near deities, they created a quasi-religious rhetoric in which houses became "shrines" to which visitors made "pilgrimages" to study "relics" and become infused with the "spirit" of patriotism.

High-minded and empyrean, this interpretive canon sidestepped the earthy details of daily life, including food production and consumption. Preservationists emphasized persons, not provisions; status, not supper. Growing and cooking food were of relatively little personal interest to the elite founders, who were generally not in the habit of cooking for themselves or their families. For them, kitchens and gardens were backstairs zones proper to slaves, professional cooks, hired girls, and servants, and food served primarily to emphasize high social status. The utilitarian finishes of food preparation spaces, with their scarred brick floors and smoke-tinted walls, seemed to them of little architectural or decorative interest. Since the male historical figures who starred in interpretive narratives rarely entered their own kitchens, stories about the food labor on which they depended could do little to help deify them, and the workaday atmosphere did not promote surges of patriotic feeling.

The early interpretation of the Mary Washington House, in Fredericksburg, Virginia, provides a characteristic illustration. George Washington purchased the house for his mother, Mary Ball Washington, in 1772. She lived there until her death in 1789, and the house passed through private hands for a century. In 1890, reports that its then-owner was making arrangements to have it disassembled and sent to Chicago to be shown at the 1893 World's Columbian Exhibition spurred 13 women from the Society for the Preservation of Virginia Antiquities to set a preservation plan in motion. They raised money to purchase and restore the house, dedicating it as "a Museum of articles pertaining to the early history of our State."[1] The interpretation turned away from the character of Mary Washington, by many accounts a woman who valued simplicity and enjoyed working with her hands, cooking, and raising herbs, vegetables, and flowers in her kitchen garden. A visitor to a fundraising tea in 1899 remarked, "the old garden is there, but little is left of Mary Washington's careful tending except the high box hedges, which must have been there when she welcomed Lafayette, in her large hat and gardening outfit."[2] The romantic image focuses on the reflected aura of Lafayette, not Mary Washington's herbs. Not until 1967, when the Garden Club of Virginia undertook a restoration of the kitchen garden, would attention turn toward food production spaces as important to the interpretation of Mary Washington. Reflecting a recent interest in updating interpretations in ways that value and elevate domestic and "backstairs" histories, a turn we see as significant, today's marketing for the house highlights the garden and touts the kitchen as a "rare surviving eighteenth-century outbuilding"[3] (Figure 1.1).

FIGURE 1.1 The Mary Washington House, shown here in the late 1920s. Early interpretation at this site foregrounded "real" political and military history and glossed over Mary Washington's cooking, gardening, and other domestic activities. Image: Library of Congress.

Industrial Exhibitions

Over the course of the nineteenth century, the accelerating pace of industrial expansion was punctuated by massive, compelling, and popular industrial exhibitions. Arising by the late eighteenth century, industrial exhibitions (also called "world's fairs" or "expositions") peaked in the U.S. with the Philadelphia Centennial International Exhibition of 1876 (attended by more than 10 million people), the Chicago World's Columbian Exposition of 1893 (with 27 million attendees), and the 1904 Louisiana Purchase Exposition in St. Louis (drawing more than 19 million). Funded and aggressively promoted by coalitions of business leaders and state and federal government bodies in public-private partnerships, these enormous cultural productions served as platforms for governments and corporations to showcase national and state achievements, demonstrate technological innovations and scientific advances, and promote new technologies and branded consumer products. For audiences, the fairs were near-overwhelming experiences of sensory immersion, demanding marathon stamina but stimulating excitement and fueling the national mass-media discourse on culture and modernity.

As vital and expanding industries, food and farming figured prominently. In machinery pavilions and agricultural halls, larger-than-life spectacles highlighted the latest patented improvements in mowers, reapers and threshers, mills and grain cleaners. The Philadelphia Centennial's Gloucester Fisheries exhibit featured a 23-foot water tank in which miniature fishing vessels "of the old and new times are afloat, illustrating different branches of the fisheries."[4] In the Kansas and Colorado building, a replica of the Liberty Bell made of corn cobs (with a gourd clapper) hung above a display of more than a thousand jars of wheat, rye, corn, barley, oats, buckwheat, and other grains, testifying to an agricultural Elysium that yielded unheard-of harvests of up to a hundred bushels per acre.[5] Consumer-focused halls introduced new products to thousands of potential customers daily. Food manufacturers outfitted lavishly decorated booths in which barkers hawked baking powders, pickles, condiments, and novelty foods. Dynamic spiels drew fairgoers into the theater of product demonstrations, taste tests, contests, and cooking shows; Pabst Brewing won its famous blue ribbon at the 1893 Chicago world's fair. Dining halls served culturally inspired menus: at the Chicago fair, guests could enjoy supper at a replica of "a tavern in Southern Sweden," or a "New England Clam Bake" steamed up on the shores of Lake Michigan.[6]

The fairs were also a venue for quasi-scholarly anthropological displays of human beings. Intended to comprise a living catalog of the peoples of the world, naturalistic "villages" were peopled with cultural performers, displaying highly staged representations of daily life that amplified the culture (and cooking) of Laplanders, Tunisians, Tahitians, Austrians, and others into exoticized versions of themselves. Significantly, for the history museums to come, the American past, too, was on display. In industrial exhibitions and fundraising events beginning with the Sanitary Fairs of the Civil War era, volunteer women organized nostalgic evocations of New England Kitchens, Knickerbocker Kitchens, Pioneer Kitchens, and Old Dutch Kitchens, outfitting them with collections of rustic antiques and preparing menus of food associated with earlier times over open hearths. Drawing on a growing nostalgia for "old-time" scenes and skills (also manifesting itself in European experiments with folk and open-air museums of rural life by the 1890s), they and other "kitchen" and "village" cooks interpreted food history to the public decades before museum "living history" techniques were imagined (Figure 1.2).

By the early twentieth century, millions of Americans had seen agricultural displays and demonstrations, tasted and tried new products, and sampled

BROOKLYN SANITARY FAIR, 1864.
NEW ENGLAND KITCHEN

FIGURE 1.2 The New England Kitchen at the Brooklyn Sanitary Fair of 1864. To raise funds to aid Union soldiers during the Civil War, volunteer women organized large-scale fairs. These events often included nostalgic kitchens like this one, intended to recall New England's colonial era. The women organized the environment to present an idealized past, including period costume, themed menus available for purchase, furnishings like the spinning wheel and open hearth with steaming kettle, and entertainment.

Source: Library of Congress.

culturally specific food at fairs large and small. Great exhibitions taught audiences that food and cooking could be entertainment, that culture and the past were subjects for a participatory form of theater, and that industrial developments in agriculture, food processing, and eating were deserving of uncritical celebration.

Domestic Science and the Home Economics Movement

Science and industry were having their impact in homes, as well. In the latter half of the nineteenth century, a generation of women who were among the first to receive formal scientific training joined with civic reformers to transform home cooks' understanding of food and nutrition, creating new standards for purchasing, cooking, and eating food. Taking up where previous promoters of "domestic economy" (like home-management guru Catharine Beecher) left off, they sought to overhaul the home kitchen with new dictates on scientific management, insisting that modern understandings of food would combat disease, poverty, and even alcoholism while elevating women's housework to a status equal to men's professions. At the same time, rural reformers were promoting the womanly domestic arts as a way to strengthen rural communities and stem the tide of young people leaving farms for the cities.

Never before had so many women had access to the tools of science. With the Morrill Act of 1862, proceeds from the sale of federal lands were given to the states for the creation of universities that would teach "agriculture and mechanical arts… to promote the liberal and practical education of the industrial classes in the several pursuits and professions in life."[7] Because a modern and efficient farm required scientific home management as well as agricultural training, land-grant colleges gradually came to offer higher education to women, channeling them into domestic science and home economics programs. Female pioneers in science found that by focusing their studies on domains traditionally assigned to women—family health, nutrition, cooking, and the stewardship of household resources—they could advance to prominent positions in the academy and reach women across the country, in all walks of life.

Their ideas had profound influence. Domestic scientists affiliated with urban reformers, attempting to inventory and improve the foodways of poor and immigrant families. Their dictates, presented with hubristic confidence, were often built as much on their own cultural biases as on scientific evidence. Dietary reformers encouraged a regimen of bland, starchy foods and meats, with a few select vegetables boiled to limpness. Seasonings like garlic, pepper, and vinegar were thought to sap strength. Domestic scientists advocated sanitation and measurement, regularity and consistency. Breaking down meals into their nutritional components and scheduling their intake as if they were pharmaceuticals—initiating an American tendency Michael Pollan has termed "nutritionism"—they encouraged people to view whole foods as quantifiable agglomerations of vitamins, starches, fats, and proteins.

Middle-class women in the first half of the twentieth century were inculcated in domestic science through home economics classes in schools, colleges, community associations, churches, and charitable kitchens. In urban neighborhoods, educated American-born settlement house workers strove to pass along the skills and values of domesticity to immigrant women and children. Meanwhile, in rural communities, farmers' organizations like the Grange offered lectures and trainings that complemented the work of the land-grant schools and other state-sponsored educational projects. Cumulatively, this had the effect of removing women's training in food preparation from the formerly dominant familial context in which culturally informed knowledge and technique passed from one generation to another; professional educators asserted control over kitchen knowledge, delivering structured assignments in tandem with an ideology of modern women as scientific managers of the home who bore primary responsibility for the well-being and health of current and future generations of workers and citizens.

The powerful legacy of the domestic scientists is an under-acknowledged influence on all American food culture but especially on food presentations in historic sites and museums. Domestic scientists interlarded their presentations with messages about culture and social responsibility, telling generations of women that properly prepared food represented values important to an orderly society: Americanness, cleanliness, health, wholesomeness, and compliance with gender expectations. Not coincidentally, early preservationists and Colonial Revival-era museum practitioners also embraced these messages. In addition, promoting the practice of cooking and nutrition as applied sciences demanded the communication modes of formal instruction: lecture, performance, step-by-step demonstration, supervised practice, and evaluation. In developing these formal teaching and presentation systems, domestic scientists originated many of the same techniques used in interpretive programs and classes today.

Farm Displays: Model Farms and Farm Vacations

The fourth strand of food and farm interpretation also reflects the deep ambivalence in the ways many Americans were responding to the changes of the late nineteenth and early twentieth centuries, as well as the strongly gendered nature of many of those responses. The creation of model farms by male elites who wanted to demonstrate the most up-to-date ideas seems quite distinct from the provision of farm vacations by farm women who found a new source of farm income in the growing American nostalgia for rural life. But both strategies took place slightly outside the commercial market for food products, nudging food and farming in the direction of display, avocation, and recreation. The two converged in interesting ways later in the twentieth century, as the model farms of an earlier period helped form the infrastructure of a later era of preservation and interpretation.

Model farms have a long lineage, linking to the feudal estates that were in many ways the templates for properties like George Washington's Mount Vernon and Thomas Jefferson's Monticello (the Mount Vernon Ladies' Association, in fact, initially considered developing the site as a model farm). As a distinctly American republic began to take shape, the owners of these large estates often used their wealth and position to showcase new technologies and ideas, combining self-aggrandizement with an urge to help others help themselves in a way that was also distinctly American. Like the land-grant colleges, the farms of ex-Presidents and other elites were subsidized endeavors, and they were as much about education and experimentation as food production *per se*. And like small and large agricultural fairs and industrial expositions, they aimed to keep food producers abreast of the latest inventions, all in an effort to keep up with the increasingly mechanized and commercialized agricultural economy. Ironically, that economy was creating deep dilemmas for small-scale producers struggling to stay competitive, but that fact only spurred reformers and advocates on to greater efforts on their behalf (Figure 1.3).

With the continued growth of the industrial economy throughout the nineteenth century, new elites appeared among the manufacturing and

FIGURE 1.3 In the late years of the Depression, Hollywood screenwriter Louis Bromfield followed the pattern of earlier "gentleman farmers" by turning three small Ohio farms into a 600-acre model farm where he demonstrated good soil and pasture management and entertained friends from the movie industry. Malabar Farm is now a state park and an active historic site; the barn pictured was built to replicate Bromfield's barn, which burned in 1993. Image: OHWiki.

professional classes, some of whom, like their more agrarian predecessors, also created model farms. By the turn of the twentieth century, the well-to-do Clark family transformed the old farm of novelist James Fenimore Cooper into a state-of-the-art dairy in Cooperstown, New York, while New York businessman William Seward Webb and his wife Eliza Vanderbilt Webb created a vast agricultural estate that they called Shelburne Farms from a patchwork of 30 small northern Vermont properties. In central Vermont, lawyer and conservationist Frederick Billings purchased the deforested farmland of pioneering conservationist George Perkins Marsh and experimented with reforestation and new methods of dairying. Other model farms were found among groups who rejected many aspects of modernization and mechanization, like the Shakers and the Amish, whose methods and results were closely watched by those who were concerned about the effects of industrialized food production on small food producers.

That essential ambivalence about the direction the economy was taking could also be seen in the turn toward farm vacations, which started in the late nineteenth century. Continuing a long history of women bringing additional money into farms through market-oriented activities, it was mostly farm women who took on the responsibility of housing and feeding visitors who wanted to "play farmer" and soak up the pastoral atmosphere of rural places. Just as it does today, farm tourism dovetailed nicely with state and private efforts to reinvigorate rural economies, as well as with the notion that it was women's work to cultivate the beauties and comforts of the home and the table for both family members and paying guests. Farm vacations were a way to expand commercial farm markets while seeming to resist them at the same time. For farmers, taking in summer boarders supplied a needed source of additional revenue that could help to keep a small farm going, while vacationers could feel that they were magically escaping or transcending the hustle and bustle of the commercialized urban world. It was a balancing act that could not be sustained as the pressures on small farms continued to build in the twentieth century, but for a time, as Dona Brown notes, "The double-edged rhetoric of farm nostalgia seemed to make everybody happy."[8]

Many nineteenth-century model farms have had afterlives as historic sites, weaving together the two sides of this type of display. In preserved Shaker villages and the thriving sphere of Amish tourism; in the properties of "great men" like the early ex-Presidents and the recreated rural landscapes of industrialists like Henry Ford in Dearborn, Michigan, and Eli Lilly at Conner Prairie, Indiana; and in the transformation of places like Shelburne Farms, Billings Farm, and James Fenimore Cooper's farm (now the Farmer's Museum in Cooperstown) into educational sites, the earlier display-oriented qualities of model farms are now fully united with the recreational opportunities offered by rural vacationing. These sites usually create a powerful aura of "pastness" around small-scale food production; their products are education and experience, not food *per se*.

Legacies and Limitations

These four strands of cultural interaction with food and farming wove together in complex ways in the nineteenth and early twentieth centuries. Each contributed to an expansive learning ecosystem in which Americans explored and absorbed messages about food, farming, industrialization, and history. Those messages ultimately constituted a body of conventional wisdom drawn upon by those who developed the first professional public history interpretations at historic sites and in museums. By the early twentieth century, the basic ingredients of a public history of food were in place. In the 1930s, sites such as Colonial Williamsburg were staging historically themed banquets and developing hearth-cooking demonstrations, many calling back the mode of nostalgic remembrance seen in the World's Fair kitchens and infusing their presentations with subtext about patriotism, health, and gender expectations. Sites without a commercial farming past of their own had absorbed and refashioned the operational practices of model farms and those who took in tourists.

Following the boom in historic site establishment between 1930 and 1950, the increasing professionalization of museum management and public history spawned further interpretive innovations. Waves of innovation in interpretation brought emphasis, in turn, on culinary, cultural, and experientially driven methods. Early on, the central focus fell on historic recipes and cooking techniques. Food historian Ken Albala has termed this highly concrete, object-driven approach "culinary history," characterized by an interest in methods, techniques, ingredients, processes, and equipment. Albala contrasts this with "food history," a more widely framed approach that calls attention to the social, cultural, intellectual, or political dimensions of food production and consumption.[9] At living history sites, interpreters pursuing a culinary history ethos mastered long-defunct trades, producing replica farming equipment and cooking utensils, and learned to cook on open hearths, pluck and dress poultry, plow with oxen, harvest grain with scythes, and press fruit for cider. Their research in period cookbooks and primary documents produced widely disseminated reprints of early recipe collections, such as the 1958 republication of Amelia Simmons' *American Cookery* (originally published in 1796),[10] as well as new research summaries such as Colonial Williamsburg's *Colonial Virginia Cookery* (1968).[11]

The "new social history" of the 1960s and 1970s brought with it interpretive methods that approached "foodways" as reflections of culture, reconstructing complex interactions among people, food, and the cultural context. Researchers pored over a wider range of primary sources, such as account books, diaries, and newspapers, to reconstruct the movements and meanings of food in a given time and place, often producing new publications that had wide influence on the field—for example, Sandra Oliver's *Saltwater Foodways*, a tome developed over decades of research to inform interpretations of the foodways of coastal New England,[12] or Jane Zeigelman's *97 Orchard*, which grew out of foodways research at the Lower East Side Tenement Museum.[13] Historian Megan Elias also used the Tenement Museum to show how interpretive points can be grounded in foodways research, illustrating how immigrants' culturally informed knowledge suggested strategies that helped them cope with times of deprivation. Elias found that a German Jewish family enduring the depression of 1873 drew food support from mutual aid societies and shifted from baking, which consumed large amounts of coal, to stovetop dishes like onion and turnip soups. Meanwhile, a Sicilian family survived the Great Depression by drawing on traditions like extending small cuts of meat with rice, beans, or bread and foraging the city for wild foods like chestnuts and dandelion greens.[14]

A third, experientially driven methodology gained new ascendancy in the current "hands-on, minds-on"-approach museum-exhibit designer Nina Simon has dubbed "the participatory museum."[15] Contemporary methods often draw on solid understandings of learning theory, providing multiple points of entry for learners—kinetic, visual, auditory—and creating new intellectual schemas and feelings of personal relevance. They provide opportunities for visitors to help with daily tasks like harvesting vegetables, hauling water, seeding raisins, or feeding chickens as well as more structured activities that might range from a few minutes cranking an ice cream freezer to a re-created tavern supper. Immersive experiences like these can carry interpretive messages in ways that strongly appeal to, and stay with, audiences. They're often reported to be the most enjoyable of all encounters with information about the past.

All three of these interpretive methodologies—the culinary, the culturally focused, and the experiential—retain an undeniable allure. Their tried-and-true tactics are so effective that, paradoxically, they can bind museums in a dull cycle of replication. Drawing on the same set of common roots in these traditions of display, once-innovative interpretation methods have been widely adopted across the museum field over time, resulting in innumerable similar experiences in historic house, village, and farm museums: hearth cooking demonstrations, Colonial tavern suppers and Victorian teas, short instructional classes, and livestock "back-breeding." There is a striking sameness to these programs, and this well-established pattern in turn shapes what visitors expect to see, feel, and do when they encounter information and experiences relating to the history of food.

Celebratory and sensuous, many history museum presentations of food labor and culture lean toward depicting regularity over interruption, full cupboards over scarcity, enjoyment over difficulty. Historically, these re-creations have focused on the well-resourced—the elite table, the lavish tea service, the groaning farmhands' board—rather than the hungry or food-insecure—the enslaved person, the sharecropper, the new immigrant, the ill or unlucky. Food quality tends to be appealing, emphasis often falling on the products of the site itself, at the peak of freshness and ripeness, rather than on produce withered or turned during transport, or goods fraudulently extended by unscrupulous merchants. Visitors

often encounter scenes of uncomplicated everyday abundance, while issues relating to labor and power may remain hidden or merely hinted at. Even where
history museums have embraced the challenge of interpreting scarcity, inequality, and difficulty, there are still challenges in moving beyond the visceral pull
of conventional presentations and escaping the tendency for audiences to see
museums and historic sites as relating only to the past.

There are signs that this is changing. The experiences of servants and
the enslaved are more often woven into historic house interpretation, while
influential sites like the Lower East Side Tenement Museum have popularized
more critical and dialogic modes of engaging with the materials of the past.
This is part of a larger shift in intent already underway in American museums,
a movement that museum thinker Stephen Weil characterized in 1999 as "from
being *about* something to being *for* somebody." Recognizing an increasing
responsibility to a socially and civically engaged public, museums have been
moving away from what some sardonically called "the salvage and warehouse
business" to become "more entrepreneurial institution[s]... providing a variety
of primarily educational services to the public."[16] The changes Weil observed,
often referred to in shorthand as "the paradigm shift," reframed museums as not
just collecting organizations, but educational institutions serving democratic
ends. They placed new emphasis on broadening audiences, diversifying
narratives, and deepening understandings. Museums are becoming places of
inclusion and of dialogue, places to examine contemporary questions in the
light of historical thinking.

But in the area of food and farming, the paradigm shift remains oddly incomplete. Institutions and community historians do understand the power of
food to broaden audience—hence the proliferation of food programming and the
experimentation with ideas like hosting farmers markets at museums. They've
also recognized the utility of food and farming topics in diversifying representation, as is reflected in the abundance of culturally specific foodways-based projects. But public historians have been less successful at delivering deepened
understandings that support public thinking and choice-making about present-
day food and farming issues—the kind of useful, relevant understanding that is,
in Weil's words, "*for* somebody." Food and farming topics still tend to occupy
interpretive positions that are *illustrative* of other themes (such as immigration or
technological innovation) rather than being *substantive* organizing principles in
themselves.

One further challenge for even the most critical and incisive food interpretation
is one shared by some of the more publicly visible areas of the food movement
itself: they take place largely in the realms of the pleasurable, the voluntary, the
educational and recreational. And they tend to rely heavily on the same kinds of
sources of support: the non-profit sector and the wallets of the relatively affluent
and educated. For public history, this means that even if the stories of people
of color and the poor are more often represented in food interpretations, those
people are still usually strikingly absent from the work of interpretation itself,

just as they tend to be absent from some parts of the food movement's organizing structure. It's not just about what we show, in other words; we also need to pay closer attention to who "we" are.

These are problems that people who identify with the food movement are grappling with more directly as the movement evolves, and the museum world is also beginning to engage more purposefully with them. They are not mere sidelines to a central focus on food; they are an essential piece of an engaged food interpretation, pointing us toward the very questions that are most important to pose and explore. It can help to have a sense of the many social and environmental justice projects that come under the heading of "the food movement" (as outlined in the next chapter). It can also help to recognize how our own skills of contextualizing and communicating can help to understand the roots of these differences and exclusions, as well as the long struggle to overcome them.

But the single most important factor—and the reason for this opening chapter's careful dissection of the roots of our own practice—is a willingness to see ourselves as already fully engaged in the food system and the culture at large. Doing this work well requires a deeply reflexive practice, demanding a rigor and honesty that may be somewhat new to the workplace culture of many sites. We need to engage with the history of our own profession's involvement with food questions, re-evaluating the tendency to present food and farming topics as narrowly focused, time-limited, nostalgic and closed-ended stories about issues that are resolved and ways of life that are over and sharply distinct from our own lives and work. Food and farming questions are ongoing democratic concerns, open-ended questions that any society will always face, as well as reflections of broader challenges specific to this time and place. We need to move beyond the legacies of older methodologies and imagine new ways of presenting food and farming as ongoing human stories—stories without endings.

Bibliographic Note

Tracing the roots of food interpretation in museums would be impossible without the large and growing body of museum historiography and criticism. Though much of the granular detail of its development lies in museum archives, where internal correspondence, training documents, and daily program schedules document its incremental development, food messages can also be read in and through the wider analyses of museum scholars. Key to our analysis here have been Stephen Weil's *Making Museums Matter* (Smithsonian Books, 2002); essays by Warren Leon, Margaret Piatt, Michael Wallace, David Lowenthal, and others in Warren Leon and Roy Rosenzweig's anthology *History Museums in the United States: A Critical Assessment* (University of Illinois Press, 1989); and Wallace's essay "Visiting the Past" in *Presenting the Past: Essays on History and the Public* (Temple University Press, 1986). Detailed discussion of the development of living history techniques in American museums can be found in Jay Anderson's *A Living History Reader: Museums* (American Association for State and Local History, 1991) and *Time Machines: The World of Living History* (American Association for State and Local History, 1984), while thoughtful critiques of living history and a revision of Anderson's timeline are offered by Scott Magelssen in *Living History Museums: Undoing History through Performance* (Scarecrow Press, 2007). More recently, a sense of urgency is fueling a field-wide discussion on updating museum methodologies; among the works advocating change are Gail Anderson's *Reinventing the Museum: The Evolving Conversation on the Paradigm Shift* (AltaMira, 2012), Nina Simon's *The Participatory Museum* (2010), and Franklin Vagnone and Deborah Ryan's *Anarchist's Guide to Historic House Museums* (Left Coast Press, 2015). A more detailed exploration of some of the roots of food interpretation also appears in Michelle Moon's *Interpreting Food at Museums and Historic Sites* (Rowman & Littlefield, 2015), while the history of the gradual separation and partial reconvergence of real and represented farming can be found in Cathy Stanton's essay "Between Pastness and Presentism: Public History and Local Food Activism," *Oxford Handbook of Public History* (James Gardner and Paula Hamilton, eds., Oxford University Press, 2017).

The phenomenon of world's fairs and industrial expositions is explored in a vast interdisciplinary literature. Erik Mattie's *World's Fairs* (Princeton Architectural Press, 1998) offers a richly illustrated overview of major international exhibitions, while Robert Rydell's *World of Fairs: The Century-of-Progress Expositions* (University of Chicago Press, 1993) and *All the World's a Fair: Visions of Empire at American International Expositions, 1876–1916* (University of Chicago Press, 2013) provide critical assessments of the interaction of world's fairs with American cultural ideals. The movement for domestic economy is chronicled in detail in Susan Strasser's *Never Done: A History of American Housework* (Pantheon Books, 1982) and Laura Shapiro's *Perfection Salad: Women and Cooking at the Turn of the Century* (University of California Press, 1986). Jennifer Jensen Wallach's *How America Eats: A Social History of U.S. Food and Culture* (Rowman & Littlefield, 2013) synthesizes many streams of cultural activity in discussions of how food culture relates to gender, race, and empire.

On model farms and "great men," see Reeve Huston, "The 'Little Magician' after the Show: Martin Van Buren, Country Gentleman and Progressive Farmer, 1841–1862," in *New York History*, Spring 2004, pp. 93–121 and Tamara P. Thornton, *Cultivating Gentlemen: The Meaning of Country Life among the Boston Elite, 1795–1860* (Yale University Press, 1989). Dona Brown's work is indispensable for understanding the nostalgic impulses within nineteenth-century tourism; see *Inventing New England: Regional Tourism in the Nineteenth Century* (Washington, DC: Smithsonian Institution Press, 1995).

WORK IN PROGRESS—AN INTERVIEW WITH DARWIN KELSEY: FROM "WHAT" TO "WHY"

FIGURE 1.4 Darwin Kelsey.

A pivotal figure in the development of agricultural history presentations in museums, Darwin Kelsey, who died in late 2016 as this book was going to press, was also among its most recent innovators, challenging the field of public history to take an active orientation to issues of critical urgency in food and farming. A leader among the groundbreaking interpretive planners who, in the 1960s, developed what has been called a "well-footnoted"[17] agricultural history presentation at the Old Sturbridge Village (OSV) Pliny Freeman Farm, Kelsey co-founded the Association for Living History, Farms and Agricultural Museums (ALHFAM) and served as an advocate and early board member of the American Livestock Breeds Conservancy, also launched at OSV (Figure 1.4).

After a stint directing the National Scouting Museum, Kelsey returned to agricultural topics in 1989, helping to establish the Lake Metroparks Farmpark, a 235-acre working farm and public park in Ohio. Shortly after launching the Farmpark, Kelsey incorporated and became Executive Director of the Cuyahoga Valley Countryside Conservancy, a uniquely structured organization whose mission is "to connect people, food, and land by increasing public awareness of how food and farming impact personal, community, and environmental health, and by inspiring personal commitment to building a resilient, sustainable food culture." Under Kelsey's leadership, The Conservancy promoted its mission through a partnership with the Cuyahoga Valley National Park, which organizes 11 working farms in a "Countryside Initiative" to demonstrate and encourage participation in sustainable farming and land stewardship. The Conservancy also organizes farmers markets, gives farm tours, offers webinars, and runs food swaps, tastings, classes, and workshops, including one for aspiring small farmers titled "Exploring the Small Farm Dream."

In 2013, Kelsey shook the foundations of ALHFAM in an address at its annual meeting. Asking why the field continued to accept or adapt definitions of living history farms developed between 1945 and 1981—definitions he believed were not just outdated, but dangerously limited—Kelsey urged ALHFAM members to "recognize that this short span of time coincides almost precisely with the most radical change in the way humans feed themselves since *homo sapiens* began."[18] Citing the litany of negative consequences of industrial food system expansion and the need for "radical change—fundamental culture change," Kelsey laid a challenge before history museums: "Couldn't—shouldn't—playing an active, intentional role in that culture change become part of the *why* shaping the *what* of most living history farms?" In the interview below, Kelsey delved deeper into the need to distinguish between *what* and *why* in order to develop public history projects in dialogue with the realities of—and alternatives to—today's food system.

When you began working on historic agriculture at Old Sturbridge Village, you created a new standard for rigorously researched, highly detailed presentations of agricultural history—a standard replicated at hundreds of other living history museums. What interpretive goals were you focused on at the time? What, if any, are living history's failures or unrealized goals?

We screwed it up. I did not have the perspective that I currently have and didn't think a lot about certain things, because nobody else was thinking about them, either. Back then, there were ideas in the air. In 1945, the idea of a living farm, a living agricultural museum, was floated, but nothing happened. In the mid-60s, John Schlebecker at the Smithsonian wanted to get living history farms going. Alexander Wall was president of Old Sturbridge Village at the time, and they were thinking about getting more serious about developing a good interpretive program in agriculture. He had a couple of new people, new PhDs, who were saying "Hey, 90% of the people here were engaged in agriculture. Why aren't we talking about it?" I went to Sturbridge in 1966 with the expectation that I was going to become the lead researcher to figure out what could be done by way of interpreting agriculture.

I was interested because I had the sense that we were living in a time of pretty radical change. People were not engaged in farming any more. They were getting out of it. I had the sense it would be good to present agriculture to people, to get them thinking about where their food used to come from and the differences from what they were experiencing today. But our

(Continued)

focus back then was on the *what*. If you look at definitions of living history farms from back then, including mine, they were really about *simulating*—the attempt to simulate the practices of some more or less specific farm, in some more or less specific place, at some more or less specific time in the past. And that's what we were focused on—getting it right. We were harvesting information with a rigor that wasn't out there anywhere else. But it wasn't about *why*. That went on for the next 50 years.

What we did back in the '60s and '70s was a game-changer. But I began to see things it wasn't dealing with, things that weren't getting communicated to people about what it was like to farm. I couldn't get my peers to talk about things I was understanding as important. Even 15 years ago, there were things that seemed to me that would be better communicated if we had real people on real farms doing real farming, and people were looking at that, engaging with it, talking about it and applying it.

Some of those ideas found expression in the Lake Metroparks Farmpark. There was no such thing as a "farmpark" in 1989 when you developed that project. Can you tell me how you hit on the idea for this new kind of educational site?

They had asked me and five other people to come and critique their concept for a historical village. Five people liked it, and I didn't. I said, "Why do you want to do this? It's been done. You've got three hundred of these living history villages around the country. Why don't you do something that's never been done?" They said, "What?" I said, "There ought to be places around the country that focus on how humans have worked with land, plants, and animals to grow things on purpose (that's John Schlebecker's famous definition of a farm)." They said, "Well, what would that be like?"

I went back to my kitchen table and worked on the concept for six months. I developed the idea that we ought to be a place that was a cross between a zoo, a botanical garden, a history museum, and a science center. We set up the notion of trying to create this thing we called a "farmpark." It was intended to get people thinking about the kind of work people did on the land before them.

You created that forward-thinking project in 1990, before today's food movement was well established. How did your thinking evolve as ideas around reforming the industrial food system gathered strength?

A lot of it has happened since Michael Pollan published *Omnivore's Dilemma*. In the years right after that, you got a host of new publications and articles and conferences on all the problems with the food system. It's no longer a weird, fringe-y thing; it's a mainstream idea. We're beginning to realize that for all the good things modern agriculture has done, there are also negative things associated with it—environmental degradation, loss of land, depleted aquifers, farmworker abuse, narrow corporate control of the food supply—I could go on. John Schlebecker has called it an "inherent pattern of problems." So, we're aware of that, and now we're trying to ask ourselves how we fix it—and we know it's really critical for society. It's about personal health, community health, and environmental health. Our food system is causing big problems. We have to change.

The Cuyahoga Valley Countryside Conservancy was developed to be in direct conversation with those ideas about change. Can you describe the Conservancy's mission?

When we talk about ourselves as an organization, we say that our purpose, our mission, is connecting people, food, and land. And we do that by increasing awareness about food, farming, and health and by attempting to inspire personal commitment, building resilience in the food culture. Not only have we rehabbed and revitalized nine old farms in the National Park, but we've also started two farmers markets in the park, and one in nearby Akron, which we own and manage ourselves. We were out there on the edge of a wave—when we got started in 2004, there were 15 farmers markets in a 16-county area of northern Ohio. Ten years later, there were over 90. We're developing collaborations with people interested in talking about change across the whole range of conversations. We say, "Come at it however you want to: health and wellness, climate change, economic development—fine." Our programming is to try to focus on these critical societal issues. Our vision is to fill northeast Ohio with thriving farming and food entrepreneurs, gardeners, and home cooks, a DIY culture that is widespread. If that happens, healthy food is an option for everyone.

The Conservancy's work involves crossing conventional boundaries between for-profit and non-profit, public sector and private. How do you manage that?

We incorporated as a non-profit in 1999 specifically to be a partner of the Cuyahoga Valley National Park, to help them figure out how to rehabilitate and revive the farms in the park, to connect them to the outside world. As a private non-profit, we can do things for them without all the red tape of being a publicly owned organization, so that's what we do. That's not to say we don't have to be careful to abide by all the rules and regs non-profits have to abide by, and we do. But we've built a three-legged stool that works together on these issues: the government, the national park, and the non-profit private sector—that's us. Then, there's a for-profit private sector called "the farmers." We are advisers to the farmers on their farming business and practices, and are on their cases to do things ethically and responsibly and sustainably. But we're also on the park's case about doing things that are really going to help the farmers.

I often describe our role here as "marriage counseling." We have to explain farmers to parkies, and parkies to farmers, because they come from different planets. Farming in a national park really is a special case—"What, you want to make a hole in the ground for a fence post? You're going to have to make an archaeological survey." What we were doing hadn't been done before, so we had to work our way through all kinds of regulatory issues that were pretty complex. It was a real exercise, but we persevered, and the park superintendent at the time was willing to push the system. We got it done.

(Continued)

We were dismissed at the outset, but after we started to make things happen, they started looking at us differently.

The Conservancy is engaged in preservation and discusses agricultural history, but really centers its work around contemporary issues. How do your projects present the past?

We don't wax very nostalgic about the past. The future is really about understanding the past and the present, what works and what isn't working, and what we can do about that. We're not about really replicating the past. It's not that there aren't ideas or lessons there, but there was a lot of screwing up there, too. America was settled in ways that really did screw up the environment—denuded the mountains, denuded the plains. Most of our programs talk about what works, who's doing what to solve problems. On the back page of all the requests for proposals that we send to prospective farmers is a quote from John Ikerd that I love: "Some folks have a hard time believing that the future can be much different, and possibly much better than the past or the present. In reality the future is almost never like the past or present. The challenge is to help shape a future that we want." I think that's what we're trying to do.

There's a saying about what we conserve and won't conserve: "In the end, we'll only conserve what we love, and we'll only love what we understand, and we only understand what we've been taught." We see that as inspiration and validation for what we're doing.

Why do you see it as so urgent that agricultural history sites get involved in educating people about contemporary issues in farming?

What most of us don't get is that the current system is destroying the life that exists in the soil. There are billions of microbes there that fertilizers, pesticides, and insecticides disrupt and kill. That's a really strong rationale for getting people to come to the kind of institutions we're talking about to think about how we produce food and what we're doing, and learn that a change is possible.

John Ikerd, one of my heroes, is a really incredible writer and speaker in sustainable agriculture. He says, for example, people do not make big changes—unless they believe (1) that what they're doing isn't working, and isn't going to work in the future; (2) that there is something that *could* be done that *would* work in the future; and (3) that it's actually *possible*, though not easy. And then, they can be inspired to go for change. I think he's right about all those things, and I think that's what we have to do. We have to help people see what the current system is doing, and how it's going to get worse, and that there are known ways to change things.

The Conservancy is disciplined about making a commitment to create a larger social impact. In your opinion, why are so many public history institutions still focused on minutiae, on getting the details right?

Because they're human. Most people start with *what*, not *why*. We think we're all about the tangible thing we deliver, but that product just validates our *why*. Look at Simon Sinek's book *Start With Why*. Organizations that we consider great start with *why*, not *what*.

Our mission statement tries to articulate what we exist for in terms of *why*. It's not just the farms in the park—that's our *what*. The farmers markets are *what*. Our education program, with over 30 different classes and workshops a year, that's a *what*. But they're there because of this need to connect people to food and land, to get them thinking about how farming and food impact them, and to be inspired to do something about it. Those *whats* are things that we have to do to make that *why* happen.

How do you know your work is having an effect? What are your indicators of change?

Culture change is slow. You don't have any monstrous change, impactful change, in the food system without the culture driving it. Slavery got outlawed, but that doesn't mean that a lot of people in certain places were prepared to greet black people as human, and they still won't. All the money and power that's invested works to keep the current system in place. People who supply the food we eat in the current system won't change unless we, the consumers, force it. You can't have sustainable farms and farmers unless people habitually prefer and will buy what they make. That's going to take a slow movement. Change isn't easy. The average age of a farmer is 58 or 59 now. If you're totally invested in the old system, you aren't interested in change. Even if you are convinced that there's a better way than your way— at 60 years old, are you going to go in a new direction? I don't think so. And that's why we're going to have to heavily outreach to mostly younger people.

On the other hand, people talk about a paradigm shift. Well, my reaction to that is that "shift happens." And it's happening, all over America.

Notes

1 Association for the Preservation of Virginia Antiquities, *Yearbook of the Association for Virginia Antiquities* (Richmond, VA: George M. West, 1896), 60.

2 Susan Riviere Hetzel, "The Mary Washington Monument," *The American Monthly Magazine* 15 (July–December 1899), 319.

3 "Mary Washington House," Preservation Virginia website, http://preservationvirginia.org/visit/historic-properties/mary-washington-house.

4 "Gloucester Fisheries, Agricultural Hall," *Frank Leslie's Illustrated Historical Register of the Centennial Exposition 1876*, edited by Richard Kenin (New York: Paddington Press, 1974), 114.

5 "Kansas and Colorado Building," *Frank Leslie's Illustrated Historical Register of the Centennial Exposition 1876*, ed. Richard Kenin (New York: Paddington Press, 1974), 116.

6 *Rand McNally and Co.'s A Week at the Fair* (Chicago: Rand McNally and Co., 1893), 168.

7 The Morrill Act of 1872, *United State Statutes at Large*, Vol. 12, U.S. Government Printing Office, 503.

8 Dona Brown, *Inventing New England: Regional Tourism in the Nineteenth Century* (Washington, DC: Smithsonian Institution Press, 1995), 167.

 9 Ken Albala, "History on the Plate: The Current State of Food History," *Historically Speaking* 10:5 (2009), 6–8.
10 Amelia Simmons, *The First American Cookbook: A Facsimile of "American Cookery," 1796, by Amelia Simmons* (New York: Dover, 1985).
11 Jane Carson, *Colonial Virginia Cookery* (Williamsburg, VA: Colonial Williamsburg, 1968).
12 Sandra Louise Oliver, *Saltwater Foodways* (Mystic, CT: Mystic Seaport Museum, 1995).
13 Jane Zeigelman, *97 Orchard: An Edible History of Five Immigrant Families in One New York Tenement* (New York: Harper, 2011).
14 Megan Elias, "Summoning the Food Ghosts: Food History as Public History," *The Public Historian* 34:2 (2012), 20–27.
15 Simon's 2010 book *The Participatory Museum* summed up a trend with roots extending back to the 1970s in which museums increasingly invited audiences to "actively engage as cultural participants, not passive consumers." Nina Simon, *The Participatory Museum* (Santa Cruz, CA: Museum 2.0, 2010), ii.
16 Stephen Weil, "From Being About Someone to Being For Somebody: The Ongoing Transformation of the American Museum," *Daedalus* 128:3 (1999), 255.
17 Jay Anderson, *Time Machines: The World of Living History* (Nashville: American Association for State and Local History, 1984), 43.
18 Darwin Kelsey, "What Is a Living History Farm? Introductory Comments," *Proceedings of the 2013 ALHFAM Conference*, Vol. 36 (2013).

2

SLOW FOOD, FAST LEARNING

Navigating the "Food Movement"

The Slow Food movement, founded in 1989 by activists concerned about cultural erosion caused by the globalization of fast food, has grown into a worldwide organization with a simple and clear proposition: to create a food system that is good, clean, and fair.[1] Slow Food's central principle is the assertion that "fast life"—the preferences for speed, ease, bulk, and convenience that support the continuing industrialization of the food system—has led to a system that damages health, environment, and community. To change that system, Slow Food argues, we can't just change the way we raise crops or prepare school lunches; we must change the values we use to make choices about food. This conception of "slowness" is about much more than cooking time; it's about taking time for research, reflection, deliberation, and inclusivity as we make personal and civic decisions that affect the food system (Figure 2.1).

This insistence on slowness stands in contrast to the general, overwhelming sense of urgency about food systems reform. Concerned activists feel prodded to rush forward, anxious to turn things around immediately. But by moving into action too quickly, well-intentioned people and groups can talk themselves into skipping the time-consuming processes of research and reflection, succumbing to "fast" thinking and hurried action. In direct opposition to their purpose, acting without first establishing historical understanding or a strong common analysis of the problems raises the risk of simply repeating many of the failures of the past. Today's activists can come to feel that our own time is just *different*, more urgent, making them oblivious to pitfalls and obstacles that slowed or ended past food movements before they could become truly transformative. Simply reviving interest in topics or skills from the past won't reverse the damage threatened by continued massive industrialization of the food system.

FIGURE 2.1 At Slow Food's international exposition Salone de Gusto, exhibitors like Hawaii's Sunshower Coffee Farm present educational displays and tastings, highlighting the unique qualities of diverse, artisanally produced food. Photo courtesy Anna Mulé.

As public historians, we inherently support "slow" values—careful inquiry, critical questioning, contextualization and comparison of evidence, considering multiple perspectives, consultation and collaboration with stakeholder and scholarly communities. By inserting the "slower" processes of historical inquiry into the urgency of the food movement, public historians can support reflexivity and more nuanced historical thinking within food systems activism, helping advocates create *lasting* change.

The Roots of Reform

The food movement has expanded dramatically in the past 10 years, permeating mainstream culture. While interest in food reform didn't come out of nowhere—food and farming activism in the U.S. dates back to the origins of the nation—it tends to crest and fall in response to changes in the food system and to people's direct experiences with the food supply. As at other times in the past, our society has arrived at a juncture in which rigorous interrogation of our food system has become a high-priority issue for a wide cross-section of the public.

Evidence that we are in the midst of a new, complex, multifaceted food movement surrounds us. In 1994, a USDA inventory of farmers markets found 1,755 operating around the nation. In 2014, that number had multiplied by almost five times, to 8,268.[2] Market growth in organic food purchasing skyrocketed as well. When the USDA began tracking acreage of land in organic production in 1997, there were fewer than a million acres of pasture and cropland in organic production. By 2011, over five million acres were managed under organic certification. Sales of organic food products rose from $3.6 billion in 1997 to more than $39 billion in 2014.[3] A 2014 survey by Consumer Reports showed that 84 percent of Americans buy at least some organic food, with nearly half buying organic products at least once a month.[4] These changes indicate an individual concern about the food supply and an interest in influencing the market to deliver alternatives.

Food systems activism happens at the community level, too. Parents organize to start school gardens or improve cafeteria lunch menus. Local land trusts arrange for tenant farmers to return preserved land to food production. Hunger relief groups lure produce vendors to "food deserts." Neighbors become shareholders in "community supported agriculture" farms (CSAs), establish community gardens, and swap seasonal cooking tips on social media. Health and community activists turn to traditional diets to ameliorate health crises like heart disease and diabetes that disproportionately affect their communities.

What's responsible for these shifts? As historians, we can point to periodic sea changes in consumer behavior and citizen action around food and farming in the American past. Campaigns have often arisen in reaction to conditions that menaced health. The prevalence of deficiency diseases such as pellagra, rickets, and scurvy among the poor in the late nineteenth century motivated domestic and nutrition scientists to search out essential compounds in food and prescribe a "balanced diet" containing recommended doses of vitamins and macronutrients. Diseases (including typhoid, tuberculosis, and botulism) communicated through the unsanitary handling of milk, meat, and produce prompted citizen advocacy to pass the 1906 Pure Food and Drug Act, overcoming 27 years of opposition to regulation during which Congress rejected more than 200 proposed food safety initiatives.[5] In the 1930s, 1970s, and again in the 1990s, consumers rallied to demand more specific ingredient and nutrition information in food labeling, much as today they are pushing for the labeling of "genetically modified" foods. Successive waves of farm-policy reform movements have swept across the decades, growing acute when economic conditions strained farmers' ability to make a living on the land. Governments and organizations have promoted home and community gardening multiple times over the past century and a half, aiming to divert food supplies during wartime, build self-reliance and strength of character in youth and the poor, or bring residents of urban neighborhoods together. The issues have varied with the moment, but concern with food and farming has never been far from the minds of the American public.

Food Reform Now

Today's food movement is notable for a potential coalescing of issues and projects formerly seen as distinct and disparate. Truly a food *systems* reform movement, the contemporary food activism scene is made up of dozens of strands of activity that share a common impetus to thoroughly rethink the values and practices underlying the way food is produced and distributed. Sometimes, though, it can seem as though there isn't much overlap in the movement's diverse agendas. Do backyard-chicken evangelists have much in common with prison-food reformers? Do biodynamic farmers share values with urban food recovery dumpster-divers?

Our answer is yes. As Jonathan Christensen has pointed out, scholarship on social movements recognizes that the character of a movement lies between the structured, hierarchically managed, stable, and relatively permanent nature of a political party or lobbying organization and the momentary fascination of a fad or cultural trend. Organized and informal at the same time, decentralized but multiply interconnected through dense interpersonal networks, social movements engage in goal-driven conflict with the status quo and the institutions that maintain it, advocating and working toward reform and change. Diverse subgroups within a movement may seek shifts in particular policies, but taken together, actors in a movement aim to produce a collective effect of widespread, coherent cultural change.[6] Despite their variations in focus, today's food activists share an implicit or explicit recognition that the current infrastructure of large-scale food production is negatively affecting one or more dimensions of environmental quality, personal health, equity, and community relationships, and all are involved in efforts to reshape and rescale the way our culture manages its food supply.

Parodists and critics tend to shallowly characterize food movement participants as solipsistic, affluent suburban elitists, but the actual movement is complex and diverse, crossing barriers of profession, culture, gender, race, partisanship, and economic position. As public historians begin to document and navigate the movement, it is important to look beyond the obvious and question dominant perceptions about who is involved in the food movement and what they care about. Below, we examine some of the major coalitions and sectors of the movement, exploring their interconnections with one another and with the history of food and farming. All of them are potential partners in exploring the intersections between public history and food systems change.

Food Producers Business communities circulate an anecdote about a chicken and a pig who decide to open a diner. As they discuss what each can contribute, the pig offers bacon and sausage, while the chicken offers eggs. After consideration, the pig says, "Forget the whole idea. You'd be invested, but I'd be *committed*." No one is more committed in questions of food systems reform than the people who grow and harvest food. Farmers, fishermen, orchardists, aquaculturists, ranchers, beekeepers, dairymen, foragers, and other primary food producers form the bedrock of the food system. As they have always been in the past, farmers are deeply and personally engaged in influencing the systems in which they work. Individually, they track industry issues, sit on commissions, teach and mentor entry-level producers, publish, experiment, and innovate. They form associations, unions, and co-operatives, and many participate with government and university research projects. Some producers are also deeply engaged in reform, leading the growing organic production sector while selling at—and managing—farmers markets, CSAs and CSFs (community-supported fisheries), or convening conferences on organic, biodynamic, and sustainable production. These producers form the core of the food reform movement. Without their knowledge, experience, skills, and resources, there can be no effective movement. The movement is for everyone, but in many crucial ways, it is *about* them.

But this sector is not monolithic, and not all food producers identify themselves with "the food movement." Many believe in the superiority and promise of conventional production methods, while others are constrained by contractual agreements to produce in a certain way for a specific buyer, or by geographical realities that limit markets and access to alternative purchasers. Then, too, they may have invested heavily, for decades, in methods rewarded (or at least sustained) by steady purchaser-supplier relationships in agribusiness. As they weigh millions of dollars sunk into land, equipment, livestock, and infrastructure against the uncertain promise of reward for change, many farmers can find little incentive to revolutionize their practice.

Whether farmers are fellow-travelers, curious observers, or adversaries of the kinds of reform advocated by those who do see themselves as part of the food movement, all are essential sources of information as well as of food, and all are potential contributors to the success of reform projects. It's possible to learn as much from those who see many barriers and potential losses in change as from those forging forward to develop cutting-edge sustainable techniques. No matter what the region or food context, food producers are essential members of any reform network.

Agricultural Laborers As we noted in the introduction, the term "farmer" tends to imply an independent, land-owning producer, when the reality is that the actual agricultural laborers who provide the human power to make farms work are themselves unlikely to own or manage a farming operation. Typically working under the supervision of a farm or ranch owner or manager, agricultural workers undertake the physical labor involved in planting, cultivating, pest and weed control, harvesting, and the operation of heavy farm equipment. Though the Bureau of Labor Statistics lists an annual mean wage of around $20,000 for farm laborers, this likely obscures lower incomes resulting from patterns of using migrant labor only as long as it's needed, casual labor agreements, unpaid internships, and dependence on undocumented laborers. The perennial tension between farming's often-narrow profit potential and its episodic demand for large volumes of wage labor has long historical roots that can be traced in family labor systems, slavery, migrancy, itinerant labor, immigration policies, wartime "Women's Land Armies," and many more agricultural labor stories.

Food Processors Also often overlooked in the simple farmer-to-consumer pairing are the millions of primary and secondary producers who have a hand in transforming raw ingredients into more processed products. Though "processed food" often gets a bad name as shorthand for inexpensive packaged food of low nutrient density, the term applies equally to the goods made by more warmly embraced secondary producers like cheesemakers, picklers and preservers, cider-makers and brewers, winemakers, bakers, butchers, and others, all of whom add value to foodstuffs through processing. Their specialty trades, many of them once found in nearly any community of size, have often been removed from view today and magnified in scale, relocated and concentrated in large industrial processing centers. Economies of scale and process automation often eliminate the need for workers to develop and practice the full range of specialized skill, further reducing processors' opportunities to master their craft, enjoy community respect and gain access to skilled-worker wages and benefits. The revival of small-scale "artisanal" processing trades in cities and small towns helps repair broken links in local histories of secondary food production. Once again, many people can take advantage of the knowledge and skill of a butcher, baker, or beekeeper, and indeed, products like craft brews and artisanal cheeses have been at the trendy edge of the food movement in many places.

But in the enthusiasm to embrace the aesthetically appealing artisanal producers returning to downtowns, it is important for food activists and the historians who work with them not to overlook how the industrial changes in food processing have stratified these trades and changed working conditions and economic outcomes for both the new artisans and the often-invisible processors who now labor in the more than 28,000 food manufacturing plants across the United States. The former often depend entirely on the tastes and affluence of an educated and upscale clientele, while the latter earn some of the lowest wages in the food industry and endure increased risk of workplace injury and harassment.

Restaurateurs, Chefs, Food Writers, and Critics The entrepreneurs and tastemakers who create and promote the culture of dining often seem to occupy the most visible and influential positions in the food movement pantheon. For example, in his history *The United States of Arugula,* David Kamp credits the impetus for the twentieth-century "food revolution" to key founding figures in cooking and criticism, beginning with James Beard, Craig Claiborne, and Julia Child. In the 1970s, a new generation of chefs and authors led the charge to integrate a growing social and environmental consciousness with food and dining. Frances Moore Lappé's 1971 *Diet for a Small Planet* called attention to the negative impacts of resource-intensive food production, while Alice Waters' restaurant Chez Panisse, opening the same year, specialized in a new "California" cuisine inspired by informal European meals, simply composed with fresh, local ingredients. A decade later, in Philadelphia, Judy Wicks' White Dog Cafe set a new standard for socially responsible food businesses. Wicks insisted on fair wages for kitchen staff, a hand in community development projects, and sustainable business practices. Along with other like-minded chefs and writers, these culinary pioneers demanded an acknowledgment that environmental health, social improvement, and food quality were inextricably linked and asserted that access to delicious and nourishing food should be not only a personal pleasure, but a human right. Meanwhile, food writers like John and Karen Hess, authors of *The Taste of America*, and Gael Greene, restaurant critic for *New York* magazine, drove advocacy for a better-tasting, fresher, more original American cuisine.

Despite the fact that their earthy food and populist rhetoric often played to affluent crowds instead of fomenting a middle- and working-class food revolution, the groundbreaking chefs and critics of the 1970s and 1980s inspired successive generations of chefs and food critics to consider more than the composition of the plate. Their descendants include chefs and food writers whose cultural import transcends the short-lived satisfaction of a dinner out. Among them are such prominent figures as Dan Barber, whose vision for dynamic and sustainable links between farms and professional kitchens resulted in an invitation to participate in a boundary-crossing collaboration with Stone Barns Center for Food and Agriculture, a historic laboratory-farm that supplies an experimental partner restaurant, Blue Hill at Stone Barns. Barber is part of a vanguard of chefs who work through organizations such as Slow Food USA and Chefs Collaborative to develop and promote local, seasonal dining and resilient economies and ecosystems. Chronicling their efforts are food writers with an investment in food systems reform, such as Michael Pollan, Ruth Reichl, and Corby Kummer.

Though access to these high-profile leading lights of the food movement is beyond the capacity of many historical organizations, chances are very good that the local food scene contains chefs and writers who are sympathetic to, and active in, food reform efforts. Chefs may be found conducting tastings and demonstrations at farmers markets or advising on state food policy. Writers may be reading at local bookstores or blogging about fresh, seasonal food. The talents and enthusiasms of chef-activists and food writers can make them powerful collaborators; many become the movement's celebrity spokespeople, making inroads with new audiences. They may also become the targets of critics who assume their epicurean interests represent the entirety of the food movement. Their energy, enthusiasm, and power to evangelize make them essential to the success of reform, but do be sure to understand their practices and philosophies when collaborating. The marketability of "local food" has given rise to some deceptive moves in restaurants and food promotion, including the false advertising of local sourcing.[7]

Restaurant and Fast Food Laborers More than eight million Americans work in the foodservice industry. Though celebrity chefs tend to dominate public imagination, the vast majority of foodservice workers earn modest to low wages and often do not enjoy the labor protections other industries offer. Since the 1970s, fast food has grown from a novelty for occasional consumption to an everyday food source for millions of Americans, multiplying its revenues nearly 30 times over.[8] Supporting that expansion are more than three million fast food workers, who have increasingly come from the ranks of adults attempting to support themselves and their families at wages that do not cover the basic costs of living. Most jobs in the sector offer no benefits and give workers little control over working hours, and the powerful companies that employ them often work against unionization efforts and other campaigns, like advocacy for a $15/hour minimum wage. Often left out of food reform networks, foodservice workers have long been a vital component of the American food system and have histories and perspectives worth exploring in interpretations of food distribution (Figure 2.2).

FIGURE 2.2 Fast food workers outside a McDonald's restaurant in Minneapolis. During a nationwide strike in April 2016, workers called for a $15/hour minimum wage, paid sick days, and the right to organize unions. Image courtesy Flickr contributor Fibonacci Blue.

Citizen-Consumer Activists Across the market table from producers and processors are the consumers who buy their goods. Citizen-consumers wield significant power in the marketplace of ideas, as well as those of products and policy. America's history of consumer activism in food politics includes hundreds of campaigns, many of them remarkably successful, including boycotts of products from colonial powers or slave states, exposure of fraudulent packaging and food adulteration by unscrupulous merchants, demands for safer food production and clearer labeling, and opposition to dangerous additives and pesticides. In private life, consumers have self-organized into buying cooperatives, established markets and food hubs, created food banks and soup kitchens, and launched advocacy organizations on issues ranging from the humane treatment of food animals to human rights, fair labor, hunger, and equity.

The dividing line between "citizen" and "consumer" is blurry, but it is important to point out that people in a polity are more than "consumers." Even people who participate very little in the market economy because they cannot purchase much, or because they cultivate their own food supply, wield political power in a democracy. It is important to affirm this concept of citizenship when evaluating proposals for purely market-based solutions. Consumers can sometimes overestimate the impact of buying power. Certainly, convincing a hospital or school system to begin buying from local producers has a significant effect at the community level, and the growth in the organic sector is evidence that purchasing patterns do have potential to reshape massive market systems. At the same time, the notion of "voting with your dollars" can be problematic for democratic activists. Those with fewer dollars face fewer choices in the marketplace, and many must prioritize survival over making statements. In addition, individual shifts in purchasing, even in the aggregate, have narrower impact than large-scale shifts in policy or the investment of public budgets. For instance, a small change in the structure of "specialty crop" farm subsidies would do far more to support produce growers than would millions of individual organic farmers-market purchases. Decisions made by each individual consumer are important culturally, personally, and locally but have limited influence unless accompanied by democratically driven change in larger political and economic systems in which people matter for reasons beyond their purchasing power. As with any presentation involving history, then, it is important when thinking about consumers' roles to balance individual actions with some consideration of broader structural forces and processes.

Health and Wellness Advocates Food and health are connected. The legacies of battles against deficiency disease and food contamination remain with us today. Not only do we still contend with outbreaks of foodborne illness (including, ironically, from the increasingly industrialized "big organic" production sector), we also face the increasing social costs of chronic diseases with dietary factors, particularly heart disease, osteoporosis, cancer, and diabetes. Health professionals, patients, and communities dealing with diet-related disease are among the most serious and committed voices in the food systems reform movement. Working in hospitals, clinics, schools, churches, health clubs, community centers, senior homes, daycare programs, and families, many take on the task of public dietary education, linking people to healthy sources of food and the know-how to prepare it. Others advocate for change in school menus, expansion of federal food support programs, food taxation and sale policies (such as efforts to ban fast food outlets or soda within municipal limits) and access to fresh food in food deserts. For this group of reformers, food is not only a political or aesthetic issue but a matter of life and death.

Social Justice Advocates Though essential to life, vital food resources have rarely been distributed equitably. While the wealthiest have long used luxury foods to denote status, society's poorest have worked to survive on whatever foods were currently accessible to them. These equity issues continue in the present, mapped onto environmental, economic, and other inequalities that are steadily widening within the U.S. and many other parts of the world. More than 23 million Americans live in "food deserts," communities defined by the USDA as "urban neighborhoods and rural towns without access to fresh, healthy, affordable food."[9] As of 2013, food insecurity, or the lack of "access to enough food for an active, healthy life for all household members,"[10] is experienced in more than 14 percent of American households.[11]

As the chapters on scale and policy discuss, enormous paradoxes and challenges are built into efforts to combat food insecurity in our modern industrial food system. Relief programs, such as federally subsidized school nutrition programs and food purchasing assistance for families and women with children, attempt to combat the worst deprivation while absorbing some of the nation's agricultural surplus, ensuring a market for farmers' commodity crops. Because of their multiple allegiances, these programs are subject to the vagaries of the partisan political process as well as to direct and sometimes personal attacks from those who oppose government-funded welfare programs. Within this matrix of issues are activists and organizations seeking to create justice through equitable access to healthy and often "culturally appropriate" food. Native American organizations seek to undo damage caused by the rapid imposition of Western processed-food diets with advocacy for food sovereignty (the ideal of full community control over the conditions of the food supply); urban activists support greater community food self-sufficiency with urban gardening, rooftop farming, gleaning, waste-food rescue, and fallen-fruit programs. All assert the belief that everyone deserves access to affordable, healthy food.

Environmental Stewards Some people support food reform not because of what they themselves consume, but because of how food production affects the land. Where the ethics of environmentalism once focused on issues like industrial pollution and endangered wild species, today's environmentalists are making the connection between farming and fishing practices and the health of lands and waters. Beginning in the 1970s, when Francis Moore Lappé's best-selling *Diet for a Small Planet* alerted environmentally conscious eaters to the outsized grain and water usage demanded by their meat-based diets, personal choices about what went onto the plate became tied to ideas about preserving natural resources. Today, opposition to intensive farming practices like the use of confined animal feeding operations ("CAFOs") comes as often from environmental activists, who recognize the potential for concentrated animal waste to cause algae blooms, fish kills, and water contamination, as from animal-rights advocates. Deforestation for agriculture reduces carbon sequestration while the expansion of industrial farming increases emissions of methane gas and the burning of fossil fuels, both tied to climate change. The application of pesticides, herbicides, and fungicides threatens water supplies and is difficult to regulate for safety, resulting in compromised human, animal, and plant health. Monoculture and seed patenting threaten biodiversity. For these reasons and more, even those who are not motivated by the pleasure of eating or the elimination of hunger have been drawn into the food movement, recognizing that a clean and healthy planet is impossible to achieve without significant changes to our current way of raising food.

Food Tourism, Festivals, and Experiences Food as entertainment, informal education, and experience is increasingly woven into travel, tourism, and recreational pursuits of many kinds. Culinary encounters have long been an aspect of traveling to new places, but the reach of contemporary media has made even everyday shopping and dining an opportunity for exploration and discovery. Discussion boards like Chowhound, crowd-sourced advice on apps like Yelp, and the offerings of more conventional mass media like the Food Channel have all contributed to this new wealth of collective public knowledge about food. Food-related festivals, from nostalgic rural fairs centered around particular local products to urban street festivals celebrating a vibrant local food scene, are often part and parcel of how places market and promote themselves, rolling food into branding campaigns and local economic development efforts. Temporary sites where people gather to eat and drink—food trucks, pop-up beer gardens, community picnics, "dinners in white" (a kind of flash-mob event that originated in France as *Dîner en Blanc*)—similarly contribute to both a sense of local place and a delight in coming across the new and unexpected.

Many of these venues and activities already overlap substantially with the work of museums and public historians, making them strong potential allies for food-related projects. Some of the caveats above—particularly about the importance of connecting with economically and racially diverse partners and audiences—apply here as well. But the very wide range of recreational pursuits involving food means that the opportunity to do that may well be found in the cycle of festivals and other events in your area.

Food Lovers, Cooks, and Gardeners Taste and quality alone motivate many people to become engaged in food activism. Home cooks, fine-diners and potluck coordinators, community and home gardeners—all are moved at least in part by the aesthetic and pleasurable claims of food on our palates and imaginations. Food systems activism draws in people who love food of and for itself, who want to grow and eat the best of what the earth can provide and to create occasions to celebrate food's cultural, social, and seasonal associations. These days, epicureans and DIYers are more socially and environmentally conscious than perhaps at any earlier time. Cooks and gardeners are becoming keenly aware of the ways in which their choices and practices can improve or degrade the land, soil, and climate. These food lovers are visible and active members of the contemporary food movement.

The loosely connected groups listed here, many and varied as they are, don't describe everyone who identifies with the food movement. Other active sectors include parents' groups, fair labor and trade activists, prison reformers, individual and intellectual property rights advocates, and countless others. The bewildering array of agendas, perspectives, and organizations sometimes seems to have no pattern; groups focused on different aspects of the food system generate a smorgasbord of organizations, books, websites, campaigns, and cultural activities. It can be difficult for people entering into food systems work to evaluate the information and proposals of so many groups, to sort reliable information from hype, or to determine which organizations or activities are most effective.

Meanwhile, engaged activists often find themselves forging ahead so breathlessly that they're rarely able to do a bird's-eye-view analysis of their own places in the reform effort relative to all the interrelated activities in the sector. Trading information rapid-fire and taking immediate action, they sometimes burrow deep into work on an issue before having thoroughly examined and understood its history or surfaced and articulated their own assumptions. This can reduce their efficacy, as they step into ancient pitfalls, ignore blind spots, and miss opportunities to expand their impact. Operating under a sense of urgency, activists fear that there is no time to articulate historical questions, search archives, and research issues deeply. They feel the pressure of looming economic and environmental crises and the challenge of creating a new generation of progressive food producers quickly. Activists push us to act fast and act *now*. But as important as it is to plunge boldly into action, we believe that the work of public historians is essential to the successful application of food activists' energy. In fact, our analysis suggests that permanent reform may be impossible without our involvement.

A Role for History

Activists do not always immediately grasp the argument that history will usefully inform the projects they're already in up to their elbows. But without historical perspective, contemporary projects are likely to break up on the shores of the industrialized food system, just as innumerable past efforts have. We are in this pickle precisely because few past food movements have resulted in lasting changes in even a single area, let alone achieved a comprehensive restructuring of the food system around safe, equitable, and sustaining principles. Historians must help activists articulate organizing questions without excluding their historical dimensions and apply rigorous processes of research and interpretation to their interrelated concerns. With their research and analytical skills, historians can historicize contemporary issues, clarify agendas, locate obscured players and hidden influences, identify key constraints, make productive comparisons, and build interpretations that link granular details and local issues to much larger historical phenomena, yielding new knowledge about which structures, at different scales, might need to be dismantled and rebuilt.

To date, much of food activism's relationship to the past has been symbolic, romantic, rhetorical, and, often, weak and ahistorical. In a strange paradox, contemporary food movements are at the same time future-focused and nostalgic. Activists often refer to past relationships with food that have been "lost," forgetting to investigate whether those relationships ever actually existed, for whom, for how long, and under what conditions. They speak of "getting back to" an unspecified past time that boasted a food system they assume was healthier—perhaps a time when fisheries were unregulated, synthetic fertilizers had not been developed, or corn syrup had not yet replaced sugar in so many foods. But that non-specific past exists only in the imagination. Healthy, wholesome, and abundant food was a treasured ideal, but rarely the norm, for most people in the American past.

Food historian Rachel Laudan ruffled feathers with her 2015 essay "A Plea for Culinary Modernism," arguing that food activists (whom she caricatured as "culinary Luddites") overly romanticize the past and should, instead of celebrating artisanal production, be advocating to improve that great boon of modernity, abundant and inexpensive industrial food. Laudan's stance on the benefits of industrialization drew fire from many activists, but her assessment of the past food supply is well supported:

> Fresh milk soured, eggs went rotten. Everywhere seasons of plenty were followed by seasons of hunger when the days were short. The weather turned cold, or the rain did not fall. Hens stopped laying eggs, cows went

dry, fruits and vegetables were not to be found, fish could not be caught in the stormy seas.[12]

Laudan insists that we recognize that the challenges of creating a reliable, healthy food system cannot be solved by attempts to replicate a past in which only industrial advancements could effectively address the plaguing issues of scarcity, safety, and perishability. The unintended consequences of those advancements created the burden we have inherited, but past food activists repeatedly failed to slow or stop the juggernaut, while sometimes overlooking the very real benefits it has created or the realities of the problems it was intended to fix.

History can help today's activists re-orient themselves to the past, cultivating a recognition that the fruits of industrialization often represented welcome victories over stubborn problems that prevented people from eating well and often. Somewhere between a too-simple imagined past and an uncritical embrace of food industrialization, public historians can draw attention to past solutions that were never realized and contribute to alternative visions that draw on data, tools, relationships, and ideas from both past *and* present. We can trace the complex histories of our food problems and help identify the root causes that keep them recurring, unsolved, and seemingly insoluble. We can surface and interrogate past models of food production, distribution, and regulation, perhaps turning up valuable ideas applicable today in modified fashion, while more comprehensively representing the consequences and costs those systems imposed.

Bibliographic Note

If nothing else, the contemporary food movement is media-friendly. Launched into prominence by a stream of popular books like Eric Schlosser's *Fast Food Nation: The Dark Side of the All-American Meal* (Houghton Mifflin, 2001), Michael Pollan's *The Omnivore's Dilemma: A Natural History of Four Meals* (Penguin Press, 2006), and Barbara Kingsolver's *Animal, Vegetable, Miracle: A Year of Food Life* (HarperCollins, 2007), food ideas also made their way into public minds through movies, magazine articles, blogs and websites. For an excellent, succinct, and practical overview of dozens of interrelated food issues and the reform efforts and organizations associated with them, see *The Food Activist's Handbook* by Ali Berlow (Storey Publishing, 2015). Philip Ackerman-Leist's *Rebuilding the Foodshed: How to Create Local, Sustainable, and Secure Food Systems* (Chelsea Green, 2011) also reaches beyond rah-rah rhetoric to acknowledge and illustrate the complexity of many food issues and provide pragmatic and scientifically informed recommendations. Pollan's 2010 essay "The Food Movement, Rising" (*New York Review of Books*, June 20, 2010) is a useful summary of the many facets of the food movement and how they overlap and sometimes clash. Scholarly and popular food writing increasingly "connects the dots" between food systems and other sectors; for example, see Margaret Gray's *Labor and the Locavore: The Making of a Comprehensive Food Ethic* (University of California Press, 2014).

Chapter 5 of this book points the way toward some helpful sources produced by government agencies, including a perhaps surprising number devoted to what we think of as "alternative" food systems. For example, the website of the National Agricultural Library of the U.S. Department of Agriculture includes extensive materials on organic production, including links to primary and secondary sources, oral histories, and current information for farmers and growers. ("In 2017" or "At time of publication" these materials can be found on the NAL's "Organic Production" page).

The tendency of history museums to romanticize the past is a frequent subject of criticism, often held in tension with the responsibility of the museum to edify and educate a democratic public. In addition to the works by Scott Magelssen, Warren Leon and Roy Rosenzweig, and Michael Wallace mentioned in the previous chapter's Bibliographic Note, see Stephen Weil's *Rethinking the Museum and Other Meditations* (Smithsonian Institution, 1990), Richard Handler and Eric Gable's *The New History in an Old Museum: Creating the Past at Colonial Williamsburg* (Duke University Press, 1997), James Gardner's "Contested Terrain: History, Museums and the Public," in *The Public Historian* 26:4 (Fall 2004), and Amy Tyson's *The Wages of History: Emotional Labor on Public History's Front Lines* (University of Massachusetts Press, 2013).

WORK IN PROGRESS—AN INTERVIEW WITH SEVERINE VON TSCHARNER FLEMING: GIVING OURSELVES SOME BALLAST

FIGURE 2.3 Severine von Tscharner Fleming. Photo: Lawrence Braun.

An organizer to her core, Severine von Tscharner Fleming has been an important figure within the contemporary back-to-the-land movement of new and young farmers (Figure 2.3). As founder and director of The Greenhorns, a non-profit organization dedicated to helping young farmers gain skills and find community, as well as co-founder of the National Young

(Continued)

Farmers Coalition (2010), she has played a key role in defining this as a movement at all. She practices a kind of activism that reflects the media savvy and
political sensibilities of many in her generation: decentralized, improvisational,
sharply aware of inequities and ironies, and determined to bring creativity to
bear on the daunting personal and systemic challenges that young farmers
face as they work to reinvent smaller-scale food economies or even just to
survive financially.

The Greenhorns' work draws deeply on history but in ways very different
from the approaches typically found at museums and historic sites. Starting
unapologetically from the present moment and the need to imagine "a longer
future," as she says in this interview, von Tscharner Fleming understands
the past not as a simple model or inspiration but as a vital way to ground
contemporary projects in realistic possibility. Those projects include *The
New Farmers Almanac* (published in 2013 and 2015) and two experimental
voyages connecting rural hinterlands with urban markets via wind-powered
transportation (Vermont Sail Freight in 2014 and Maine Sail Freight in 2015,
see Figure 2.3). Reflexive, curious, and keenly attuned to the ways in which
the new back-to-the-landers, like older agrarians before them, have already
seen themselves romanticized and their work depoliticized or co-opted, von
Tscharner Fleming pushes us toward a core set of questions about what it
actually means to tell "stories without endings."

*When I think about your work in relation to farming history, it strikes me that
history's in a lot of what you've done, but I think specifically of things like the* New
Farmers Almanac *and the Sail Freight voyages. What would you point to as the
most successful invocation of history out of those projects?*

I guess it really depends on how you define success. I feel like with our
cultural work, each different medium that we choose seems to attract,
engage, animate a different sub-section of our community. And I think a big
part of the reason for having such a diversity in terms of the output and forms
is that different forms and fora engage different people.

So for instance, Sail Freight is really accessible. You don't have to write
or read. You can just walk up to it. And that has meant a really interesting
cross-section of post-oil, peak-carbon people and transition-minded people.
It's meant historians, maritime history buffs, boat buffs, your general waterfront
wharf rats. It's meant art students and hipsters and just people who are at
the farmers market or passing by. It's people who are interested in pedestrian access or waterfront issues or planning issues for whom the waterfront
is this crucial access for pedestrian engagement. With the first Sail Freight,
a lot of it had to do with the diversity of products, how many value-added
products there are that are completely non-perishable and "look, we can do
this in two weeks!" And Maine Sail Freight was a lot more ambitious in terms
of our communication goals. So we're now kind of like hey, you know, let's
look at the terms of trade over the course of history, how have the terms of
trade changed, how can we look at the sailboat as an example of a colonial

technology and examine the characteristics of a colonial economy in terms of how we're exporting high volume low-value goods to be processed and creating wealth elsewhere? And how can we, in thinking about what our new economy looks like in the new farmers movement, learn our lesson in those broad seams of history and characterize what kind of an economy we're working towards and what the characteristics of that economy will be?

And the same thing with the *Almanac*. Once we have our core group up to a certain level of literacy and familiarity around the form and that this is going to be a miscellany and there's going to be historical snippets and that there's these different parts of our American agricultural history, then it feels like we can kind of iterate and go further down the rabbit hole basically, in terms of pushing the discourse frankly beyond *Animal, Vegetable, Miracle* and *Botany of Desire* and "grow organic vegetables" as this kind of win-win middle-class rhetoric.

It's a process of politicization, and the fact is we know so little history as a group, as a young generation, and then furthermore as young farmers, a lot of us are coming from environmental science backgrounds or anthropology backgrounds or English major backgrounds. We're not all coming to this with a history of land tenure and landed power or the history of colonization or the history of slavery that close to the frontal lobe.

Can you think of other examples where you encounter something in history that isn't an inspiration, but it might actually be a model for something to avoid?

Well, I think it's a pattern language. And that the purpose of historical thinking is to elongate our notion of the present and the implications of the present on the future, and to invoke, therefore, a longer future. Let's embolden ourselves with the stories of these mariners who navigated the planet with dead reckoning and recognize that opportunism—we don't have to be telepathic, we just have a little bit of foresight, and that foresight has the potential to really reward us over the longer time.

Another part of that is tuning in to—this is one of the big phrases from our project—"tune in to the logic of the landscape." So you know, those guys were shipping slaves from Africa and they were coming across on the Azores and loading up on molasses and oranges and rum and slaves in that triangle. And clearly we're not interested to do that kind of a triangle now. But the approach to geography and the winds and the trade routes and the ecology as the driver and impetus—tuning in to the logic of the landscape and of the ecological system and looking at, especially when it comes to farming, where are the most hospitable to human habitat places and then overlay on top of that, okay, so where are there commodity systems that are failing and then how can I lay over a geography of affordable land, plenty of water, likely to be a good market, other young farmers nearby, maybe a college town—then you start thinking in exactly the same way as those mariners about resettlement. And in this case it's not based on a

(Continued)

virginal continent absent of humans. It's more of a retrofit kind of a way to operate. But the thinking and the reckoning and the kind of pointing and figuring, those are crucial skills for young farmers as they're getting started.

It becomes a way of thinking that serves our survival, as young farmers, I think, but I do really see that as survival of humanity and that young farmers are expressive of and intuitive in a way that's just the beginning, I hope. I think the fact that there's all these young people who are operating outside of capitalism—well, they're inside capitalism but their motivations make more sense, like sensibility or sense of purpose or precautionary sensitivity or evolutionary sense, than they may make dollars and cents!

Can you say something about the sources or aha moments or the entry points to history for you?

Well, I'm trying to make sense of how we got here and how we might go forward, completely as a navigational tool. Here I am such an agrarian and so motivated to be in the agrarian world, and yet such a major amount of the history of agrarianism seems to be this conflict between servitude, exploitation, and producerism, and then this yeoman, slightly artificial, groovy idea that we all are into and that lives alongside that contradictory history of stealing land and slavery and exporting cotton and institutions that drove those different frameworks and what the outcomes are of different settlement patterns. What makes the U.S. different from Brazil and why did the Mexican revolution succeed and what's the character of the democracy in places where more access to land exists? And just on and on and on, all these questions like what are we shooting for? Where do we want to go? And how do we find justice vis-à-vis this intersection between humanity and ecology? Because it's not simple and it's not easy and it's confusing, and especially when you're being belittled all the time by the status quo, by the Monsanto media, essentially. And I felt like in 2009 and 2010 we were dancing around selling a story that was very simple, very rosy-cheeked, you know, happiness fits right inside a gourmet restaurant, right inside of capitalism, right inside of white power, and we were absorbed as a narrative immediately because we were able to sex it up and frame it in to that system and then you know, you get into *Vogue* and you get into the *New York Times* and you can be stylish. But obviously it's not the whole story!

And a lot of the people who are doing this work frankly have educational if not other privilege to back them up as they try to sniggle their way in with informal lease agreements and lots of dogged self-exploitation. Then there are the larger structural injustices of student loan debt and having babies and the nice person who gave them an informal lease dying and the kids wanting to cash in and gentrification and all of these factors just start playing themselves out against the magic of those young farmers and their initiative and vision and boldness and passion.

Is there anything else I should have asked you about how you use history in your work or how you think about history?

I guess a really basic one would be that a major critique of organic farming, small-scale farming, family farming, high-labor farming is that it's backward. So I think being able to really clearly articulate how it's not backward and what backward was, that we're knowledgeable and literate about backward, and which processes back then worked better than what came in-between and which phases of in-between were then discarded for other reasons. And that there were periods when there was an equivalent mania about apps except it was a mania that was to do with steam-cars. And just give ourselves some ballast.

Notes

1 "Food, in this formulation, should be good tasting and good for the health of the people who grow it and eat it. It should be clean—free of toxins and disease, and produced in a way that does not damage the environment. And it should be fair—sold at accessible prices for all consumers, and offering fair working conditions and compensation for those who produce it." "Our Philosophy," *Slow Food USA* website.

2 United States Department of Agriculture Economic Research Service, "Number of Farmers' Markets Continues to Rise," United States Department of Agriculture Publication No. AMS 173-08 (2008).

3 United States Department of Agriculture Economic Research Service, "Organic Production," United States Department of Agriculture website.

4 Consumer Reports National Research Center, "Organic Food Labels Survey," March 2014. http://greenerchoices.org/wp-content/uploads/2016/08/CR2014 OrganicFoodLabelsSurvey.pdf.

5 Ilyse D. Barkan, "History Invites Regulation: The Passage of the Pure Food and Drug Act of 1906," *American Journal of Public Health*, 75:1 (1985), 18–26.

6 Jonathan Christensen, "Four Stages of Social Movements." *EBSCO Research Starters,* EBSCO*host* (Ipswich, MA: EBSCO Publishing Service, 2009). For an intriguing parallel with two earlier eras of similarly "intersectional" social movements in which food reform played a key role, see Jeffrey Haydu, "Cultural Modeling in Two Eras of U.S. Food Protest: Grahamites (1830s) and Organic Advocates (1960s–1970s)," *Social Problems* 58:3 (August 2011), 461–487.

7 Food writer Laura Wiley's investigative series "Farm to Fable" (*Tampa Bay Times*, April 13, 2016) sent ripples through the restaurant world by exposing a number of such deceptive messages at Florida restaurants, farmers markets, and other outlets.

8 In his 2001 investigation of the fast food industry, Eric Schlosser reported "In 1970, Americans spent about $6 billion on fast food." In 2015, the National Restaurant Association projected $201 billion in "quickservice" restaurant sales (National Restaurant Association, "Positive Outlook for 2015, National Restaurant Association website," January 27, 2015; Eric Schlosser, *Fast Food Nation: The Dark Side of the American Meal* (New York: Houghton Mifflin, 2001, 3)).

9 United States Department of Agriculture Marketing Service, "Food Deserts," USDA website.

10 United States Department of Agriculture Economic Research Service, "Food Security in the U.S.," USDA website.

11 United States Department of Agriculture Economic Research Service, "Food Security Status of U.S. Households in 2013," USDA website.

12 Rachel Laudan, "A Plea for Culinary Modernism," *Jacobin*, May 22, 2015.

SECTION II

Research Foundations

3

THE TRIPLE TOP LINE

A Different Way to Think About Food and Farm History

The biggest obstacle to interpreting the history of food may be that we think we already know about it. As Chapter 1 showed, the legacies of past assumptions, ideologies, nostalgias, and reform movements have contributed to powerful narratives and images that have the ring of established truths. And these have created remarkably durable images, especially of what a farm is and how the history of food production and consumption has unfolded in different places.

The second big obstacle is that once we start thinking about it more seriously, we often realize that we actually know very little and that piecing together a better-informed sense of how we've ended up with our current industrialized food system is an immensely complicated task. This chapter works to chart a path between these two positions—the big unconscious assumptions and the challenge of seeing familiar foodscapes in different ways. We propose building an interpretation that keeps issues of *scale* front and center and that starts from a particular set of questions about *environment, economy,* and *energy.*

To help organize an interpretive approach, we suggest a "top line" narrative that can help to frame interpretation around those questions. This approach is keyed to the timeline in the Appendix and emphasizes the fundamental disjuncture between an economic system based on ideas about limitless growth and a set of physical resources—particularly agricultural lands and the other resource bases that provide our food—that are, by their very nature, limited. Many contemporary advocates of a less purely profit-driven model of economic life speak of a "triple bottom line" that takes into consideration social equity and environmental health as well as economic growth. We are advocating here that museum interpreters, educators, and exhibit designers should think about a similar "triple *top* line" when developing an interpretation of food and farming histories.

The narrative that emerges follows the same general shape as the mainstream histories with which most people are familiar. But it sets those histories on a somewhat different foundation, inviting us to see them with new eyes. To engage most actively with contemporary dialogues about food, we need an interpretive framework that clearly examines the results of food's location within three big interlocking contexts: capitalism as an economic system, industrialism as a method of production, and fossil fuel as an energy source. And we need to think hard about what that means at the very different scales of production and consumption that make up our food system.

While this chapter aims to set out a useable framework for rethinking food and farm history, it also recognizes that even more than most histories, this one is very much in the process of being pieced together, in dialogue with many kinds of people listed in the previous chapter—food producers, advocates, consumers, researchers, environmentalists, policy makers—who are working to rethink our collective relationship with land, food, energy, and each other. Public historians and museum interpreters have much to offer in this process: ways of considering the available evidence about the past, an ability to frame good critical questions, and skill at moving often-fragmentary historical materials into an accessible narrative shape. But the point here is less about creating finished, authoritative knowledge than about finding ways to share our processes of inquiry with others who are grappling in real time with the same big questions. The gaps in our own knowledge and the challenges of overcoming them may actually be an asset in this case. They provide opportunities for public historians and museum interpreters not only to model skills, but also to see our work as part of a collective effort at addressing urgent social and environmental questions.

The Mainstream Narrative

Here is the outline of the big story about food that we think we know. It begins with the very long time span of human life on the planet and narrows to the U.S., particularly the northeast, the region of the U.S. where small-scale farming first "declined" and therefore where a great deal of effort has been expended to understand, defend, and revitalize it.

Humans have been around for more than 200,000 years, and for the vast majority of that time they have subsisted by hunting wild animals and gathering wild plants. The question of when, why, where, and how people began intentionally cultivating and domesticating wild species is a fundamental one for archeologists and anthropologists, and it is far from settled. But current research suggests that agriculture developed in a number of places around the world starting about 12,000 years ago and that it spread from at least ten independent centers of development, the earliest being in the Middle East, eastern China, Mesoamerica, and Polynesia.[1] Although cause-and-effect relationships are difficult to pinpoint, it seems clear that farming is historically linked with expanding populations, increasingly sedentary settlement patterns, and specialized, often hierarchical social and political arrangements. More complex food systems, in other words, have long been linked with changes in the scale on which humans live.

By the Middle Ages, 700 or 800 years ago, the dominant form of subsistence in Europe consisted of mixed-crop cultivation and animal husbandry within a generally feudal system of land ownership, a model that diffused around the world as Europeans began to build colonial empires after the sixteenth century. Just as important, *ideas* about this kind of agricultural society—the link between individual land ownership and political power, the notion of the natural world as a resource to be exploited by human ingenuity, an emphasis on intensive productivity and a particular kind of work-discipline, and a kinship system that gendered farmers and landholders as male and passed along land through the male line—spread with European colonialism. In sometimes-contradictory ways, those ideas contributed to the building of settler societies like those in North America. Settlers' aspirations toward land ownership sometimes helped fuel anti-colonial and democratic movements, while the monopoly on landholding by males of European descent helped suppress other models of agriculture and subsistence, particularly those of indigenous and enslaved people who had long practiced a flexible and effective mix of hunting, gathering, farming, and food preservation tailored to their particular environments and climates. In the pre-Contact era, agriculture was embraced unevenly by different indigenous groups, but even where it was widespread and sophisticated, it was widely misunderstood by colonizers because its cyclical, seasonal, lineage-based patterns of settlement and occupation were so radically different from that of the Europeans.

By the start of the nineteenth century, the main components of today's dominant agricultural system were becoming established in much of North America and certainly in the northeastern U.S.: northern-European-style farming within an economic system increasingly driven by market-oriented considerations and pushed by the new tools, desires, and expectations of industrialism. Colonial American farmers were never as fully self-sufficient as our nostalgic images of them have sometimes led us to believe.[2] But until the early nineteenth century, farmers' decision-making about crops and prices was shaped far more by immediate and local factors (like weather and personal relationships) than by what more distant markets would bear. By the time more commercial markets began to come to the fore in the early nineteenth century, however, agriculture was already a maturing rather than an expanding sector in the northeast. Small-scale, locally or regionally oriented farming seemed slow and unproductive by comparison with the heightened efficiency and economic opportunity of industrial production, prompting many younger people to go into industry, seek larger farms along the advancing western frontier, or at the very least embrace the logic and methods of the new industrial economy (Figure 3.1).[3]

The familiar narrative about older farming areas in the American northeast is that they fell into decline once farmers moved west to larger, more fertile

FIGURE 3.1 Narratives about progress and decline helped to construct both anxiety and nostalgia around small farms in the American northeast starting quite early in the nineteenth century. For many people over the past 200 years, a sight such as the much-photographed Jenne Farm in Reading, Vermont, invokes a simpler bygone era and masks continuities and adaptations within the region's farm economy. Image: Jitze Couperus.

farms. The case of New England gives us a useful way to see this dominant narrative in action. The taken-for-granted history of New England is that its soils are generally poor and rocky, which led ambitious farmers to move, often after tapping out the limited fertility of their original farms and leaving behind an iconic landscape of old stone walls running through the newer-growth forest that has reclaimed formerly cleared hillsides. This familiar story isn't entirely untrue—New England *did* lose farmland and farmers over the course of the nineteenth and twentieth centuries—but it's not entirely true, either. The region's soils are mixed, but acre for acre, its farms are actually among the most productive in the country—just on a smaller scale.[4] In fact, New England's overall farm production actually increased right through the nineteenth century, not peaking until 1910.[5] But a closer reading of the historical record shows that farmers in the region have continued to farm productively and worked to maintain the fertility of their land as best they could. Starting about 200 years ago, though, they were doing it within an economy that increasingly demanded more productivity and seemed to provide the tools to achieve it.

Westward expansion and increasing industrialization and productivity make up, to a very large extent, the familiar mainstream story that is told about the

American food system. That story is interwoven with the history of farm policy, which will be explored in Chapter 4, and it helped create the nostalgia for older, smaller-scale kinds of farming that we have already seen as a contributing factor to the ways in which agriculture tends to be presented at historic sites. Farms got larger and more specialized; management of food production became more scientific and interlinked with large-scale markets; yields were increased through new technologies and human-made "inputs"; canals, railroads, and finally trucks and airplanes helped expand food markets and networks of distribution as the age of muscle power gave way to steam and then to the petroleum that dominates not only transportation but many aspects of how we live—and eat—today. In the Cold War decades of the mid-twentieth century, this cluster of methods went global, giving rise to what has been termed the "Green Revolution." For humanitarian, economic, and geopolitical reasons, many non-industrialized countries adopted the technologies of high-input industrialized farming, exponentially increasing yields and helping establish a framework for the globalized food markets that exist today.

The overall movement toward higher productivity and longer-distance food systems is also intercut with countless examples of people resisting the logic of large-scale, market-driven agriculture. But over time, the "alternatives" have repeatedly failed to carry the day. In the U.S., as elsewhere, indigenous groups have fought largely unsuccessful battles to hold onto their foraging, hunting, and farming territories. Nineteenth and early twentieth century agricultural "improvers" and reformers advocated for small farmers to adopt new scientific methods and approaches, without recognizing how these were already changing the rules of the game so that farming on a small scale was less and less viable. Activism and political movements sparked by farmer resistance, perhaps most notably in the "Populist" fervor of the late nineteenth century, have tended to founder on the big question of whether capitalism needs to be rejected or merely reformed. In the South, both white champions of small-scale agriculture and black farmers struggling to stay on the land were ultimately undone by markets and policies—including price supports for commodity agriculture and soil-conservation measures that reclaimed "submarginal" land from farming—favoring more industrialized pro-duction. Small-scale foodways have often been relegated to the status of curiosities, encountered by mainstream diners only at cultural festivals or urban ethnic restaurants. Seemingly radical ideas from the early twentieth century, like the "organic" approach proposed by Sir Albert Howard, actually drew on deep peasant farming traditions from Europe, Asia, and elsewhere, but these remained on the fringes until the more comprehensive environmentalism and neo-agrarianism of the 1960s and 1970s. Even now that it has been more widely embraced, the logic of industrialism and capitalist markets has made itself felt: the mainstreaming of organic food has been dubbed "big organic" by critics who see it as merely a somewhat kinder, gentler version of industrialized commodity farming.[6]

By the turn of the twenty-first century, the dominant system seemed to have become "too big to fail." It is supported on every side by policy, infrastructure,

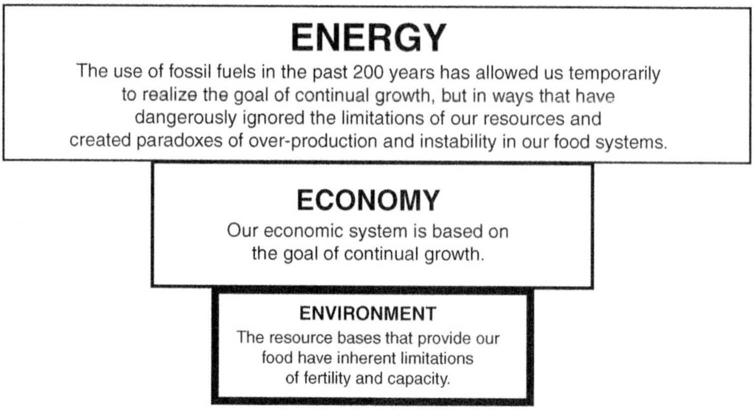

FIGURE 3.2   A "triple top line" interpretive framework shows the links among an inherently limited resource base, an economy based on growth, and an energy source that has allowed for a spectacular but temporary and dangerous era of expansion.

the advertising industry, learned habits of convenience and mobility, and a long history of efforts to provide safe, abundant, and affordable food for all. The story that we know is essentially a winners' version: technological improvements and efficiencies trumped less-effective methods, creating winners and losers along the path to a modern, reliable food system (Figure 3.2).

A Counter-Narrative

Today's food movement may represent the most extensive moment yet of questioning the "too big to fail" and "get big or get out" logic of that system. The contemporary movement draws on earlier critiques and alternatives but also on an ever-greater body of evidence about the environmental, social, and economic costs of industrialism, especially how the greenhouse gases it pumps into the earth's atmosphere are destabilizing the global climate. Our massive, heavily capitalized and subsidized, technologically sophisticated food system—hugely dependent on fossil fuels and responsible for enormous amounts of greenhouse gas emission—may have become too big to survive rather than too big to fail, threatening our survival rather than ensuring it.[7] This brings us back to the shift in viewpoint that is the starting point for this book. We are proposing that public historical interpretation of food and farming should be based in a counter-history of agriculture that can speak directly to the impulses and questions of audiences who are recognizing those problems and seeing food as one important way to start addressing them.

   This counter-history retells the familiar story of agricultural expansion and technological progress from a different angle. This is not just the historian's usual response of "Well, it's actually more complicated than that." Rather, it places the whole narrative on a different foundation and questions the consequences of many aspects of modernity, industrialism, capitalism, and fossil fuel use. Questioning them does not mean discounting them entirely or denying that they have produced many advantages for humans, but it lets us see these big contexts more clearly and avoid the trap of assuming they are inevitable and unchangeable. It takes a longer view of short-term gains and asks about their longer-term consequences. And it calls attention to the expansive impulses at the heart of the modern world and the way those impulses have been linked with ever more sophisticated technologies and ever more ambitious projects (like "ending hunger" and "feeding the world").

The counter-narrative helps uncouple farming from ideas about both progress and civilization, on the one hand, and purity and naturalness, on the other, that have historically been attached to it, and have proven to be powerful—and deeply contradictory—in Western imaginations. It calls into question not just dominant model of food production but the whole human-centric way of understanding the non-human world it is built on. It upends the hierarchy that puts people at the top of the food chain, with mammals a little lower, cold-blooded animals and plants lower yet, and micro-organisms barely present in the model except as problems to be eradicated. And it exposes the very uneven ways in which the benefits of industrial agriculture have been and continue to be distributed, even within well-meaning attempts to address those inequities.

The counter-narrative also presents food production as a much more collaborative venture among humans and other species, in which visible and charismatic creatures like draft horses and baby lambs are much less central than pollinators or the microbial beings that enable soil fertility as well as processes like digestion and fermentation. From this perspective, the scientific agriculture of the past two centuries is not so much a triumph of human inventiveness as a sudden loss of knowledge about how to assist and work within the cycles of growth and regeneration already happening all around us. These cycles are extraordinarily complex in their details but quite simple in their broad outline: nutrients move from one form to another, produced by the breaking down of matter and consumed by growing plants as well as by animals and people. Food production, in this view, produces food for far more species than just humans and the animals that humans eat.

By becoming overly reliant on imported nutrients of any kind—but particularly in the form of potent human-produced, fossil-fuel-based fertilizers—farmers break that cycle of nutrient exchange and ultimately weaken the capacity of their land to support growth without increasing levels of intervention. As soil grows less fertile, farmers need to import more and more nutrients, creating another cycle that is interwoven with indebtedness and new vulnerabilities (for example, the need for human-made pesticides and genetically modified species to fight off pests that the soil and plants themselves are no longer robust enough to resist). As other food sources like fisheries become unreliable due to over harvesting, ocean acidification, and climatic changes, we are beginning to see the same cycle repeating itself on marine vegetable and fish farms.

This artificial-nutrient cycle is also intimately connected with an economic one set in motion by the shift to commercialized and mechanized food production. In the American northeast, that shift began around 1800, linked to the rise of industry and new capital markets that continued to expand to national and now global scales. The feedback loop in this cycle goes like this: New technologies and the opening of new and initially more fertile land enabled farmers to achieve greater efficiencies and higher yields, while expanding markets in cities provided them with more customers for their products. The combination had the effect of driving prices down, something consumers welcomed. But lower prices meant farmers had to produce more in order to stay solvent, which prompted them to embrace yet more technological fixes, which helped increase yield even further and ultimately lowered prices even more. By the late nineteenth century, many American farmers were already chasing a receding horizon of profitability and struggling with what R. Douglas Hurt has called the "problems of plenty." If farmers wanted to stay competitive in regional and national markets, they could no longer charge enough to cover their own costs of production.

The chapter on policy will show how government intervention has repeatedly attempted to offset the effects of this cycle of over-production and falling prices by trying to bring supply and demand into balance (for example, through price subsidies to farmers or buying up some of the surplus food that is an inherent byproduct of the industrial system). But even during the New Deal era, when federal agricultural policy tried to address the worst effects of over exploited land and risky commodity markets, few voices advocated for actually reversing the trend that led to larger scale and more mechanization. By that point, and especially as oil became America's dominant energy source by the middle decades of the century, food production and distribution were big business, with the interwoven petroleum, chemical, transportation, equipment, processing, distribution, and advertising industries working to protect and extend their stake in what was for them a highly profitable sector. Individual farmers, even those who still attempt to operate within this very large-scale system, have seen their own share of the profits continue to erode. That has contributed in turn to the cycle of farmers leaving the land, children not following their parents into farming, and the remaining landowners swallowing neighboring farms and becoming even larger and more specialized and mechanized—and more heavily indebted—as they pursue that ever-receding horizon. It is difficult to say yet whether the current food movement will amount to a serious challenge to this pattern, but the cyclical nature of the challenges it faces—and the collapse or co-opt of so many earlier attempts at reform and reinvention—are crucial pieces of the historical story that public history can bring more fully into contemporary settings. In a nutshell (and as the diagram in Figure 3.2 shows), the triple top line narrative we advocate in this book can be summarized as follows.

- The resources of land, sea, and non-human species that provide our food have inherent limitations of fertility and regenerative capacity, which many modes of food production have successfully worked within for millennia.
- However, with the advent and expansion of capitalism as an economic system starting around 500 years ago, those limitations came into tension with the assumption that a healthy economy was one that could continue to expand and become more profitable indefinitely.

- There was a general balance between environmental limitation and economic growth until the start of the fossil fuel era about 200 years ago. At that point, humans began to access vast reserves of carbon-based energy that had been accumulated over hundreds of millions of years. This windfall seemed to promise that endless economic growth could actually be achieved by injecting exponentially more energy into systems—including food systems— that had necessarily been smaller until then. Fossil-fueled expansion made another huge leap when a petroleum-based economy started to become the norm worldwide after World War II.
- In our own time we are seeing growing evidence of sweeping changes in the world's climate as well as economic and political instabilities often sparked by shrinking resources and widening inequalities. More and more people are connecting the dots of environment, economy, and energy and questioning the long-term effects of changes that seemed to make sense in the short term. And as they search for ways to answer those questions, more and more people are beginning with food (Figure 3.3).

FIGURE 3.3   As more people confront the staggering amounts of waste in our industrial food system, "food rescue" and gleaning projects like City Harvest in New York City increasingly work to divert unsold food to hungry people. Historians can help add depth to discussions about the many problems of scale, including the counter-intuitive relationship between overproduction and food insecurity. Image: U.S. Department of Agriculture.

All About Scale

In thinking about how to interpret food history in public, it seems important not to let our own questions and accounts be absorbed into the dominant narrative and the profit-driven logic that it embodies. It is also important to acknowledge that not everything about modern industrial food production is detrimental and that there is no single perfect model for farming in a way that harmonizes fully with the natural world. Agriculture itself is invasive and artificial, whether practiced on a small or large scale. But that question of scale is paramount. Industrial capitalism's tendencies toward over production and consolidation were kept in check to some extent in the era of muscle, wind, and steam power because it was not yet possible to move and store most kinds of food over long distances. The pollution and waste endemic to today's system occurred much less, or not at all, at smaller scales. The established European model of farming, with its assumptions of human superiority and emphasis on cultivating land as intensively as possible, was exported through colonialism and expanded as industrialism and capitalist markets developed, but it was turbo-charged by petroleum, and it has in turn contributed a good deal to the spike in greenhouse gas emissions over the course of the past century.

This is the basic fact that the contemporary food movement works to address, and in many ways, that work is all about scale. As more people come to realize the problems and vulnerabilities inherent in the very large systems that developed over the course of the twentieth century, a common response has been to try to shorten the distance from source to plate and bring more transparency into the processes of getting there. A previous generation of food and farm activists focused largely on organic methods, but by the turn of the twenty-first century, organic, too, had become big business, fully a part of the industrial food system rather than a true alternative to it. By the first decade of the twenty-first century, "eat local" was the new rallying cry for people attempting to create true alternatives, with local food widely seen as emblematic of freshness, shorter supply chains, smaller carbon footprints, and more ethical production and consumption based on an awareness of relationship and seasonality rather than purely commodified transactions.

But localness, like nearly everything else about food and farming, proves to be a slippery concept when we look at it more closely. For one thing, it's difficult to draw precise boundaries around "local," especially when it comes to the logistics of providing "local food" to large numbers of people. Suburban growth around most modern cities has taken much of the farmland that supplied urban food markets before automobiles became dominant in the mid-twentieth century, and the need to cover longer distances now adds copious "food miles" to products from small-scale producers in more distant hinterlands. Meanwhile, even dedicated "locavores" resist giving up some non-local foods. In the "Global North," this has been particularly true of coffee, tea, chocolate, and tropical fruit. Meanwhile, many parts of the "Global South" that produce those foods are also the source for the many migrant farmworkers whose low-wage labor is nearly as prevalent in the local-food sector as in mainstream industrial agriculture. Local food economies are often assumed to operate separately from larger ones, but that assumption masks the many ways that smaller scales are tangled in the same wider circuits of labor and exchange that local-food advocates are trying to escape or reform.

A second big problem with the emphasis on localness is that the hyper-local "foodsheds" many locavores have envisioned as the way of the future seldom existed even in the past. Even if they had, they don't necessarily offer the best or most realistic model for a future that includes a much larger and more urbanized population, a very different kind of economy and society, and a rapidly changing climate. Even in colonial America, most farmers were not the entirely self-sufficient homesteaders we sometimes imagine.[8] That image was constructed, in part, for strategic or ideological reasons. For example, Thomas Jefferson extolled the virtues of the yeoman farmer as part of a defense of his particular vision of American democracy, a theme that New England champions of agriculture picked up in the pre-Civil-War years as they tried to stem population loss and argue for the importance of free (rather than enslaved) agricultural labor. The image was refined and reshaped by later ideas about farming, which were sometimes romanticized or nostalgic but just as often pragmatic, aiming to show the value of modernizing and experimenting with new crops, markets, and techniques.

As people in today's food movement gain experience and think through issues of scale more thoroughly, a focus on regionally scaled food systems seems to be gaining favor, superseding the earlier intense focus on "100-mile diets" and visions of wholly self-sufficient towns and homesteads. This emerging region-based vision perhaps more closely mirrors the actual scale of pre-World War II food systems and offers a particularly useful point of connection with interpretations of past food issues.[9]

So scale is very much an open question for the contemporary food movement. In many places, "the local" is being scaled up and integrated into larger systems, but it is hard to know what the most economically and environmentally "sustainable" scope might eventually be and how they might differ from region to region. How can re-scaled systems avoid following the same logics of intensification and consolidation—so clearly shown in the rapid rise of "big organic"—that have led us to the dominant industrial model? This is not a merely logistical or economic question. Those processes have historically been driven by the powerful urge toward growth, expansion, and "advancement" inherent in modern thinking. The whole notion of "scaling back" or "scaling down" in a serious way runs counter to the way most modern people assume the world should work. The idea of living at a smaller scale may lose its appeal when consumers realize it means sacrificing much of the convenience, stability, affordability, and variety that our globalized industrial food system has led us to expect. It's one thing to choose local tomatoes in season at a farmers market, but something quite different to accept that some foods are *only* going to be available seasonally (or not at all). Resistance to scaling down is also driven by worry that only large-scale industrial food systems are capable of "feeding the world," a globally scaled idea that is related to perfectly justifiable human fears of hunger and scarcity. Advocates of scaled-down food systems must find ways to contend with public tastes, desires, fears, and assumptions that often run very deep.

This is one of the places where history can help. Just because we once ate more regionally in most parts of the U.S. does not mean we can—or should—simply return to that particular scale of food production and consumption. Nor does it mean that knowledge about past food systems holds any straightforward lessons about this (or any other topic) for the present and the future. But our work as interpreters of history does offer at least two big benefits to current attempts at re-scaling.

First, we have data about how pre-petroleum-revolution food systems worked and how people operated within them. We can never know exactly how food tasted in the past or precisely how people felt and thought about it. But we have many clues, as well as skills that let us build larger contexts for the often fragmentary data the historical record presents. Here is one example: In the fall of 1853, a country doctor named Lucius Cook wrote a letter to his local newspaper describing his great success in growing carrots on three-quarters of an acre in the small western Massachusetts town of Wendell. His letter was subsequently reprinted in *The New England Farmer*, one of countless American journals devoted to the improvement of agriculture in the mid-nineteenth century. Digitized a century and a half later, it appeared in a Google search for "Wendell farmers" and provided a nugget of information for a local history project that was trying to construct a new genealogy for today's food movement based on a "triple top line," scale-focused re-reading of the region's agricultural history.[10] The time period—the middle of the nineteenth century, when the manufacturing economy was beginning to siphon off workers and enthusiasm around New England—and Lucius Cook's identity as a doctor—a member of the town's very small professional population—both suggest that Cook was attempting to demonstrate to his rural neighbors that there was wisdom in scaling up and becoming more specialized in their farm production. Although we don't know anything more about his agricultural activities (except that he had previously failed to turn a profit with two previous crops of turnips), it is not hard to locate him within the very widespread movement to shore up the farming sector and bring Yankee farmers more actively into the economy of a new century.

A second advantage for today's public historians is that we have the benefit of hindsight, which lets us see and assess consequences that people of the past could not. In the tidbit about Lucius Cook's carrots, for example, we can hear echoes of local and regional debates about whether small farmers should pursue new techniques and ambitions. Between the lines of Cook's celebration of his bumper crop, we can sense the silent presence of the skeptical or resistant neighbors he was probably trying to convince of the wisdom of pursuing more commercially oriented, less diversified farming. Our hindsight allows us to see that they were perfectly right to be skeptical and that Cook was over optimistic about their ability to flourish in ever larger markets. But we can also see that he and other "improvers" were not mindless modernizers. Rather, they were people genuinely concerned about the economic and civic health of the places they lived. This hindsight doesn't lead toward any firm conclusions about a perfect scale or solution. But it lets us look at both past and present more carefully, with a sense of what the stakes and outcomes have historically been in aiming toward particular levels of growth or economic scale.

Closer attention to the nuances of these kinds of debates over time shows that the supposed decline of New England and northeastern agriculture was a much slower, more uneven, contested, and incomplete process than is commonly supposed. In fact, its period of sharpest decline wasn't actually until after World War II, when interstate highways, larger supermarkets, sprawling suburbs, and other developments that came with the expansion of the fossil-fuel-powered economy at mid-century really ate into both the available farmland and small farmers' ability to turn a profit. This is not a simple tale of loss but a more complex story of continual and often highly successful adaptation and engagement with market demands and changing energy sources.

Like a good deal of the discussion about contemporary food issues, this strategy approaches scale as an open question and challenges the idea that the most desirable food system is the one that runs most efficiently at the largest scale. But it doesn't necessarily reject larger-scale or longer-distance food production out of hand. Interpreting food history in this more critical light can help us see more clearly the cases where it may in fact make more sense to opt for economies of scale—for example, to trade specialized crops between regions or countries as has been happening since the colonial period. But it also helps us to see where the race toward ever greater efficiency and yield has worked against farmers and other producers, creating "problems of plenty" and an endlessly receding horizon of profitability. This perspective can allow us to tell a much more complex story that offers many points of connection with today's rescaling efforts.

Those two skills—trying to understand how things looked and were experienced in the past while using our longer perspective to think critically about causes and consequences—are the historian's stock in trade, and museum interpreters and public historians often already do them very well. We don't have to become advocates for a particular cause or project in order to participate in discussions about rescaling contemporary food systems. We just need to find ways to attach our interpretations to these ongoing and open-ended projects that already encompass a good deal of discussion about local and regional economies, cultures, histories, and "sense of place"—all topics that are also central to the work of public history and museums. To conclude this chapter, we offer two examples of complex questions that can be rendered more approachable by a focus on how the scale of our food system has expanded over time.

Talking About Scale (I): Cows and Carbon

One frequently heard criticism of the industrial food system—and its historical partner, the Western diet—is that far too much land, water, and grain are devoted to raising meat, particularly beef cattle. Manure run-off from CAFOs and emissions of methane and nitrous oxide caused by conventional cattle farming are now widely recognized as contributing to many environmental problems including water pollution and greenhouse gas production, while a diet heavy in red meat contributes to a range of health problems in humans. Vegetarian and vegan reformers argue that it would be far better for us, for other species, and for the planet if people stopped eating meat.

While it's certainly true that a "Supersize Me"-style menu of non stop fast food burgers isn't likely to improve anyone's health, the questions around meat are more complex than the all-or-nothing position of many anti-meat-eating activists. At smaller scales and on the kinds of grass pasture that cows are naturally adapted to eat, manure is an invaluable fertilizer rather than a toxic waste. At that scale, the methane produced by cows belching is readily reabsorbed by grasses that convert it to nutrients. In places where there is limited soil fertility, pasturing cows and other ruminants has long been a crucial way for humans to turn plants—particularly grasses, which people aren't able to digest—to nutritious food, essentially by using animals as a middle step. Grazing animals also trample grass (which is carbon-based) deep into the ground, further helping fertilize the land but also moving carbon out of the atmosphere and sequestering it in the soil, which has a much greater capacity to store it. This additional benefit—what some are now calling "carbon farming"—is sparking greater interest within efforts to slow or mitigate climate change. As farmers struggle to defend small-scale livestock practices in parts of the world where industrialized food is still gaining a foothold or to relearn them in places where it is well established, animals are often a crucial component in cycling nutrients, maintaining productive farmland, and perhaps moderating the climate as well.[11]

There are certainly other philosophical and even spiritual arguments to be made against eating animals. But many of the most commonly cited issues are actually problems of scale rather than problems with meat *per se.*

Talking About Scale (II): Hunger and Waste

It can be difficult to absorb the idea that many of the stubborn problems in the industrial food system are actually caused by over production and over abundance rather than by shortage. We see the realities of hunger and unequal access to healthy food in our own communities; we hear stories of farmers struggling to stay on their land; the logical assumption is that scarcity is somehow at the root of these problems. Yet many people are also aware of the staggering levels of food waste in our system, a fact that clashes with the perception and reality of lack.[12] It can be difficult to accept that the same system that provides such a highly varied, affordable, and seemingly secure food supply at the supermarket simultaneously produces tremendous waste, actual deprivation for some people, and an insoluble puzzle for farmers unable to recoup enough to meet their costs of production.

Food insecurity and agricultural over production are strangely twinned within our industrial food system. The triple top line approach can help to clarify how they came to be so closely paired, particularly after the Great Depression. That was the decade in which the internal contradictions of a capitalist and increasingly industrialized food system became starkly visible to millions of people. With the free market in free fall but farmers already producing as much as they possibly could in an attempt to stay ahead of ever lower prices, the U.S. was treated to the spectacle of food producers throwing away products they couldn't sell even as streets were filled with hungry people lining up for free food—what one observer caustically called "breadlines knee-deep in wheat."[13]

Outrage over this juxtaposition was partly responsible for federal food assistance programs becoming linked with programs designed to keep farmers afloat. Hunger and over production are two problems that help to solve each other—or at least to mask deeper questions about what happens once an industrial capitalist food system reaches a certain scale. Those questions can be unsettling, and thinking them through requires a willingness to re-examine the nature of our economy itself. If food waste is mostly a result of the enormous scale at which we're attempting to feed ourselves, why has so much more effort historically gone into producing more food even more efficiently than into rescaling the system or recapturing the waste within it? Are food pantries, community meals, and food rescue efforts enough, or do these projects—laudable and indeed essential as they are for addressing the immediate problems of hunger—continue to obscure the contradictions that were perhaps easier to see when they first sprang into visibility during the Depression? Historical thinking contains no neat answers to these big puzzles, but it can help to lay bare the steps along the way to the perplexing situation that so many producers and eaters struggle with in the present.

Bibliographic Note

The scholarly literature on the history of agriculture, industrial and otherwise, is enormous and growing quickly. One very serviceable general account of American farming is R. Douglas Hurt's *American Agriculture: A Brief History* (Iowa State University Press, 1994), which includes chronological discussions of different regions of the U.S.. Hurt shows, although sometimes between the lines, how the industrialization and commercialization of farming has led to many of the big problems that the contemporary food movement works to address. Hurt's *Problems of Plenty: The American Farmer in the Twentieth Century* (Ivan R. Dee, 2002) traces the origins of those problems in more detail. For a more pointed critique, the works of Wendell Berry are still compelling and cogent; his 1979 essay "Energy in Agriculture" (in *Bringing It to the Table: On Farming and Food*, Counterpoint, 2009) is a pithy statement about the effect of fossil fuels on agricultural production. Paul Conklin's *A Revolution Down on the Farm: The Transformation of American Agriculture since 1929* (University Press of Kentucky, 2009) and Deborah Fitzgerald's *Every Farm a Factory: The Industrial Ideal in American Agriculture* (Yale University Press, 2010) chronicle the effects of the shift into a highly industrialized agriculture in the U.S.. Harvey Levenstein's books on food history, *Paradox of Plenty: A Social History of Eating in Modern America* (University of California Press, 2003, covering the period from 1880 to 1930) and *Revolution at the Table: The Transformation of the American Diet* (University of California Press, 2003, covering 1930 to the 1990s) offer a densely packed and readable history of the demand side of American food systems.

Beyond these specific historical accounts, there is a broader scholarly and activist critique of our big assumptions about both agriculture and modernity, shaped very much by the insights of Michel Foucault and others who have tried to see outside those assumptions. One good starting place for experimenting with this way of thinking is Anna Tsing's essay "Unruly Edges: Mushrooms as Companion Species," which somewhat playfully proposes a fungi-centered history of agriculture, colonialism, and racial/gender relationships (in *Environmental Humanities* 2012, available online). Works from the field of "Big History" (for example, by David Christian, Fred Spier, and Cynthia Stokes) similarly seek to expand our frameworks for thinking about human and ecological histories and help to put the very recent development of industrial capitalism into perspective. One work that fits between the grand scale of ecological time and the more recent history of Euro-American agriculture is Richard Manning's *Against the Grain: How Agriculture has Hijacked Civilization* (North Point Press, 2005), which questions the costs and benefits of agriculture, particularly in forms centered around cereal crops like corn and wheat. Extending this critical approach in many directions are the many popular books by activists and "food movement" authors like Wes Jackson, Anna Lappé, Marion Nestle, Michael Pollan, Vandana Shiva, and many others.

On questions of scale, David Bell and Gill Valentine's *Consuming Geographies: We Are Where We Eat* (Routledge, 1997) is a still-valuable source from the late 1990s that examines food issues at various scales from the individual to the global. Bell and Valentine touch on the use of the term "glocal," coined by Roland Robertson, to push back against the idea of the global as a big homogenizing force and the local as a small particularizing one. "Glocalness" is one way of expressing the now-commonly accepted scholarly idea that globalness and localness are intimately intertwined and continually act on each other.

We can trace the "mainstreaming" of local food through publications like the March 2007 issue of *Time* magazine, whose cover declared "Forget Organic. Eat Local." Books like *Animal, Vegetable, Miracle: A Year of Food Life* (Barbara Kingsolver, Harper Perennial, 2009) and *The Town That Food Saved: How One Community Found Vitality in Local Food* (Ben Hewitt, Rodale Books, 2001) captured the new enthusiasm for the hyper local. Almost as quickly, there began to be a questioning and refining of the term and its application. *Choices*

("The Magazine of Food, Farm, and Resource Issues" from the Agricultural and Applied Economics Association) published a 2010 theme issue on "Local Food—Perceptions, Prospects, and Policies," which sets out some of the main questions in a useful way and asks how localness intersects with other scales, particularly those of the state and the region. Drake Bennett's July 22, 2007 article "The Localvore's Dilemma" in the *Boston Globe* is another good summary of the complexities of industrial, organic, and local food choices.

Much recent scholarly and popular writing on food touches on issues of scale in one way or another. Several of the works mentioned in the bibliographic note to the previous chapter are also relevant here, particularly Hurt's *Problems of Plenty.* James McWilliams' *A Revolution in Eating: How the Quest for Food Shaped America* (Columbia University Press, 2005) examines the emergence of regional foodways in colonial America and makes an argument that increasingly abundant food supplies were crucial to the formation of a specifically American political consciousness by supporting expanded and vigorous populations and fostering cross-regional trade of surplus foods. Margaret Gray's *Labor and the Locavore: The Making of a Comprehensive Food Ethic* (University of California Press, 2014) exposes the largely invisible presence of migrant farmworkers within the local food realm, while Julie Guthman's work, especially *Agrarian Dreams: The Paradox of Organic Farming in California* (University of California Press, 2004), explores the problematic "scaling up" of formerly small-scale alternative ways of producing and selling food. In *Stuffed and Starved: The Hidden Battle for the World Food System* (Melville House, 2012), Raj Patel shows how the big paradoxes of over production have also been "scaled up" to the global level, making "hunger, abundance and obesity…more compatible on our planet than they've ever been" (11).

WORK IN PROGRESS—AN INTERVIEW WITH BRIAN DONAHUE: RETHINKING THE BACKSTORY

FIGURE 3.4 Brian Donahue.

(Continued)

Brian Donahue has created a unique niche for himself as someone who operates with equal competence in the worlds of hands-on farming, historical scholarship, and land policy and advocacy (Figure 3.4). He dropped out of college in the 1970s to learn to be a farmer, and in 1980 was one of the co-founders of Land's Sake in Weston, Massachusetts, a non-profit community farm that was the subject of his first book, *Reclaiming the Commons: Community Farms and Forests in a New England Town* (Yale University Press, 1999). He also worked as Director of Education at The Land Institute in Kansas. When he eventually returned to Brandeis University to finish his B.A., M.A., and Ph.D., he focused his research on the New England farm landscape over time, producing careful studies of the Concord area that became not only a multi-award-winning book—*The Great Meadow: Farmers and the Land in Colonial Concord* (Yale University Press, 2005)—but also an important component of planning for the restoration of a Revolutionary-era agrarian landscape at Minute Man National Historical Park. He currently teaches American Environmental Studies at Brandeis.

A key component of Donahue's work over the past decade has been his involvement in two important regional studies of past, present, and possible future land use: *Wildlands and Woodlands: A Vision for the Future of the Massachusetts Forest* (Harvard Forest, 2005) and *A New England Food Vision: Healthy Food for All, Sustainable Farming and Fishing, Thriving Communities* (Food Solutions New England, University of New Hampshire, 2014). Written to be accessible to a wide audience, rooted in careful consideration of land use and food production in the region over time, and cognizant of the many conversations going on around issues of economic and environmental justice, climate change, housing, and labor as they relate to food, these two studies offer an intriguing parallel to the kind of engaged interpretation we are calling for in this book. In this interview, he discusses the permeability of the business/education line in the relationship between historic sites and farmers.

We're trying to bridge a couple of things with this project. One is this incredibly slow, meticulous, lifelong project of learning about history and building historical knowledge about farms, about forestry, all of that stuff. And then the urgency of environmentalism and activism and concern about changing climate.

I would say that I'm not sure how urgent things are. I mean, it feels urgent and we feel like we need to make change and do things, but of course we've been at this long enough to see a couple of go-arounds on this. Everyone who came of age in the 1970s and remembers what that was all about, and then to see it all go quiescent—by "it" meaning, you know, back to the land, growing more local food, and getting more energy locally and all that stuff, to see that fade away for a couple of decades and then come back in some ways so strong—yes, there's a great urgency to it, but on the other hand you do have to take the long view. And when people ask how this is all going to happen and what needs to happen now, in the next five years—I don't know! Who could have predicted in 1979 or 1980 that all of a sudden the price of oil would collapse and all the urgency would go away? And who could have predicted in the mid-1990s, late 1990s, that all of a sudden local food would become mainstream, at least conceptually mainstream, even though that's not how all our food is grown, obviously. But still, it's now a concept that it's not just a bunch of hippies and health food people. And that was unpredictable!

Thinking about where we interject history into that, and especially historical scholarship and the kind of very fine-grained work that you've done in Concord, where does that fit in relation to discussions about policy and change?

At a kind of intellectual framing level in terms of the stories we tell, in terms of large lessons that we can take from the past of farming, say, in New England and the way the land has been treated, I think there are several big messages. One large lesson is that farmers are not people who just despoil land. That's a very deep strain in conservationist thinking, going all the way back to the agricultural improvers of the nineteenth century, that your common everyday farmer didn't know what they were doing and were basically wrecking the land. They were under some constraints, sure they made some mistakes, but they were maybe more sustainable and cared more for their land than they've typically been given credit for in academic and scholarly circles.

The second big lesson in New England is, I do believe, that that side of farmers' nature was always in tension with strong market demands and aspirations to succeed economically and become part of the middle class, and then just the imperatives of the market once you're enmeshed in it. And that that is often quite destructive, or at least it doesn't care whether you take good care of the land or not. And so we have a period in New England where it's pretty clear that the land was over exploited and degraded, particularly in the nineteenth century, much too much land cleared, and it was one of the things that helped drive the early conservation movement with George Perkins Marsh and Henry Thoreau and the rest of it. So there's a whole lesson in there of ecological problems that were driven by a voracious market.

And then a third story has to do with the success of farmers who stayed in in the late nineteenth and early twentieth century finding urban markets and ways of using the land that fit pretty well, and market gardening and dairy and fruit production and poultry and so forth. There's kind of a heartening story there, even though ultimately in the twentieth century it then couldn't compete with national-scale industrial production.

So there's an intellectual framework we're starting to develop that needs to be better developed, that informs what we might be trying to do with sustainable agriculture today and farming in the future in New England, and puts us at the end of a story that isn't just about "Oh, they built the Erie Canal and New England agriculture collapsed," because if that's true, we've got an uphill battle trying to do anything with this land today, and I think there's a more encouraging but instructive story back there.

(Continued)

If you're thinking about historians developing knowledge that is of potential interest to actual working farmers in the present, what should they know about actual working farmers in the present?

There's kind of a complicated answer to this, and it's something farmers need to know about themselves, and historians or anyone who's working on these programs. You know—how do I put this? Sometimes I think organizations that are working with farmers want the farm to pull its own weight economically, and the farmers do too and so it's kind of backwards from the way we often think about it, but there's kind of an expectation that if the farm is somehow subsidized that it isn't real, that the real farmers out there make money.

I've come across this with many organizations that say, okay, we've got a historic property and we're going to have farming in here, but we're not going to subsidize it forever. We want it to be part of the real world and eventually it's going to make it or break it based on it being a business. Well, most of the real farmers aren't making it as a business. The history of American farmers is farmers exploiting themselves and most of them going out of business in order to provide cheap food for this larger industrial economy. It's never benefited farmers, and a lot of them have just stayed in it by self-exploiting or by some kind of subsidy where—you know, you find these guys who are the most hard-driving farmers, the guys who survived the late twentieth century because they're so incredibly hard-driving, and they have the most free-market ideology you can imagine, and then usually, at least around here, you turn around and find out that most of the land that they're farming now they're leasing from some town conservation commission for like $25 an acre. There's a huge public subsidy just protecting the land. They're no more market farmers than anyone else.

So that I guess what I'm coming around to is that if you look at the commercial part of the farm enterprise and the educational side and the interpretive side as kind of one enterprise where there's going to be a bunch of different income streams and we're going to acknowledge from the beginning that yes, we want the farm enterprise to be run in a businesslike manner and to be as economically successful as possible but we don't have false expectations that it's going to make it. Because then we set up a clash between these farmers who are driven by that imperative and all the other stuff you want to see happen. You want it to look a certain way, you want it to not make noise at certain times, you want it to not smell, whatever it is, if you're going to put these things together then you've got to support it and subsidize it and that's *not a bad thing*. We haven't made it fake when we do that.

If I look at the future of New England farming, it's a huge wide range of farming that's partly family farms, a lot of hobby farms, part-time farmers, educational farms, people's gardens, it's a whole spectrum, and it's got to be supported in a whole lot of different ways to achieve different social and environmental benefits. And it cannot come down to "the farm has to support itself by growing potatoes at a price that makes it in the market." So I think there's a wide-ranging way of trying to answer your question. If we've got farmers who are in a role within some historic or conservation property and we want them to play a specific role, fine, we've got to make it possible for them to do that and succeed at it and not just by getting out of their way and saying, "You're going to make it." And that's not going to be easy because a lot of these farmers are going to have the mindset, the ideology in their heads that they *should* be making it—they're a business—which is kind of this strange schizophrenia in farmers as to what they really are.

And a very old one.

A very old one—it's this old tension. And so we've got to break farmers out of this too. And it's the same with a lot of things. It's like hunters—we have to see hunters as playing an ecological role, reducing deer populations—there's a whole spectrum of things that have to do with land stewardship.

Well, and undoing those dichotomies that were created when the market did reach its fullest flower around the turn of the twentieth century or whenever.

Right—we've got the cheap food or the cheap wood production over there, and then we've got the nice part of the landscape over here, and where the people live over here, and we're trying to make them all somehow not clash with each other instead of seeing them as part of some kind of organic whole.

That's really helpful. Because there is that expectation that, oh, it's a business, how can we parachute that into the non-profit world. But what you're saying is that there has to be support flowing in that direction toward farmers all the time.

Yeah. And I think that's a good thing and that what we need to do is shape it. God knows the amount of subsidy that flows to industrial farming is enormous. So if we value these other kinds of farming that's for producing good food, yes, but it's for healthy food, it's for getting people to eat in a healthier way, it's for having a landscape that's attractive that we like to live in, it's for understanding our past—all that stuff has value. And farmers are just one piece of how that can be delivered to people.

What do farmers most need to know about historians?

Farmers do not want to be romanticized. So I think that their initial instinct on meeting a historian who supposedly knows something about agricultural history and is "Oh boy, here's someone else who knows all about oxen and bringing in the sheaves" and all this stuff that's irrelevant to the real world of farming and that's very in-amber, stagnant, romantic. And so it would help to meet some real historians who have a more dynamic understanding of history that's a little more nuanced and lively and aware, perhaps.

Notes

1 For an overview of current archaeological thinking about the emergence of agriculture, see T. Douglas Price and Ofer Bar-Yosef, eds., "The Origins of Agriculture: New Data, New Ideas," *Current Anthropology*, 52:4 (October 2011).

2 James McWilliams explores the many cross-ties among cuisines in colonial regions along the east coast of North America in *A Revolution in Eating: How the Quest for Food Shaped America* (New York: Columbia University Press, 2007).

3 In addition to McWilliams, *A Revolution in Eating*, see Hal Barron, *Those Who Stayed Behind: Rural Society in Nineteenth-Century New England* (Cambridge and New York: Cambridge University Press, 1984); Martin Bruegel, *Farm, Shop, Landing: The Rise of a Market Society in the Hudson Valley, 1780–1860* (Durham and London: Duke University Press, 2002); Christopher Clark, *The Roots of Rural Capitalism: Western Massachusetts, 1780–1860* (Ithaca: Cornell University Press, 1990); Brian Donahue, *The Great Meadow: Farmers and the Land in Colonial Concord* (New Haven and London: Yale University Press, 2004); J. Ritchie Garrison, *Landscape and Material Life in Franklin County, Massachusetts, 1770–1860* (Knoxville: University of Tennessee Press, 1991); and Steven Stoll, *Larding the Lean Earth: Soil and Society in Nineteenth Century America* (New York: Hill and Wang, 2002).

4 Michael M. Bell, "Did New England Go Downhill?," *Geographical Review*, 79:4 (October 1989), 464. For other discussions of the misperceptions surrounding agricultural decline in New England, see Barron, *Those Who Stayed Behind*; Michael Bell, "Stone Age New England: A Geology of Morals," in *Creating the Countryside: The Politics of Rural and Environmental Discourse*, E. Melanie DuPuis and Peter Vandergeest, eds. (Philadelphia: Temple University Press, 1996), pp. 29–64; and Brian Donahue, "Another Look from Sanderson's Farm: A Perspective on New England Environmental History and Conservation," *Environmental History*, 12:1 (January 2007), 9–34. While direct comparisons can be difficult given the wide variety in types of land and land uses, levels of subsidy, etc., a National Agricultural Statistics Service summary of 2015 farm productivity in U.S. states shows Massachusetts and Connecticut producing at per-acre levels similar to much more agricultural states like Iowa, Georgia, Wisconsin, and Florida, and greatly outpacing some others like Washington, Oregon, and Montana. See www.nass.usda.gov/Quick_Stats/. This is all the more striking given that most New England food producers receive relatively little of the federal subsidy that supports commodity crop production, most of which goes to much larger farms elsewhere in the country.

5 Donahue, "Another Look from Sanderson's Farm," 20.

6 Julie Guthman has very thoroughly explored this process in her work, most notably *Agrarian Dreams: The Paradox of Organic Farming in California* (Berkeley, CA: University of California Press, 2004).

7 The industrial food system's complexity and breadth create challenges in pinpointing actual amounts and percentages of greenhouse gas (GHG) emission that can be attributed to it. The U.S. Environmental Protection Agency has estimated that agriculture accounts for 10% of the nation's GHG production, but transportation and refrigeration are not included in this total ("Sources of Greenhouse Gas Emissions"). The United Nations Food and Agriculture Organization says that livestock alone create 14.5% of anthropogenic GHG ("Major cuts of greenhouse gas emissions from livestock within reach"); other studies focusing solely on livestock (for example, *World Watch*) put this figure much higher (Robert Goodland and Jeff Anhang, "Livestock and Climate Change: What if the key actors in climate change are...cows, pigs, and chickens?"). The Research Program on Climate Change, Agriculture and Food Security of CGIAR (the Consultative Group on International Agricultural Research, an international consortium of organizations and agencies concerned with food security issues) takes a more comprehensive approach, factoring in things like food waste, deforestation, and biofuel production (Simon Bager, Bruce Campbell, and Lucy Holt, Sonja Vermeulen, "Food Emissions"). A 2007 *Boston Globe* article (Drake Bennett, "The Localvore's Dilemma," July 22, 2007) traces some of the reasons that doing a "Life Cycle Assessment" of food's carbon footprint is so complex. It is clear, however, that industrialized food production, processing, and distribution is a very significant contributor to GHG production globally.

8 See McWilliams, *A Revolution in Eating*, especially the final chapter.

9 Re-regionalizing efforts can be found around the U.S. and elsewhere. New England and the northeastern U.S., perhaps because of this region's relatively small size and

long history of concern for the vibrancy of its agricultural economy, seem particularly active in this regard. The Northeast Sustainable Agriculture Working Group (NESAWG) is a collaborative 12-state project started in 1992. More recent efforts include two studies that work toward models of more sustainable regional agriculture, *A New England Food Vision* (Durham, NH: Food Solutions New England, 2014) and *New England Food Policy: Building a Sustainable Food System* (American Farmland Trust, Conservation Law Foundation, and the Northeast Sustainable Agriculture Working Group). The Sacramento Regional Food System Collaborative in California, the Regional Food Systems Working Group of Iowa, and the Center for Regional Food Systems at Michigan State University are other examples of regionally scaled projects. For an overview of the rationale for creating and studying food systems at the level of the region, see Kate Clancy and Kathryn Ruhf, "Is Local Enough? Some Arguments for Regional Food Systems," *Choices: The Magazine of Food, Farm and Resource Issues*, First Quarter 2010.

10 See the Landcestor Project website.

11 A classic anthropological text, "Mother Cow," explores this situation in rural India in the early years of the "Green Revolution" there, arguing that the Hindu taboo against eating cows actually stems from the necessity of keeping cattle alive so that they can continue to provide essential resources like milk, dung (for fuel), and draft power for very impoverished farmers who would otherwise be tempted to eat them when other food was not available. See Marvin Harris, *Cows, Pigs, Wars and Witches* (New York: Random House, 1974).

12 A U.S. Department of Agriculture study found that 31 percent of all food produced in the U.S. in 2010 was wasted in supermarkets and homes, in addition to food that goes to waste in the field or on the loading dock. See Jean C. Buzby, Hodan Farah Wells, and Jeffrey Hyman, *The Estimated Amount, Value, and Calories of Postharvest Food Losses at the Retail and Consumer Levels in the United States* (Washington, DC: USDA Economic Research Service, Economic Information Bulletin No. EIB-121, February 2014). Many reports on food waste do not take pre-retail wastage into account; for a preliminary study focusing on food waste at the pre-retail stage, see "Left-Out: An Investigation of the Causes and Quantities of Crop Shrink" (commissioned by the National Resources Defense Council, 2012).

13 Corrington Gill, *Wasted Manpower* (New York: W.W. Norton, 1939), p. 138. The phrase became the title of Janet Poddendieck's well-known study *Breadlines Knee-Deep in Wheat: Food Assistance in the Great Depression* (Berkeley, CA: University of California Press, 2014 [1986]).

4

A PRIMER ON POLICY

Compared with a demonstration of how to save heirloom seeds, a cider tasting at a revived nineteenth-century orchard, or the chance to sign up for CSA vegetable shares at a historic farm, interpreting food policy can seem dry and uninviting. Even when it doesn't, it may be confusing (why do we subsidize commodity crops so heavily, anyway?), contentious (who's right in the fierce dispute over labeling genetically modified foods?), or both. Unlike the immediacy of much food-related interpretation, it can also seem distant—something that happens elsewhere, seemingly of little relevance except in agricultural states or during occasional food scares, and not the first point of entry for interpreters hoping to engage audiences through food.

Yet in many ways, an engagement with policy is where the rubber meets the road in connecting historical interpretations with contemporary food issues. In the preceding chapter, we argued for the importance of connecting local stories and places with a triple top line narrative that creates a very broad framework for thinking about our food systems. That "macro" level includes the market, particularly in its globalized manifestations. But it also includes government, in all of *its* manifestations—national policies that have historically supported the scaling up of food production while trying to mitigate some of its effects, state-specific regulations that have shaped more regional food economies, even local ordinances that govern health regulations at festivals or restrict nuisance suits against farmers manuring their fields. Policy is an important piece of the linkage between the micro and the macro.

Some awareness of past and present food policy, then, can be a crucial tool for interpreters. This chapter and the interview that follows present some ways of thinking about policy as a vital component of food interpretation. Rather than aiming toward a comprehensive overview of food and farm policy history in the U.S., we try to show how the broad outlines of this story emerge from the responses of food producers, consumers, politicians, advocates, and others to particular opportunities and dilemmas, particularly those created by a large-scale, market-oriented food system. Grasping those outlines can help interpreters contextualize local and regional stories more coherently and can even offer a bridge to talking with visitors about the logistics of historical practice itself (for example, "Why can't we just sell the food we grow at our site?"), making policy interpretation truly a porous interface between past and present.

Before moving on to the overview, we offer two additional reasons why this topic is not only intriguing but also central to a revitalized food interpretation. First, although audiences may not immediately be drawn to food policy as a topic (or may even be resistant to it), they probably have more immediate and intimate knowledge of policy issues than they realize. Most people are aware of national, regional, and local debates and controversies around food safety, labeling, prices, and the related subjects of farmland development, environmental protection, and resource use more generally. This awareness may come with strong and perhaps politicized opinions, creating challenges when approaching these topics interpretively. But it also creates an opportunity to deepen an existing conversation about causes and consequences and to link visitors' individual experiences with broad questions about our food system.

And a related larger point is that if it is done carefully and well, interpreting public policy can help foster more informed community opinion about food and other issues. As Anne Effland argues compellingly in the interview that follows this chapter, far from being something dry and technical enacted by distant politicians and anonymous bureaucrats, policy is really a reflection of the multiple, often competing interests within a democratic society. At its worst, public policy can be unduly influenced by particular powerful interests. But at its best, it addresses and tries to balance those different positions in ways that are constantly in flux and that very often invite some level of public participation. The fact that many people feel so disconnected from the sources of their food is a result of the yawning gaps between food producers and consumers that have opened up over the course of the nineteenth and particularly the twentieth centuries. As those gaps have widened, general public participation in debate over food policy has lessened and become much more focused on the eating side of the equation. But today's resurgence of concern about what's happening all along our food chains creates an opening for increased civic involvement in a fuller range of policy discussions. Food interpretation at historic sites can help to make room for deeper understanding of the collective decisions of the past and the politics and passions surrounding them, potentially catalyzing more active and thoughtful engagement with these same questions and processes in the present.

A Capsule Overview of American Food Policy

Americans debate about many things when they debate about food policy: ideas about safety, nutrition, and health; approaches to environmental use and stewardship; the ethics and practicalities of labor and labeling practices; differing levels of faith in new technologies and free markets; and much more. Much of the time, though, people really seem to be debating the proper function of government itself and the extent to which it has the right—or the responsibility—to intervene in economic and social life.[1] This is particularly noticeable in federal policies relating to food, since intractable dilemmas at smaller scales often get pushed to the federal level for some kind of resolution or ruling. This overview follows the long and extremely bumpy road toward the sometimes contradictory roles that the American government now plays in regulating food production, marketing, and consumption.

That road has always run parallel to the growth of both commercial markets and many kinds of non-government organizations involved in food issues. In the early years of the nation, these organizations provided much of the infrastructure for the kind of research and development work eventually supported by government. For example, a Society for the Promotion of Agriculture, Arts, and Manufactures was established in New York in 1791 to keep up with debates and experimentation in farming and other areas. (In the realm of agriculture, members explored everything from the latest cast-iron plows to the possibility of domesticating elk and moose.) This group and its successors laid the groundwork for the later involvement of the state, which established the New York State Agricultural Society in 1832.[2]

In the early through mid-nineteenth century, the energies of both private and public entities were mostly devoted to the project of expanding commercial food economies through technological innovation and the opening up of new land for settlement, with new transportation infrastructure (roads, canals, and eventually railroads) facilitating wider trade and settlement. The pursuit of market-based growth was already a double-edged strategy even in this early period, with longer-settled areas like the northeast beginning to find themselves left behind in the rush toward westward expansion, mechanization, and larger scales of production. As that happened, some private organizations emerged to take an interest in revitalizing food production in the older regions. Those functions in turn became absorbed into government around the turn of the twentieth century, helping to give food policy its somewhat contradictory tasks of supporting continued commercial growth while also trying to offset some of its more problematic effects.

The westward-moving frontier is a foundational element in the telling of American history, and its effects were as hotly debated in the nineteenth century as they have been by historians ever since. East-west tensions over the frontier developed quickly. The addition of new territories and states changed the balance of power and the allocation of resources in the U.S. and sparked disputes over whether public lands should be sold for the highest price possible or distributed in more egalitarian ways. By the middle of the nineteenth century, those regional stresses were re-mapped along north-south lines, with people in both slave and free states seeing the new territories as proving grounds for differing political and economic visions. During the antebellum years when federal politicians were attempting to work out these conflicts within a still-united government, southern lawmakers fought successfully to keep farm policy at the state level, fearing that federal intervention in agricultural decision-making would compromise southern control over this crucial sector of the South's economy. But the southern states' secession from the union in 1861 created an opportunity for northern advocates of national agricultural policy and oversight. Building on pre-war gathering of agricultural statistics by the Patent Office, the federal Department of Agriculture was created in 1862 and elevated to cabinet status in 1889.

Even as the Civil War intensified, two additional pieces of important legislation in 1862 helped create the framework for the active federal role in food production that we know today. The Homestead Act was based on the ideal of universal access to new farmland while the Morrill Land-Grant College Act was designed to strengthen links among government, the expanding field of higher education, and agricultural experimentation and innovation. The land-grant model, which gave states federal lands that they could use or sell in order to establish agricultural or other vocational colleges, expanded on existing public and private infrastructure that supported the pursuit of scientific farm methods. Although they were intended to strengthen the farm sector in an industrializing economy, the agricultural colleges, with their experiment stations (added in 1887) and cooperative extension services (1914), contributed greatly to the processes of further mechanizing food production and making it more capital-intensive, pushing along that receding horizon of profitability for smaller producers.

This was just one of the paradoxes of growth that began to be felt much more sharply as the nineteenth century went on. As American agriculture scaled up and expanded into new parts of the continent, new gaps opened between supply and demand and between the costs of production and the prices the market would bear. Attempting to keep up with competitive pressures, food producers found themselves facing ever higher levels of debt and up-front costs (for example, railroad rates that many felt were extortionate). In response, some banded together in cooperative and political organizations that occasionally became national in scope. These movements straddled many regional, ideological, racial, ethnic, and other fault lines as they struggled with the question that still faces us today: to what extent could the "problems of plenty" be addressed by tinkering with the same economic and technological systems that produced them? But although the producer-led agitation of the late nineteenth century was fragmented in many ways, groups like the Patrons of Husbandry (also known as the Grange), the Farmers' Alliance and Colored Farmers' National Alliance, and the People's Party (or Populists) did succeed in shaping the national agenda at times, proposing various solutions that later found their way into federal legislation.

Government also began to be more involved in food safety issues after the Civil War. The USDA's Division of Chemistry, conceived in the mold of the older agricultural "improvers," was drawn into consumer safety issues in the wake of high-profile food scares and more general concern about trust and transparency in ever-longer supply chains. One of the earliest of these followed the introduction of "oleomargarine" in the 1870s. Invented in Europe as an inexpensive substitute for butter, this product sparked a long-running controversy that was fought through state and federal legislatures for decades. The conflict was grounded in part in dairy farmers' concerns over competition but also in an enduring "butter mystique" that made the new engineered food one of the earliest targets for a range of broader fears about the emerging industrialized food system.[3] Later debates over milk pasteurization, slaughterhouse sanitation, and the supposed "backwardness" of rural life reflected the same uneasy combination of faith in scientific progress with uncertainty about what was being lost and gained in modern industrial life. In 1906, the Pure Food and Drug Act expanded the powers of the USDA to regulate food safety labeling and content, and in 1927, a new agency, the Food and Drug Administration, was created to carry out this work (Figure 4.1).[4]

FIGURE 4.1   As concern over food fraud and tampering grew in the late nineteenth century, culminating in the passage of the first federal food purity laws in the 1906 Pure Food and Drug Act, product manufacturers and advertisers increasingly trumpeted the value of "purity" in food, drink, and cleaning products. Image courtesy University of Washington.

After a tremendous amount of economic turbulence in the late nineteenth century, American agriculture enjoyed a relatively stable two-decade period in the early twentieth century when food prices and production costs were at last in balance. After World War I, however, prices once again dropped sharply, setting off an agricultural depression that caused widespread distress in rural places well before the 1929 stock market crash. There was growing consensus among farmers, politicians, and researchers that the problem was systemic and needed to be dealt with in a more fundamental way.

The New Deal programs of the 1930s over rode lingering doubts about whether the federal government should intervene directly in agricultural markets, although some of the more far-reaching provisions of the early New Deal legislation— particularly those that addressed the environmental degradation caused by industrial farming practices—were quickly challenged in court and changed toward regulating imbalances in supply, demand, prices, and income (conservation was not written back into federal farm legislation until 1985, although it has made steady gains since then). The Agricultural Adjustment Act of 1938 established a role for the federal government in monitoring the supply of certain key commodity crops— initially corn, cotton, and wheat—and helping to smooth out the financial bumps caused by fluctuations in prices and demand. The 1938 act also called for the passage of a new comprehensive piece of federal legislation, which became known as the Farm Bill, roughly every five years. In that same year, the Federal Food, Drug and Cosmetic Act strengthened the provisions of the 1906 legislation and created the framework for regulation in subsequent decades.

Since the 1930s, this general commitment to federal intervention in food safety and markets has remained in place, although new technologies and products continue to pose challenges for consumers and regulators and there has never been a clear consensus on how best to address the receding-horizon problem inherent in an industrialized capitalist food system. Policy fixes for that problem have included price supports for particular commodity crops, payments and subsidies to farmers, and occasional restrictions on production. The federal government has also warehoused, marketed, distributed, and offset agricultural surpluses in a variety of ways, including distributing them—or providing funding to purchase them—as foreign and domestic food aid. The U.S. food stamps program has been coupled with the surplus production problem from its beginnings, although as with other policy solutions, the specific mechanisms for getting food to hungry Americans while creating markets for unsold commodities have varied widely over time. Initiated in 1939 as a New Deal answer to the twin crises of bread lines and depressed prices for farm products, the program expanded tremendously during Richard Nixon's presidency, in the same years that federal agricultural policy was moving away from the New Deal template and toward a much more market-driven approach.

As the petrochemical, food processing, and fast food industries grew with the expansion of the "Green Revolution" in the 1960s and 1970s, U.S. food prices went into free-fall and government policy shifted toward supplementing farmers' income rather than attempting to regulate or moderate the market. An alarming moment of inflation in the early 1970s spooked consumers and politicians and helped solidify the idea that one of government's key roles was to keep food affordable. The percentage of disposable income that Americans spend on food has continued to fall steadily since then, even as the number of calories we buy for our bucks has increased.

Low food prices have often been extolled as one of the great benefits of an industrial food system, but a good deal of the food activism of the past two decades has been devoted to drawing attention to the hidden costs of those low prices, from tax-funded subsidies for commodity farming to widespread health problems caused by cheap and ubiquitous low-nutrition foods. Over time, anti-hunger efforts have become separated from discussions about agricultural surpluses, and few people still connect those particular dots when thinking about the problem of hunger in America. But the food stamps program still resides within the Farm Bill, and in fact it absorbs the lion's share of the funding in that legislation—80 percent of the total in recent bills.[5] This little-known legacy of earlier policy battles and social reform efforts is a particularly striking example of how our food system simultaneously produces scarcity and over abundance.

This overview has given short shrift to policy on international and global scales, including the 1948 General Agreement on Tariffs and Trade (GATT), which established the shape of international trade in the postwar decades and its successor agreement that created the World Trade Organization (WTO) in 1995 as a more fully globalized system of exchange. As trade agreements have continued to expand, so has the scope of resistance, with many food movement projects tackling issues of fair trade or migrant labor in transnational and global scales. There have of course been debate and conflict over trade, tariffs, labeling, safety, and many other issues across national lines for as long as there have been nation-states.

We would argue, though, that the great majority of these, whether national, international, or global, are based on the same fundamental attempt to mediate and mitigate the effects of expanding markets and the opportunities and anxieties that go along with them. Today's international debate over genetically modified organisms is not precisely the same as the controversy over the introduction of margarine in the 1880s, but its underpinnings *are* the same: attempts to use scientific discovery to create affordable food for all; public concern over the safety of "unnatural" foods; and a host of national, ethnic, regional, and other food cultures and economies whose tastes and histories inflect their responses on smaller policy levels (for example, in the banning of GMOs or the push for labeling places of origin). Policy remains one of the central realms where food issues are fought out and negotiated, as the interview that follows makes clear.

Bibliographic Note

Most of the general history included in this chapter is drawn from two very good basic sources: R. Douglas Hurt's *American Agriculture* (already noted in previous chapters) and Anne B.W. Effland's succinct summary of "U.S. Farm Policy: The First 200 Years" (*Agricultural Outlook*, March 2000, published by the Economic Research Service of the U.S. Department of Agriculture and available online). Effland breaks American farm policy into four overlapping phases that have emphasized land distribution and settlement (1785–1890), improving productivity (1830–1914), regulating markets and disseminating scientific and economic information (1870–1933), and providing direct support for farmers caught in the gap between supply and demand (1924 to today). "A Historical Primer on the US Farm Bill: Supply Management and Conservation Policy" by Devan A. McGranahan, Paul W. Brown, Lisa A. Schulte, and John C. Tyndall, *Journal of Soil and Water Conservation*, 68:3 (May–June 2013), 67A–73A (available online) is an excellent short history of the various big concerns that have been acted on in various (sometimes contradictory) ways through the Farm Bill over time. The USDA also provides numerous summaries and highlights, most of them available online, to accompany new Farm Bills; for example, "Agricultural Act of 2014: Highlights and Implications" includes sections on all of the standard elements of the bill but also on organic agriculture and local and regional foods, a clear response to the still-growing interest in those areas. Harvey Levenstein's *Paradox of Plenty* (also previously noted) is a very good source for the consumer-side experience of policy questions, including domestic food aid and food stamps.

Many books on contemporary food policy and controversies can help to make links with the historical policy record and clarify the often-muddled world of policy debates today. For a balanced and accessible short book that explores food policy through the lens of selected high-profile controversies, see *Agricultural and Food Controversies: What Everyone Needs to Know* by F. Bailey Norwood, Pascal A. Oltenacu, Michelle S. Calvo-Lorenzo, and Sarah Lancaster (Oxford University Press, 2014). Parke Wilde's *Food Policy in the United States: An Introduction* (Routledge, 2013) gives a very solid overview of contemporary food policies and issues, while a glossary of agricultural terms, programs, and laws assembled for the use of members of Congress engaged in creating policy is also very useful for general readers (Agricultural Research Service, "Glossary of Agricultural Terms," 2017 edition, U.S. Department of Agriculture, available online). The Food and Drug Administration's website includes a very extensive and well-researched set of materials on the agency's history. Marion Nestle's *Food Politics: How the Food Industry Influences Nutrition and Health* (University of California Press, first published in 2002 and updated in 2007 and 2013) is a detailed and accessible account of the more nitty-gritty aspects of food policy and politics. Nestle, a biologist and nutritionist, exposes some of the big contradictions underlying American food production and policy and shows how the food industry's fundamental dilemma—how to get people to keep eating more when most of us already eat too much—translates into distorted messages in the advertising and political realms.

WORK IN PROGRESS—AN INTERVIEW WITH ANNE EFFLAND: POLICY IS ABOUT SOCIAL CHOICES

FIGURE 4.2   Anne Effland. Photo credit: Dan J. White.

The gaps between historical interpretation and real-life action and advocacy around food issues in the U.S. are perhaps nowhere more noticeable than within the Department of Agriculture, where a fairly robust presence for historians in the middle decades of the twentieth century has dwindled to a single position: that of Anne Effland (Figure 4.2). Although housed in the Office of the Chief Economist and classified as a social scientist, Effland is very much a historian. In her 25-year career at the USDA, she has produced an impressive body of work focusing on federal farm and rural policy; rural labor, women, and minorities; and the institutional history of the USDA itself. She combines the skills of a scholar with the public historian's ability to communicate across a wide range of audiences that include people within the federal government, other historians, and broader publics. Among her award-winning projects are "Farm Bill Side-by-Side" summaries that quickly clarify and compare the details of this massive and important piece of legislation very soon after its passage.

Her work at the USDA gives her a unique perspective on the question of how public historians might most effectively interpret food and farm policy. In this interview, she makes a case for the vitality and human dimensions of policy, as well as the crucial role of policy-making within a democratic society.

Your work as an agricultural historian has been mostly oriented toward people who are actually making agricultural policy. And you've made a really strong case for why the historical perspective can be really important and useful there. How might that historical perspective be useful not just within government but also in explaining government out in the wider world?

I think the most critical piece for those who might be trying to interpret the play of policy outside the realm where it's made would be to identify the context you would be interpreting within. You've got a time period, a region, a type of living history farm, maybe a type of farm; if you're a historical monument it might be a particular event in time, if it's public programming it might be around an event, or it might be related to a span of time in a particular place. So you need to identify what that context is that you're going to want to interpret in, and then looking within that context, where could you have an impact? Where might be the places where you could bring together policy on a much more individualized or localized level? And that's where this kind of breadth of context comes in, because it's perhaps not as easy for someone who's not working within policy, but if you do start thinking about how people live their lives—did they acquire their land by way of some sort of public land distribution policy? Did they participate in extension programs? Were they politically involved trying to influence legislation through some farm organization? So along those kinds of lines, within the particular context where they're working.

And I would want to urge that it's seen from the perspective of not just what government does to the people in the place and time but also how *they* influence, if they're organized or if they respond to local leaders or—you know, build in some agency, a reminder of democracy to a certain extent.

Would that be your answer to a non-farmer saying "Oh, that's just dry, boring policy stuff"? Or is there more that you might say to make a case for the vitality of this as a subject?

What I would add to that from the non-farmer perspective is—one of the key things for getting past that dry, confusing, disconnected view is to step away from the technical details of what's actually in the programs and how the programs were created and the details of the politics of the policy creation towards a broader sense of what policy *is*. It's a way of making social choices about how we're going to allocate resources within our society, within our democratic organization. So you take a kind of bigger historical picture. Why do we have farm policy? What is this about? And the origins of farm policies are actually a pretty interesting human story about access to land, about access to resources to raise families to where you live, to have a kind of independence that goes with owning your own business, in a sense, which is what farming really is, controlling your own life. So there are a lot of places where you might get at this.

Ag policy is about social choices for farming systems, it's about allocating social resources to food production, and to people who produce the food. So it's got two sides to it. And over time it's become more weighted perhaps towards the people who eat the food, use the food and resources, away from those who produced it. So for mostly urban consumers, the farming side seems kind of distant.

In an individual site or event context, you can disentangle the sides or the multiple angles on a particular policy that's associated with that event. So for

(Continued)

example, you might look at a family farm site and talk about the things that helped change the way farm families linked up with the rest of the economy and how that affected the roles of the people in that family.

For example, you will have children moving out. Why are they moving out? They have an opportunity to be educated, they have an opportunity to choose other occupations in other places and then you can link to individual people's own family stories of that, because aren't many families that are far enough away from a rural background to not know some member who left, or some member who many have left unhappily but within a generation the experience is different from that first disconnection. So you can make connections about why individuals might have left and what happens to them over time, and the positive and negative of that. It's a matter of being able to interpret more sides of an individual experience, I think to get more to the details of what life was actually like in small-scale farming, who survived and who didn't, why they did, why they didn't, and what the longer-term outcomes are. It's also possible to look at policy in terms of how some farmers were able to survive when they might not otherwise have been able to *because* they have these broader markets.

When you look at it in that framework, there's a point of connection with the contemporary, with questions about labor, about family mobility, about who actually produces the food.

Yeah, and that's tricky from a policy perspective, a bit of a tricky subject to navigate, and maybe the way you do navigate this is to keep it very individual. And so you don't want to create a story where you talk about victims and oppressors, even though there may be elements of that in the story. On the one hand, this is a story from the perspective of agricultural employers concerned about continued access to a labor force. And on the other hand, it's a story about agricultural workers who are able to move and then choose to move into other parts of the economy and what that means about the immigrant experience.

So obviously, there's not a final end to these stories, ever. Maybe I have more faith than the average person, but at least in a democracy it's kind of an interplay between policy, the effects of policies, and new policies to deal with those effects. It's just sort of back and forth. And when you have the opportunity to tell a historical story, you can bring that in in a way that doesn't often come in when people experience these policy issues in an events context.

So the view of what is and isn't best can be different over time. Not to put a rosy picture on all these dislocations, because of course they're terrible and tragic and in the moment they create a lot of hardship and distress, but again, it's being able to have this historical story that gives the opportunity to see it in a bigger context, which can help when thinking about policy for individual people in their current day, just thinking about it with this breadth of time perspective.

I'm curious how you situate yourself as a researcher, the neutral researcher providing good reliable rigorous data within the federal government, in this very politicized realm and an urgent moment.

Although there are many good critiques of the scientific research system within the USDA, I'll speak from my personal experience: there's a high value placed on this ability or discipline of separating science from policy, and on the idea that science, including social sciences, is a neutral pursuit in that there are rules of evidence, there are rules of research, that can create this discipline that separates the policies from this, if you don't mind my sounding a little pretentious, what I think of as the search for truth—to identify what is and isn't true, and being scrupulously honest about it as much as any individual person is capable and presenting the results of that research in a way that's replicable by others. That's the core of science.

And it's difficult to remain in that core and there are many pressures from outside, and in particular I would say working within government, a lot of the pressure does come from outside to link that search to political or policy decisions. But within government, the discipline is there to provide the research and allow others who are politically eligible to make those policy decisions.

So that it's a difficult thing and it's hard if you believe strongly in particular issues. But it is possible to do your scientific research and work and maintain an internal integrity in that, separate from your own personal views or advocacy or whatever you do outside of that. My experience is that the bulk of the researchers that I work with do operate in that way and are relieved to be in a position to be able to work in that way, because that is the difference between science and politics.

When we're thinking about public historians, they are essentially the ones who are charged with taking good historical scholarship and moving it into the public realm. So I'm just curious whether you have any thoughts about that. I think you've articulated really well how you maintain that kind of rigor within the framework that you work in. What would you say to people who are more on what we think of as the "front lines" where they're having to speak to these things?

It depends of course upon where you're doing your interpreting. If you are associated with an organization that has an advocacy perspective, then you're going to be a lot less free to educate the public in multiple views. But if you're at a government-type installation or something that's got a clear neutral educational purpose, and in fact it seems to me—policy is in and of itself not neutral and it's descriptive of social decision-making. If you're able to see that, if you begin to see policy from that perspective, it gives you the breadth from which to take these multiple viewpoints. So just because you're interpreting a mine disaster in southern Appalachia as a rural labor issue, there may not be a very sympathetic story on the mine-owners' side, but there may be stories, not just the miners', but also the managers', the local managers', there are a lot of things that go into why positions exist as they do.

So from my perspective the best possible way to bring policy in is to not avoid it but to see it as this social decision-making story. And anyone who has current events experience knows that social decision-making is a very complex process with multiple points of view. So I think my recommendation

(Continued)

is not to avoid but to remind people of what policy in fact is. We don't live in a country where there's the state and the people, and the state does to people what those who influence the state believe it should. It may be that there are more and less powerful and influential groups; that's certainly not deniable. But there's also, as I've mentioned before, agency within the least powerful groups that can be interpreted as well as the multiple motivations behind those in more influential positions, so that it doesn't become a black and white story. I mean, it takes some doing but it seems to me that the key is to see this as social decision-making and not as this group against that group.

I know that incorporates a highly optimistic view of our political system, and not everyone would agree with me on that! But from the perspective of finding a neutral place where you can begin to think about how to interpret in an educational way that broadens people's thinking about particular issues and events, that's the way to go at it.

One of my graduate advisors forced me always to "name names" is how he put it. Nothing ever happens without individual human beings doing things, at least in political history. And so you can't say "this office did something," because an office doesn't do things, the people within the office do. You end up identifying and, in some senses requiring the individual actors to be responsible for what they've done, even if they're no longer living. But they themselves made choices about how they would respond to certain events, etc. So it forces you to go beyond a simplification like "it happened in this office, and therefore the government did this." So in some cases you have evidence of collusion and widespread activity that is detrimental to another group. In other cases you have individuals who take advantage of their power to force things through. But those are two different kind of evidence, two different descriptions of events. And so the historical discipline of having to look at details of how stuff happened really opens up the realities of life in other times that we take for granted in our understanding of life in this time. It takes that way of looking at things and places it back into the historical context and really opens up the ways you can start to try to understand what actually happened and why.

I think it needs to be clear that policy is an iterative process and it includes both intended and unintended or vested consequences and then it continues on. So properly identifying what happened, in this detailed a way, facilitates critiques and better policy. It shouldn't be seen as making excuses, it is an effort to try to truly understand what brought about these consequences that weren't expected, and then what we would do to fix these pieces. It is in and of itself a very historical process, which makes it a very appealing area to study. But it shouldn't be divorced from experience because it has a great influence on how individuals are able to make their own choices in their lives.

Notes

1 The authors of the recent F. Bailey Norwood, Pascal A. Oltenacu, Michelle S. Calvo-Lorenzo, and Sarah Lancaster, *Agricultural and Food Controversies: What Everyone Should Know* (Oxford University Press, 2014, p. 3) reach the same conclusion, locating the contemporary fault line along the question of whether people trust government more than they trust large-scale corporations (the basic liberal position) or vice versa (the more conservative stance).

2 Ulysses Prentiss Hedrick, *A History of Agriculture in the State of New York* (New York: Hill and Wang, 1969[1933]), pp. 113, 115–116.

3 See Richard A. Ball and J. Robert Lilly, "The Menace of Margarine: The Rise and Fall of a Social Problem," *Social Problems*, 29:5 (June 1982), 488–498.

4 The FDA was housed within the USDA until 1940, when it was moved to the Federal Security Agency, a Roosevelt-era cabinet-level agency that combined many of the New Deal programs dealing with health, environment, conservation, and education. This agency became the Department of Health, Education and Welfare (HEW) in 1953 and is now the Department of Health and Human Services (HHS). The FDA remains within its mandate.

5 By the USDA's own reporting the Agricultural Act of 2014 was projected to cost $489 billion overall ("Agricultural Act of 2014: Highlights and Implications," accessed online at www.ers.usda.gov/agricultural-act-of-2014-highlights-and-implications. aspx), but the *Washington Post* followed a somewhat broader accounting method and arrived at the figure of $956.4 billion (Brad Plumber, "The $956 Billion Farm Bill, in One Graph," *Washington Post*, January 28, 2014). The two sources agree, however, on the 80 percent figure for food assistance (now known as the Supplemental Nutrition Assistance Program or SNAP). It is surprisingly difficult to find solid historical scholarship on the history of domestic food assistance in the U.S., but the sections of Levenstein's *Paradox of Plenty* that deal with this topic do include some nuanced discussion of the politics of the food stamp program over time (see pp. 62–63, 145–159, and 256). For a general (if uncritical) overview, see Julie A. Caswell and Ann L. Yaktine, eds., "Supplemental Nutrition Assistance Program: Examining the Evidence to Define Benefit Adequacy" (Washington, DC: Institute of Medicine and National Research Council of the National Academies, 2013, pp. 29–32. Available online).

5

A PRIMER ON PRIMARY SOURCES

The same kinds of primary sources that underpin any public historical interpretation are also important for interpreting food history: material culture, maps and photographs, town and city directories, census data, legal documents, print media, oral histories, and so on. There are also some key specialized sources relating to food production and consumption, and this chapter will focus on some of those. Some of them will already be familiar, while others, like agricultural censuses, may be new to many people. They range from the vivid and intimate—a cookbook splotched with food stains next to a favorite recipe—to the most seemingly impersonal reams of bureaucratic statistics. Across the spectrum, though, any sources we might tap for this topic—including living people—present specific challenges that stem from the histories of food production and policy traced in the preceding chapters.

Many of these food-specific sources *seem* particularly transparent, whether they are documenting the number of bushels of corn grown on an upstate New York farm in 1880 or the flavors of ice cream served at a California soda fountain in 1960. But they inevitably reflect ideas—often powerful and passionately held—about progress and tradition, safety and danger, place and identity, what's natural and unnatural, what's right and wrong. As with any primary sources, we need to keep those perspectives in mind alongside the information being conveyed about food itself. There is a great deal to be learned about gender, social class, race and ethnicity, and other "social history" concerns by doing that, but if we bear in mind the "triple top line" framework of environment, economy, and energy as we gather and interpret sources, we can also illuminate moments of change, adaptation, and challenge as they happened in specific times and places along the road to a fully industrialized food system—and perhaps away from it again.

Government Data

Because food supplies, trade, public health, and taxation have long been matters of pressing concern to governments, the collection of information relating to food production and marketing has a long history. There are rich troves of data to be explored in many kinds of government records, whether focused directly or indirectly on food, on both the production or consumption sides of the equation. There is so much data available, in fact (especially after the era when government became centrally involved in food policy and regulation), that it can be overwhelming. Unless you're embarked on a really comprehensive project—for example, an exhibit on agricultural history for a state museum—we suggest that you not try to gather and absorb all of the available materials, but rather try to create "anchor points" that can be integrated with the top line framework as well as with more specific data (for example, from oral histories, genealogical materials, or detailed records of what was produced at particular farms or eaten at particular restaurants).

Your search for anchor points might begin by learning something about policy and regulatory histories for the specific scale and area you're interested in. See what you can find out about the founding of boards, commissions, or departments of agriculture or food regulation. (A quick search on Wikipedia or the relevant agency's website can often net this basic information.) How does the timing of their establishment seem to fit within the triple top line narrative? Were states, counties, and towns responding to opportunities for growth, anxieties about decline, or a sense that new technologies, markets, and products needed to be embraced or offset (or perhaps both)? Were these agencies part of the state- and county-level infrastructure that developed in the eastern part of the country in the early nineteenth century and formed some of the basis for later, more sweeping federal oversight of food production and marketing? Or did they emerge from that federal involvement, as in the case of many of the land-grant universities? What areas of public life did the people involved in creating these agencies come from—politics, education, food production, social reform? Knowing even a little about this can help you contextualize the kinds of studies, policy, and regulations they sponsored and the kinds of problems and opportunities they were trying to address.

Once you have some sense of the policy landscape, so to speak, try to identify key studies or bodies of data for your area and time period of interest. It is fun and sometimes productive to search more generally for online data sources, but having some key targets in mind can help to focus your particular inquiry. One good way to do this is to pay attention to footnotes and bibliographies in secondary sources about those times and places. For example, studies of farming in colonial Massachusetts tend to refer frequently to a 1771 valuation of property that was done for taxation purposes. While cryptic and incomplete compared with the level of detail in later agricultural censuses, this 1771 survey nevertheless opens a window onto the farming, milling, and land-clearing activities of specific colonial-era families. As with a great many other historical statistical resources, it is now available online, in this case through a digital project based at Harvard University.[1]

Another useful anchor point can be some general statistics about the food being produced and sold in your area in different time periods, along with population and income or real estate values at the town, county, or state level. Plugging these into the Timeline of U.S. Food and Farming History in the Appendix may help you to see some new connections or form some new questions that your project might explore. For example, the Shapiro House at Strawbery Banke Museum interprets the history of a family of Ukrainian Jewish immigrants residing in the city in 1919. In developing the interpretation, researchers overlaid city maps and demographic data onto family oral histories, identifying concentrations of Jewish households and gardens along with important community resources such as kosher butchers and mikvehs (ritual baths). The resulting interpretive plan adds context and dimension extending far beyond the habits of an individual household to create a richer picture of the effects of one immigrant community's food needs on the reorganizing of the city's business and social networks—a cross-cultural phenomenon still shaping cities and towns (though featuring participants of different national origin) today.

The Federal Agricultural Census is an excellent source for information about food production and marketing. In addition, it sometimes lets us drill down to a much more granular level that focuses on individual towns, people, farms, and other food-related enterprises. Agricultural information first became a formal part of federal census-taking in 1840. The U.S. Agricultural Census was conducted in tandem with the decennial census until 1950, after which it changed to a five-year schedule in years ending with a "4" or a "9," and after 1978 in years ending with a "2" and a "7" (making the 2012 version the most recent one as of this writing). The data from the 1840 Census are minimal, but separate agricultural schedules for 1850, 1860, 1870, and 1880 give us wonderfully specific information about particular farms and their products. If you have access to the full census returns through Ancestry.com or some other avenue, you should be able to locate "Non-Population Schedules," which include the agricultural schedules.[2] Search the Internet for "Agricultural Schedules: 1850 to 1900" to find copies of the blank forms for those years plus the explanations and instructions issued to census takers, which will give you a sense of what information was being gathered.

The 1890 agricultural schedule was even more detailed than its predecessors, but the results were lost to fire along with most of the rest of the 1890 Census, and the raw data from 1900 and 1910 were destroyed by Congressional order, leaving us only the collective information from those and subsequent years. Even that data is extensive, although lacking in the richly individual information of the 1850–1880 censuses. Figures are often broken down by county and listed across particular time ranges, yielding useful comparisons that can serve as anchor points. All of the federal reports have now been digitized by the National Agricultural Statistics Service (NASS) of the U.S. Department of Agriculture and the Albert R. Mann Library at Cornell University. Some states have also conducted their own agricultural censuses in various time periods, and those can help fill some of the gaps in the federal data.

Primary sources relating to farming are relatively concentrated within the USDA. Because domestic food aid has been such an enormous part of the Farm Bill, many historical sources relating to nutrition guidance and food insecurity are also to be found in USDA-generated materials.[3] But other food-related material from the federal government is far more dispersed, reflecting the ever more fragmented character of the American food system as well as its complex relationships with commercial markets, trade, environmentalism, and public health. Studies and statistics relating to fisheries, for example, have historically originated in the U.S. Fish Commission, established in 1871, and its successor agencies within the Department of Commerce and Labor and (since 1939) the Department of the Interior, where issues relating to fisheries—commercial, recreational, and ecological—remain housed within the Fish and Wildlife Service.[4] Meanwhile, food safety was moved from the USDA's portfolio in 1940 and has been housed in agencies focusing on health, education, and human services since then. The Food and Drug Administration (FDA), which deals most directly with food regulation from a consumer perspective, is currently part of the Department of Health and Human Services. Issues relating to environmental health and degradation have been dealt with in rather piecemeal ways, through government efforts focused on forestry, natural and cultural preservation and recreation, resource protection, and industrial practices.[5] Most of the contemporary agencies covering these areas have gathered and made available archival materials—the USDA and FDA are particularly strong in this regard—in addition to primary sources being available elsewhere.

One final type of government data worth mentioning here is the soil map or soil survey. Produced by various agencies and entities, including the agricultural extension services of land-grant colleges and universities, soil maps and surveys provide detailed data about types of soil across the U.S. The USDA's Natural Resources Conservation Center houses the Web Soil Survey, a worldwide digital map of soil types that is fully searchable. While it takes specialist knowledge to interpret this kind of map fully, most of us know enough about the difference between loam and clay to gain a general sense of where the prime agricultural land and the less fertile areas are in a given area. This can be a very useful starting point for thinking about questions of land access, use, and cost, as well as an opening for talking with farmers, ranchers, foresters, conservationists, and others about how and why the land base in a particular area has been utilized in different ways over time.

One word of caution: the conventional approach to soil surveys has been to determine the most sensible and rational use of particular soils. But as we have seen in the preceding chapters, ways of measuring efficiency and capability have often been strongly shaped by particular understandings of land as a resource to be exploited for maximum yield or profitability. So a soil survey—or any official designation of land based on its potential productivity—is a double-edged tool, to be approached critically. If we read it in one way, it can tell us about the potential of certain places to grow certain kinds of products well. Looked at from another angle, it shows us some of the assumptions that have helped to marginalize some kinds of places and practices of food production that the food movement often seeks to rediscover and support.[6] No matter how we use a soil map or survey, though, it can be a way to start linking our historical inquiries with some of the actual physical resources that are ultimately the foundation for all of our talk about food.

Menus and Cookbooks

Menus and cookbooks are familiar sources, often readily available in local and personal collections as well as in the growing number of online databases. These sources can be a vivid way to connect the micro with the macro. The appearance of different ingredients and modes of processing, packaging, or presenting food reflect changes in the scale and industrialization of food systems as well as economic shifts and ideas about the old and the new, the familiar and the exotic. Menus and cookbooks themselves also emerged in the same time period and were shaped by many of the forces that produced our modern ways of living and eating: the growth of cities and an urban—and then suburban—middle class; the expansion of commercial markets starting in the eighteenth century; changing gender roles and modes of work; and new technologies sparked by scientific invention and industrial production.

Cookbooks reflect all of those trends in detailed and often fascinating ways. A title like *Science in the Kitchen: A Scientific Treatise on Food Substances and Their Dietetic Properties, Together with a Practical Explanation of the Principles of Healthful Cookery, and a Large Number of Original, Palatable, and Wholesome Recipes* (published in 1893) clearly signals its allegiance to the scientific thought that underpinned the emerging fields of home economics and nutrition around the turn of the twentieth century. In contrast, *Mary at the Farm and Book of Recipes Compiled during her Visit among the "Pennsylvania Germans"* (1915) just as clearly emerges from the nostalgic reaction to "progress" and the desire to reconnect with older foodways.[7] Its fictional narrative follows a young teacher returning to the countryside to learn womanly culinary skills at the side of her elderly aunt. (On the way to the family farm in her uncle's horse-drawn wagon, the heroine is described as "enjoy[ing] to the full the change from the past months of confinement in a city school, and miss[ing] nothing of the beauty of the country and the smell of the good brown earth."[8]) Many cookbooks combine old and new. *Joy of Cooking*, first published in 1931 and revised in subsequent decades, provides detailed instruction in how to cook using newly available tools like the pressure cooker, but it also includes chatty instructions for traditional ways of preparing food ("There are, proverbially, many ways to skin a squirrel, but the following one is the quickest and cleanest...").[9]

An edition of *Joy of Cooking* sits on many cooks' shelves; *Science in the Kitchen* and *Mary at the Farm* are more unusual but can be found online in the collection of 75 volumes in Michigan State University's "Feeding America: The Historic American Cookbook Project." There are extensive collections of cookbooks in university and public libraries and archives around the U.S., often at land-grant universities with a long history of collecting materials relating to food. "Feeding America" focuses on the "long nineteenth century," with cookbooks spanning the years from 1798 to 1922. Other collections emphasize different time periods or specialize in particular regions. Digitization is still uneven among these collections, with some of the premiere repositories (for example, Harvard University's Schlesinger Library, which holds more than 20,000 cookbooks and much more in its culinary collections) still requiring an in-person visit to see most of their materials.

Menus have been more widely digitized to date, perhaps because of their scanner-friendly format. Again, institutions with a particular connection to food history have tended to be at the forefront of both collection and digitization. The Culinary Institute of America has made about 10 percent of its more than 25,000 historical menus available online, and Cornell University, the University of Washington, University of Houston, and University of Nevada Las Vegas have also produced significant digital menu projects. Given the regional or era-specific focus of many of these, it can be worth searching these collections to see if there is a body of digital material from the area you interpret, or that might serve as a direct comparison with more local menus.

Some of the more sophisticated online menu and cookbook collections offer the ability to search by date, location, style of food, or even individual ingredients, a particularly useful feature when documenting the ways that changing food systems affected what was actually appearing on people's plates both at home and when dining out. "Feeding America" has an ingredients search filter, while the New York Public Library is working toward full searchability of all of its 45,000 menus from the 1850s through the 1970s. The library's ambitious "What's on the Menu?" crowd-transcription project is enlisting volunteers to "extract all the delicious data frozen as pixels inside [our] digital menu photos," providing an intriguing model for the creation of new shared knowledge about the history of food.[10]

Agricultural Journals

Food and farm writing intended for a wide popular audience has been an important component of American discourse about food for a very long time, from early agrarian writings to Progressive Era effusions about returning to a simpler life to contemporary food blogging.[11] One specialized type of source within this tradition is the agricultural journal, which flourished in the mid-nineteenth century and reflected many of the ideas being put forward by the modernizers and "improvers" of the day. Expanding side by side with the printing industry, the agricultural press was able to reach unprecedentedly large audiences with ideas about how to thrive in changing agricultural markets. Even though only a minority of farmers subscribed, farm-specific journals like the *Cultivator*, the *American Farmer*, the *Southern Agriculturalist*, and countless smaller publications reached somewhere around 350,000 farmers, mostly in the north, by the time of the Civil War.[12] More general titles like *Niles' Register* and *De Bow's Review* had a wider readership and also contained much that related to rural and agricultural matters. Many of these have already been digitized, and more continue to become available all the time; selected issues or whole runs can be found at Google Books, the Internet Archive, the Library of Congress, and many other digital repositories.

These sources are more useful for understanding the eastern part of the U.S. and the middle of the nineteenth century than other times and regions. But they have unique, if somewhat uneven, advantages. They are often wonderfully fine grained, with discussions of very specific places, people, methods, and outcomes. As with the tidbit of information about Dr. Lucius Cook's bumper carrot crop, found through a Google search in a now-obscure regional journal, small items from the agricultural press can add detail and precision to broader narratives. They also give us a sense of the complexities of the arguments, visions, and passions of the day. They can reveal contingencies often subsumed in the smooth dominant narrative of agricultural history as Americans tried to understand how their systems of food production and exchange, their modes of working, and their rural places were changing—for better and worse—in response to industrialization, urbanization, and expansion. Just like today's "food movement," the agricultural journals present a dizzying range of opinions, positions, and solutions. But they also show us the real depth of concern and engagement around issues relating to food, land, labor, and the values that were being attached to them (Figure 5.1).

Seed Catalogs

The arrival of a seed catalog in the winter mail was once an important annual event in farm homes. These trade publications presented lists of the plants and seeds offered for sale by mail-order horticultural companies. Circulating by the late eighteenth century and proliferating by the mid-nineteenth, they are a detailed source of information about the plant stock available at a given time and place and the expectations and values of the people who sold and purchased it. Among the insights seed catalogs can produce are the dissemination of plant varieties across regions and climatic zones, the migrations of plants from one consumption category to another—for instance, the span of time in which an herb ceased to be thought of as medicinal and became a "pot" or "sweet" herb for flavoring food or the point at which a tomato variety fell out of commercial favor and became a home gardener's hobby vegetable. Catalogs also hint at the adoption of technologies, practices like the application of insecticide and fertilizer, the availability of specialized tools and gadgets, and even the standardization of seeds themselves as this crucial part of the food system became more scientific

FIGURE 5.1 The lavishly illustrated covers of seed catalogs from the late nineteenth through mid-twentieth century make excellent subjects for visual analysis. This cover of the 1896 catalog from J. A. Everitt hints at state boosterism (the U.S. map is captioned "the center of population is a few miles southeast of Indianapolis"); the adoption of modern glass greenhouses, as seen to the right of the child's head; and a mix of products for all markets including commercial corn varieties, garden produce, and flowers. The child's ruddy good health and sailor suit (associated with physical activity) underscore the vision of families thriving on robust yields. "Annual Catalogue of Celebrated Seeds," Indianapolis, Ind. J.A. Everitt, 1896. Image contributed by U.S. Department of Agriculture, National Agricultural Library, via Biodiversity Library.

and commercialized. Ordering and planting instructions offer some clues to the phenology—the study of natural cycles of weather and life—of past eras, a particularly salient kind of data as we struggle to understand the currently changing climate. Like cookbooks, catalogs conveyed gendered messages about proper activities for women and men, dividing flower and kitchen gardening from the work of field cultivation, and encouraging women to learn the art of flower arranging in order to speak with the "language of flowers."

The falling cost of printing and increasing commercial competition drove catalog publishers to develop ever more appealing marketing strategies for named varieties, giving rise to bright color illustrations and hyberbolic monikers using words like "perfection" and "giant." The effects of depression and war, too, became visible in the seed supply, as plants were touted for their incredible yield and American stocks praised over European stocks that had become impossible to import. Because seed catalogs existed to move product, they demand critical evaluation. Their enthusiastic and prescriptive language reflected sellers' and growers' wishes and hopes every bit as much as their real experiences.

After 1960, the distribution of seed catalogs began to fall. Though a niche market for home gardeners remains, particularly among aficionados of organic seeds and heirloom plant varieties, the heyday of the seed catalog has ended. Many local, county, and state libraries and museum collections hold seed catalogs distributed in their own regions, and some excellent collections are available online. They are invaluable in planning a garden re-creation, identifying plant varieties likely to be in use at a specific time and place, understanding how people put plants to use in kitchens and medicine chests, and rediscovering small-scale cultivation techniques now lost from commercial practice. Read critically, they also offer a way to connect with questions about changes in scale, methods, weather, and expectations as the industrialized food system developed in the nineteenth and twentieth centuries.

Material Culture

The implements of older methods of food production are all around us. Seafood restaurants hang old fishing nets and wooden lobster traps on their walls; rustic and rural eateries display a rusting plow or harrow in the front yard; antique glass canning jars on a shop or restaurant shelf signal quaintness and a kind of DIY aesthetic that has now become trendy with the adoption of Mason and Ball jars for countless new uses from hip cocktails to nightlights. Meanwhile, old tools proliferate in museum collections, especially in smaller local museums where the contents of everyone's barn seem to end up in the basement of the historical society. For better and worse, most people are at least vaguely familiar with these objects, making material culture a potentially useful point of connection for critical engagement with food history.

However, as Chapter 1 has shown, material culture has often historically been the *first* (and sometimes only) point of entry for public interpretations of food history. And that means that this type of primary source is already heavily shaped by long-standing modes of interpretation ("Here, take a turn at the butter churn") that work against the kind of questioning we are advocating in this book. The advice we have offered so far—try to work against the nostalgia for past foodways, don't assume an inevitable progression from simpler past methods to more sophisticated present ones, look for ways to connect interpretation with questions about environment, economy, energy, and scale—applies in spades when it comes to artifacts, because audiences (and interpreters themselves) may so quickly default to those older patterns.

If you have a collection of hand tools or objects used in farming, fishing, or food preservation, think about how you might use it in counterintuitive ways rather than letting it send the too-simple message "This is how they used to do it in the old days." Tools intended for use with muscle power can be excellent ways to engage with questions about energy sources and changing economies: How long would it take a person with a scythe to mow an acre of hay, as opposed to a horse-drawn mower or a fossil-fuel-driven one? What can you find out about when those transitions took place for specific farms in your area and also about which food producers continued using less energy-dense methods even after more powerful ones were available? Typically that pattern was dictated by wealth—those with more capital could afford to invest in newer and more expensive technologies—but that doesn't necessarily mean everyone thought the changes were positive. And it doesn't mean that change was always one-directional. Did people go back to plowing with horses during the lean years of the Depression? Can you find evidence of back-to-the-landers in various periods—the Progressive Era, 1960s commune dwellers, today's neo-agrarians—who chose muscle-powered farming methods for economic or philosophical reasons? As with any good social history, keeping your antennae tuned to moments of transition, exclusion, resistance, and creative adaptation will let you tell a much more nuanced story about food over time. And that story—with the artifacts that support it—will open toward the kinds of questions and projects in which audiences and community partners are likely already engaged (Figure 5.2).

Living People as Primary Sources

People involved in food production and consumption—current and former farmers and fishermen, cooks, bakers, restaurateurs, and others—can also be sources of information and ideas. Recording oral histories and exploring family collections are tried and true methods for linking past to present, personalizing, enlivening, and often extending information found in the kinds of materials discussed above. Even more importantly for reinvigorated food interpretation, connecting with living people lets us blend the usual activities of collection and research with partnerships and active engagement in present-day food issues, helping to support more civic- and community-oriented projects.

FIGURE 5.2 Canning jars, currently in vogue for everything from cocktail shakers to pincushions and nightlights, illustrate the widespread presence of material artifacts from earlier eras of food production and preservation. These objects may help to invite audiences into discussion about how and why food technologies and practices have changed—and why they sometimes change back again. Image: Patrick Truby.

Oral historians, ethnographers, and others experienced at this kind of work are well aware of the caveat mentioned at the start of this chapter: we need to approach all primary sources with an eye to the positions and perspectives of the people providing the information. This task becomes more challenging with living people who have the potential to respond to and perhaps challenge your interpretations. And the same things that make food an engaging starting point for community projects—its universality, its intimacy, its many entanglements with politics as well as with sensory and emotional memory—also mean that people's ideas about it tend to be strongly held and often unique to themselves. The methods worked out by people who work with food tend to be a complicated blend of their own experiences, intuitions, and visions with information gleaned from a multitude of other sources—educational programs, scientific studies, professional and social networks, writers, and more. Honoring and representing an interviewee's idiosyncratic approach while situating it within a broader comparative context requires diplomacy, sensitivity, respect, and careful thought. But in many ways this is the nitty-gritty of knowledge co-creation about our food systems, and it is at the core of the facilitating role we envision for public historians in dialogue with food systems activity.

This chapter has highlighted some key sources, but the list is by no means complete. Other primary sources well worth investigating include architecture, particularly the socio-spatial organization of food production, preparation, and dining spaces, as well as the archeology of food, farming, and dining. We have aimed to orient public historians and museum interpreters to an expanded resource base, while suggesting approaches for accessing, assessing, and using some of the general and specialized sources that help us to understand the history of food. But as the following interview with Valerie Segrest suggests, finding ways to bring these sources into dialogue around food issues in the present is what will make them more meaningful and relevant to our publics. This dialogic approach reminds us that our own work is also shaped by particular positions, tastes, and visions that are time- and culture-bound. Our skills in interpreting primary sources are just one piece of the larger task of creating spaces and projects where people with a wide range of perspectives on food—and all that food connects to—can come together to reflect and converse.

Bibliographic Note

Chapter 5 has focused directly on primary sources themselves, but there is also an extensive literature of secondary material that suggests good ways to contextualize and interpret such information. A good general starting point on using primary sources to inform food interpretation is Sandra Oliver's compact Technical Leaflet "Interpreting Food History," *AASLH History News* 52:2 (Spring 1997), 1–8.

Probably due to their ubiquity, cookbooks have been considered by a number of scholars. Works bringing a critical lens to the nature of these sources include Jane C. Busch's "Learning by Pinches and Dashes: Using Cookbooks as Historical Research Documents," *AASLH History News* 52:2 (Spring 1997), 22–25; Alison P. Kelly's "Choice Receipts from American Housekeepers: A Collection of Digitized Community Cookbooks from the Library of Congress," *The Public Historian* 34:2 (Spring 2012), 30–52; and Kennan Ferguson's "Intensifying Taste, Intensifying Identity: Collectivity Through Community Cookbooks," *Signs* 37:3 (Spring 2012), 695–717. Book-length works that treat cookbooks in some detail include Barbara Haber's *From Hardtack to Home Fries: An Uncommon History of American Cooks and Meals* (The Free Press, 2002), Laura Shapiro's *Perfection Salad: Women and Cooking at the Turn of the Century* (Farrar, Straus, and Giroux, 1986), and Susan Strasser's *Never Done: A History of American Housework* (Pantheon, 1982). For an intriguing lay perspective on historical recipe research, Laura Schenone's memoir *The Lost Ravioli Recipes of Hoboken: A Search for Food and Family* (Norton, 2008) highlights, in a moving personal voice, many of the challenges of working with recipes and oral traditions handed down in families and immigrant communities.

Histories of restaurants provide a good deal of context on menus as sources, helping shed light on why and how their presentations of food were shaped. Rebecca Spang traces the Parisian origins of fine dining outside the home and its gradual adoption in the U.S. in *The Invention of the Restaurant: Paris and Modern Gastronomic Culture* (Harvard University Press, 2002); picking up the story, Paul Freedman's piece "American Restaurants and Cuisine in the Mid-Nineteenth Century" analyzes operations, cuisine and clientele at several northeastern restaurants (*New England Quarterly* 84:1 (March 2011). Chapter 4 ("Dinner is Served") of Margaret Visser's sweeping history *The Rituals of Dinner: The Origins, Evolution, Eccentricities, and Meaning of Table Manners* (HarperCollins, 1992) discusses the social evolution of restaurants and expectations for bourgeois behavior in them. Though localized in its focus, William Grimes' *Appetite City: A Culinary History of New York* (North Point Press, 2009) has the advantage of discussing a lengthy time span, from the opening of the city's first coffee houses in 1813 to the age of Mario Batali, Daniel Boulud and other larger-than-life celebrity restaurateurs of our own time, offering glimpses along the way of most of the nation's major restaurant trends. Jennifer 8. Lee's *The Fortune Cookie Chronicles* (Hatchett, 2008) is an accessible and fascinating exploration of the origins and spread of Chinese restaurants in the United States through the twentieth century. Samantha Barbas focuses on twentieth-century trends toward "home cooking" and "mom-and-pop" restaurants in her article "Just Like Home: 'Home Cooking' and the Domestication of the American Restaurant," *Gastronomica* 2:4 (2002), 43–52.

Menus and seed catalogs are examples of culinary ephemera, a wider set of sources that have been treated in both historical studies and studies of graphic arts and design. William Woys Weaver's *Culinary Ephemera: An Illustrated History* (University of California Press, 2010) is a wide-ranging work that takes in not just menus but also product labels, tourism brochures, advertisements, and other sources. In his associated article "The Dark Side of Culinary Ephemera: The Portrayal of African Americans," *Gastronomica* 6:3 (Summer 2006), Weaver also discusses ways in which graphic imagery promulgated and reinforced racial and ethnic stereotypes.

Material culture interpretation boasts a rich body of literature, and (due in part to the legacies of farming museums) much of it centers on the implements of food and agriculture. Debra Reid's *Interpreting Agriculture at Museums and Historic Sites* (Rowman & Littlefield, 2017) treats the material culture of farming at some length, expanding on her article "Tangible Agricultural History: An Artifact's Eye View of the Field," *Agricultural History* 86:3 (Summer 2012). Specific works like Alison J. Clark's "Tupperware: Product as Social Relation" in *American Material Culture: The Shape of the Field*, Ann Smart Martin and J. Ritchie Garrison, eds. (Winterthur Museum, 1997) or Abigail Carroll's *Of Kettles and Cranes: Colonial Revival Kitchens and the Performance of National Identity* offer examples of kitchen and farm objects used to interpret meaningful narratives.

Taking a step outside the professional and scholarly literatures on sources and artifacts, public historians interpreting the tools and technologies of food production may want to investigate the field of "appropriate technology" as a possible source of information and inspiration. Drawing on the "small is beautiful" and renewable energy movements of the 1970s, adherents of appropriate technology favor muscle- and renewably powered, environmentally responsible, and decentralized methods and machinery. While they focus largely on alternative modes of rural economic development outside already industrialized countries, they are also in dialogue with efforts in the U.S. and elsewhere to relearn and apply smaller-scaled technologies in the food sector and many other areas. Tillers International in Scotts, Michigan, is an organization that has productively blended present-oriented development projects with deep study of past technologies, including in a small on-site museum of their own, while the FarmHack movement also creatively uses and adapts older technologies for today's small farms. In addition to being sources of information for public historians and museums thinking about ways to link artifacts of the past with questions in the present, people involved in relearning, teaching, and disseminating these smaller-scale methods are potential partners who may find value in historians' own knowledge and skills, illustrating the productive possibilities at the blurred edges of past and present.

WORK IN PROGRESS—AN INTERVIEW WITH VALERIE SEGREST: FOOD, HISTORY, AND HEALING

FIGURE 5.3 Valerie Segrest.

A nutritionist, educator, and enrolled member of the Muckleshoot Indian Tribe, Valerie Segrest specializes in local and traditional foods of the Puget Sound region, serving her community by coordinating and managing the Muckleshoot Food Sovereignty Project (MFSP) (Figure 5.3). Native movements for "food sovereignty" (the right of communities to determine their own healthy and culturally appropriate food needs and to control their food supply) build on ideas articulated in the 1990s by La Via Campesina, an international peasant farmers advocacy group. These issues take on added import when considered in light of Native tribal sovereignty, the principle
(Continued)

underlying the right to tribal self-government. For Segrest and other Native food sovereignty advocates, preserving access to traditional foodways, lands, and cultural continuity are interconnected issues. As Segrest notes, food and water rights were integral to the treaties made by tribal governments; leaders felt an imperative to ensure that "we'd be able to flourish physically, culturally, and spiritually for centuries to come."[13]

In food, Segrest finds a "living link" with land and ancestry, discovering in traditional eating practices a means of connecting contemporary Native communities to a sense of place, cultural identity, and better health. With the Muckleshoot Food Sovereignty Project, Segrest builds community food security by maintaining knowledge about, and access to, traditional cultural foods, using intergenerational explorations of food as "an organizing tool." The MFSP offers workshops, contributes articles to the tribal newspaper, facilitates discussion programs and the sharing of cultural teachings, and suggests health-supporting protocols like eating a traditional meal once a week and designing school, senior, and community center menus around local and seasonal food availability. Here, Segrest demonstrates how combining sources including community consultation, oral history, and archival research contributes to the survival of traditional practice, as she reflects on the deeper meanings she finds through connecting contemporary people to longstanding traditions, "remembering what we already know" to continue the tribal stewardship of the food system.[14]

Please tell us about how you began work with the Muckleshoot Food Sovereignty Project. What motivated you to begin looking at foodways of the past, and how did you work with the community and archival sources to surface long-held knowledge?

My background is in nutrition; I chose to study nutrition because of the high prevalence of health problems in tribal communities—things that I know are totally preventable diseases, like diabetes and heart disease. If you just change your diet, you can prevent those things from manifesting in your life. But I also know, as a historian, that the current diet we were eating has been superimposed on tribal communities, and that 150 years ago, there was *no* recorded incidence of diabetes, for example. So I started asking my community what was happening, what had happened. A lot of people mentioned to me that there was a time when the cultural transmission of food teaching had been severed. My family is a great example of that; we never received those teachings. 150 years ago, our people were eating over 300 different traditional foods. Today, we eat only between 13 and 20 of those foods. At the time [I began working on the MFSP], I was doing a project with the Burke Museum. They had a database of archaeological sites where they had found plant foods and shell middens around the region, and that's where that number of over 300 traditional foods comes from.

So how do we revive those foods, and what happens in the process of reviving those foods, when we get people involved? What I found is that people are really hungry for knowledge, that when we can put a traditional foods diet into a modern context, it helps people develop a sense of identity, a sense of who they are and where they come from, and how they navigate the two worlds we walk in as Native people. There is potential for incredible healing to happen in that journey. So the MFSP aims to create a culturally relevant nutrition curriculum. We also look at places where food can be grown, or used to be grown, and how we can engage people in revitalizing those food efforts. Finally, we recognize that food is an interface between every department we've created on our own governmental level, as well as in government-to-government relationships, so we try to develop strong partnerships with our tribal Wildlife Program, with the state Department of Fish and Wildlife, with schools, county, and state bodies. Whatever efforts are going on out there, we want to work with them—we don't try to reinvent the wheel.

What are some of the major activities of the Muckleshoot Food Sovereignty Project?

We do a lot of work around salmon right now. It's a hot issue. Genetically engineered salmon is now before the FDA, to decide whether this [the introduction of genetically engineered salmon into the food supply] will happen. Tribal people were never invited to the table to discuss whether it was even appropriate to create a Frankenfish in our food system, which would be the very first GMO animal integrated into our food system. As far as our culture, we organize our life around salmon. It is not separate from who we are. Our bodies have been built for thousands of years on our relationship with that fish. We brought it to our tribal council's attention, and passed a resolution against the legalization of GMO fish. We took that resolution to the Affiliated Tribes of Northwest Indians, and they passed it. Now it has been passed at the National Congress of American Indians level, which means that the entire Indian Country opposes the production of GM salmon. But it still hasn't been discussed on the FDA level at all. FDA employees have straight-up said "Do we even need to talk to tribes?" Yes! That food is our cultural and intellectual property.

We deal with things like that, but we also take groups of people to huckleberry meadows, showing them how to identify the plant, talking about how this food is anti-diabetic, discussing different ways of accessing and harvesting and processing this plant. And we coordinate with food policy councils and governmental organizations to help build our regional food system.

How can traditional cultural knowledge help support the development of a healthier contemporary food system?

I can't tell you how many times I sit in food policy meetings and discussions where I say, "Remember, we have an ancient food system here that feeds a lot of people." Maybe a lot of us don't eat those traditional foods, or know how to harvest or hunt or fish, but there are people that still do. We really try to not talk in a past tense. Ours really is a living culture, and just as our

(Continued)

ancestors were very innovative, we also use what's innovative at the time. I had a carver once tell me that people told him "it's not very traditional to use a chainsaw," but he said "if my ancestors could have used one, they would!" I'm not coming from a stance that says "let's decolonize our food system," because I'm not insisting on eating only pre-Contact stuff. We can celebrate kale, and peas, and tomatoes just as much as we can celebrate huckleberries, fir teas, and stinging nettles. How do we take the best of both systems and create an abundance that feeds the future? We need to honor the past food system that fed people for a long time, and still feeds people very well today.

How do you show that knowledge from the past can still be relevant to contemporary people and the challenges they face? How do you link food awareness across the generations?

Everything we do, we personally invite an elder to come and witness and work. I worked with over a hundred youth this summer developing herbal first aid kits with 12 items of traditional medicine, made with wild plants available right outside your door. What I hear time and time again are concerns that "our youth are rowdy, they're troublemakers, they don't care"—but when I talk to them from the standpoint that if we take care of ourselves and our tribal knowledge, if we learn about these traditions, if we hold ourselves in a good place, then they will be going out in the world to heal somebody— then, I don't have enough for them to do. Something turns on inside of them. This is the knowledge they're so hungry for—that direct connection to their ancestors in a real-time way. And that's what it was for me, too. While I was studying that database at the Burke Museum, one day I was walking in downtown Seattle, near the site of my community's traditional village site in Pioneer Square, and I was munching on a handful of hazelnuts from the farmers market. That day, when I went into the database, I read something saying Muckleshoots had been harvesting and eating hazelnuts for 300 years. I was like, "Yes! My ancestors were eating hazelnuts hundreds of years ago!" and I don't think I could feel any closer to them than I did in that moment. Here I am, eating this food that my ancestors built their lives upon.

But there's also a science behind it. I have a medical degree, and I also talk about the genetics and epigenetics that are embedded in traditional foodways. For instance, rose hips are a traditional food that is very high in Vitamin C, and it comes out at a certain time of year, so it's important to eat it then. So for youth, these understandings that connect to science are very relevant to them and to their practice.

Just about every museum and historic site in North America is situated in a landscape with a Native history and sometimes a continuing Native presence. When they teach about food and foodways, what should the people interpreting those places know about representing ancient foodways and the issue of food sovereignty? What would you say to them?

I would say, "Watch your language." Avoid the past tense, because the more we seem to celebrate a culture as if it were gone, the more invisible we become. People say things like "Native people *used* to use nettles"—actually, I do, I'm here, and I use nettles all year long. We haven't disappeared. We still practice those traditions, and using present-tense language encourages people to recognize that we still exist in the world. Terms like "food desert," for instance, can be pretty derogatory toward folks in the Southwest, like the Paiute and the Shoshone, who I grew up with. They see the desert as a thriving, rich landscape that they get abundant food from. There's a lot of food in the desert. Don't use past tense, and don't use derogatory remarks.

Also, I would encourage people at those sites to diversify what they think of as food. Get your head out of the pasture, and look into the woods that surround your farm. Look for the fir tips, look for the mushrooms on your forest floor. Those were also foods that were cultivated here. The forest is full of food! In Seattle, they just started a food forest in Beacon Hill, and one article called it "Seattle's First Food Forest." Ah, no, there was a forest here from long ago, and it was a food forest. That's what's going to help get equity in our food system—using culturally appropriate language to bring everyone to the food table.

Equity is an important issue. It seems like the face of the food movement is often thought of as a white, middle-class, urban, or suburban face, but once you begin looking around, it becomes clear that people in all communities are concerned about food, from different cultural standpoints. Do you see your food work as equity work?

I think this is what's so exciting about food sovereignty: the chance to educate. Native people have histories that many people don't know much about at all. What we learn in school about the way things went down in the past is not true. It's very generalized and it's very shallow. And when Native people are heard talking about our food system, the opportunity that presents itself is an opportunity for the truth to be told. We can't deny that there was a rich food system that created a rich social network.

One of the main pillars of our culture, one of the holiest things you can do, the most heart-centered demonstration of generosity and honor and balance on the land, is to feed somebody, to cook a meal. That's what you do. When you have a stranger in your home, someone that's not feeling well, you feed somebody. And that's the center of *everybody's* tradition—not just Native Americans, but all over the globe, you feed somebody. The beauty that's represented there!

And with all the implications that can come out of this, the effect is that we can *be* heard and *feel* heard. Food is what binds us together and gives us common ground. That's what I think is really encouraging about the food movement. I think we can get really caught up in talking about inequity and invisible people, but we are in it together. There *are* a lot of issues and losses, runoff from farms getting into our rivers, challenges in revitalizing our fishing industry, destruction of forest habitat. Fish, which has fed people in the

(Continued)

Northwest for 10,000 years, is suffering from abuse and damage to the fisheries. We are the generation that has to watch that, and we could be the generation to watch the last salmon go up the river. So we're dealing with some really serious moments. We don't have time to pick people apart. We have to come together.

When I first started getting up and speaking in public about these issues, I was so nervous: "What do I have to say? I'm just a kid!" One of my teachers looked at me and told me "It's not about you." Instant relief. It's *not* about me. It's about the food. It's about the work that needs to be done. When you do that work, have faith in it, believe in it, it will take care of you. We can sit and talk about "This isn't fair to me," or "The middle-class white folks are getting all the money to do all the work," and that may be true, but when you have a chance to sit at the table, you are reminded that we're there. We are bringing something very important to the table, because we talk about food as much more than a commodity. It is a gift, it is a teacher, and an amazing community organizing tool. This is why I wanted to be a nutritionist—I didn't want to just count numbers in food, but to see the spirit of it. When we get out in the landscape to see a plant, an animal, a fish, I see how we receive healing in that process, feel that reciprocity. That's what the nutrition world is starving for.

Notes

1 See "1771 Massachusetts Tax Inventory," http://sites.fas.harvard.edu/~hsb41/masstax/masstax.cgi. Because online addresses are often subject to "link rot" over time, you may need to re-search for these resources. In general, we are including specific titles of resources and documents here rather than URLs (web addresses) for all of them.

2 As of this writing, Ancestry.com includes a category for "Selected U.S. Federal Census Non-Population Schedules, 1850–1880." You can search for it directly under the census for the relevant year or search for specific farmer names and look for entries in the non-population schedules for those people.

3 A search within the USDA website for "history nutrition guides" should produce several useful collections and pages relating to the evolution of government food guides dating back as far as 1894.

4 The U.S Fish Commission's *Annual Report to Congress*, published from 1871 to 1903, and its annual *Bulletin of the United States Fish Commission* (1881–1903) are the fisheries equivalent of the USDA's compilations of agricultural census data. Both are available online as of this writing, as are some of the volumes of the foundational 1884 study *Fisheries and Fisheries Industries of the United States* produced by the U.S. Fish Commission in its early years.

5 For example, the U.S. Forest Service was created in 1905 with a mandate of preserving natural habitat and forest resources. Its work overlapped to some extent with that of the National Park Service, established in 1916 to safeguard places deemed significant to national memory and character. In the 1930s, New Deal legislation created a number of conservation-focused programs, many of which disappeared when the immediate crises of economic and environmental collapse seemed over. As noted in the preceding chapter, the 1933 Agricultural Adjustment Act (the original Farm

Bill) included a provision for supporting conservation efforts by farmers, but this function was stripped from the 1938 act that superseded it, and conservation was not reintroduced to the Farm Bill until the 1980s. The Environmental Protection Agency is a relative newcomer, created in 1970 as an umbrella organization dealing with many of the scattered concerns about the health of human and non-human species and environments, but issues relating to food production are not included in its purview, an indication of the difficulty of piecing back together a sense of interrelatedness in food, health, economic, and environmental issues. Energy-related issues are more fragmented yet and are only beginning to be linked with food concerns; the 2002 Farm Bill was the first to include a section focusing specifically on energy. The 2008 Farm Bill included more funding for energy programs, including some controversial support for biofuel production; the 2014 bill reauthorized these expenditures and also built on energy efficiency and renewable energy initiatives.

6 For an excellent example of how to read these kinds of sources critically, linking them with the kinds of questions in the triple top line narrative, see E. Melanie DuPuis, "In the Name of Nature: Ecology, Marginality, and Rural Land Use During the New Deal," in *Creating the Countryside: The Politics of Rural and Environmental Discourse*, E. Melanie DuPuis and Peter Vandergeest, eds. (Philadelphia: Temple University Press, 1996), pp. 99–134.

7 *Science in the Kitchen* was written by E.E. Kellogg and published in Chicago by the Modern Medicine Publishing Company in 1893. *Mary at the Farm* was written by Edith M. Thomas and published in Norristown, Pennsylvania, by John Hartenstine in 1915. The inscription in the digital copy of the latter in the *Feeding America* collection is dated 1968 and shows that the book was given as a gift from one woman to another in that year, perhaps reflecting a renewed interest in "old time" foodways in this later era of reaction against more industrialized food.

8 Thomas, *Mary at the Farm*, 14–15.

9 Irma S. Rombauer and Marion Rombauer Becker, *Joy of Cooking* (Indianapolis: Bobbs-Merrill Company, 1964 edition), 453.

10 "About 'What's on the Menu,'" New York Public Library website.

11 The anthology *American Georgics: Writings on Farming, Culture, and the Land* (Edwin C. Hagenstein, Sara M. Gregg, and Brian Donahue, eds., Yale University Press, 2011) contains a wonderful selection of these early agrarian writings. Dona Brown's *Back to the Land: The Enduring Dream of Self-Sufficiency in Modern America* (University of Wisconsin Press, 2011) draws heavily on the prolific writings of back-to-the-landers around the turn of the twentieth century.

12 Hurt, *American Agriculture*, 149. For a more in-depth exploration of the reach of these publications, see Sally McMurry, "Who Read the Agricultural Journals? Evidence from Chenango County, New York, 1839–1865," *Agricultural History*, 63 (Fall 1989), 1–19.

13 Valerie Segrest, "Welcome," Muckleshoot Food Sovereignty Project website. http://nwicplantsandfoods.com/muckleshoot.

14 Valerie Segrest, "Food Sovereignty: Valerie Segrest at TEDX Rainier" (presentation at TEDX Rainier, January 23, 2014).

SECTION III
Moving into Action

6

A FRESH APPROACH TO FOOD
AND FARM INTERPRETATION

The last section laid out a set of tools for developing new perspectives on the local histories embedded in our food system—the "triple top line," considerations of scale and a capsule framework for understanding food and farm policy and some of the specialized sources that can help us interpret food history. These tools are useful, but only if we put them to work. How can we use them to craft refreshed farm and food interpretations—presentations and experiences that support more nuanced thinking about how our society has tackled the perennially challenging task of feeding itself equitably, healthfully, reliably, and sustainably? How can these tools help our communities address food questions that link past, present, and future? This chapter presents recommendations for a staged process guiding the strategic planning and implementation of civically engaged food interpretation in museums and public history sites—interpretation designed to "stick" and serve its constituencies well into the future.

Somehow, despite good intentions and ever-present interpretations of food and farming, we seem to keep failing to forge these links. We've identified two important reasons for this. The first is related to the "just do it" mentality of many food activists. Driven by the urgent need for change, public historians often find themselves responding to a sense of pressure to *act*, taking advantage of a cultural moment that drives audiences toward historical content about food. Individual interpreters, educators, and program planners, perceiving potential connections to the food movement, have already had a visible influence, launching new initiatives and developing projects from within their existing areas of authority. Museum practitioners offer new cooking classes and partnership events, post activities on social media, invite farmers and chefs in for experiments with historical preparations, and introduce more food events into the annual calendar. They've achieved some remarkable successes—enlarging and diversifying audiences, re-branding fusty-sounding programs, and drawing clear lines of relevance between museum activities and contemporary food questions.

But, speaking generally, these efforts are still in danger of being dismissed as "flavor of the moment" projects. Because they tend be overlaid on or squeezed into interpretive plans established decades ago, they don't carry the same institutional weight as the foundational interpretive messages that pervade audience experience and link in multiple directions to other key content. Interpreters invested in food issues can find their work cast as a colorful add-on to core interpretive goals, but not an essential component of those goals. Operating alone or as a "skunkworks" where new ideas are developed outside the mainstream, individuals, isolated departments or divisions, or small groups do not have the leverage to command large expenditures, shift resources, make major changes in collections use and display, or meet the other requirements of a powerful and coherent interpretive experience. This limited scope of operation means that these atomized efforts will usually fall short of creating memorable public experiences with food in history or lasting commitments to the topic within organizations. As we've joked while compiling this book, "we won't solve this with a cornbread recipe." No single program or exhibit, no matter how well developed, can deeply embed an engaged approach to food issues in an organization.

The second reason public historians hold back from creating dialogue between past and present is the readiness with which we tend to revert to the entrenched habits of recent professional practice, which are themselves shaped by the legacies of much deeper patterns of presentation and communication. Obsessing on the "what," in Darwin Kelsey's terms, rather than the "why," has not encouraged us to envision how historical presentations of food could be reorganized to better serve audiences in the present. Classic presentation genres—exhibition, period installation, demonstration, re-creation, living history—tend to set audiences up for concrete and often aesthetic comparisons: for instance, warm milk frothing from a cow's udder into a pail looks, feels, smells, and tastes different from milk in a plastic container at the grocery store, inviting a comparison at a purely sensory level. But the varied set of conclusions a visitor might draw from that experience is unlikely to generate critical and structural comparisons between past animal husbandry practices and dairying economies with the hidden complexities of the dairy industry that produces low-cost plastic jugs of milk today. Standing at the edge of the chasm between the pretty (or gritty) "pastness" of historic sites and exhibits and the busy, multifaceted, confusing, and contentious world of present-day food issues, we as practitioners of history feel nervous about making the leap ourselves, let alone urging audiences to jump with us.

The good news is that, once we decide to move forward, we are already well equipped to bridge these two kinds of content. Interpreting food systems doesn't require that we reinvent public history from scratch—just that we take a serious and strategic approach that anticipates continuous experimentation. The staged approach we suggest here promises to help overcome the seemingly opposed professional values of "just do it!" urgency and reluctance to engage in current events. Recognizing that history organizations are complex, with multiple and diverse audiences, participants, and obligations, we advocate working with and within governance, management, and community structures to align vision, resources, personnel, activities, and outcomes. This approach—serious, collaborative, and inclusive—has four components:

1. A guiding philosophical orientation that includes an embrace of the contemporary and a commitment to shared inquiry
2. A cultivation of organizational support to ground new interpretive goals in institutional structures, mission, and strategy
3. An interpretive planning process that supports themes related to the triple top line and incorporates critical criteria for transformative food interpretation
4. A stylistic approach marked by creativity, imagination, and experimentation, illustrated by examples of current projects

These four components overlap and shade into one another yet also represent distinct arenas of thought and action that deserve careful attention before launching a new interpretive project.

Guiding Principles

Embrace Contemporary Questions

If you've read this far, the notion that historical thinking can be used to engage and investigate contemporary topics should come as no surprise. It is really the paramount principle of this approach. Yet, some practitioners still feel hesitant to engage in contemporary food politics and policy—a lack of confidence related to an uncertain, on-again off-again relationship of public history, civic responsibility, and democratic action.

But today's public historians are increasingly turning to professional traditions that see historical thinking and evidence from the past as resources that can be applied to current questions and choices across a variety of civic and social realms. For example, the planners of the Chicago-based National Museum of Public Housing see their museum-in-progress as "a powerful lens for thinking about the intersection of public responsibility and the creation of home" and a place to challenge narratives about public housing and reveal ways in which "social and racial equality remains closely tied to housing issues in the present." These practitioners, like many of their peers, are challenging the belief that being professionally responsible means maintaining a distance from matters relating to civic decision-making and public policy.[1] As public historians find good ways to problematize it, the history of food production can be explored and examined in similar ways.

Shared Inquiry

This second principle asserts that transformative interpretive projects require processes of shared inquiry. This approach, now widely endorsed by museums and public historians, is seen in the recent proliferation of crowd-sourced exhibitions, pop-up installations, dialogic tours, and open collections. But there are particular reasons to adopt shared processes when re-interpreting food production and consumption. In a very real sense, the history of food systems is a history that doesn't exist yet in a readily accessible form. Despite its accessibility as an entry point for thinking about issues of economy, energy, environment, and equity, those stubborn issues remain daunting and unresolved, and we soon find ourselves a long way from the cozy territory of baby chicks and heritage tomatoes. New investigations may destabilize audiences' taken-for-granted assumptions or stances—and also our own. Acknowledging the unsettled nature of the questions and the unfinished project of searching for answers is an important component of rethinking food interpretation. As museum professionals and practitioners of public history, we must demonstrate a willingness to ask probing questions about the nature of our economy, seeking perspectives and responses from as many different participants in the system as possible to develop the fullest available picture. This is where we move beyond food as a starting point and encounter the complex and sometimes challenging implications of what we've started.

The inherent subjectivity of food experience guarantees the existence of multiple perspectives, including some that organizational staff are unable to imagine. Creating impact on audiences and on the food system demands the forging of new relationships and the ability to think creatively and expansively. Unless we remain open to working with a variety of views, we won't surface the full range of realities and considerations operating in the food system and will rely on our sometimes-inadequate old learning, resulting in unbalanced or shallow interpretation projects. This task of relearning is not easy or straightforward, for exactly the same reasons that it is so important: struggling with accepted truths, it is open ended and engaged with the present-day world. Seeing ourselves as partners with our audiences and visitors in this process is not only a way to invite them into the work of building new historical knowledge but an important acknowledgment of our own participation in the civic processes of rethinking and reshaping the living systems on which we all depend.

Cultivating the Organization

Once philosophical foundations are in place, the next step in building an engaged approach to food interpretation is to cultivate the organizational structures and systems that will support it now and in the future. Complex and hierarchical, bureaucratic and managerial, museums and other historical organizations are designed to foster stability in perpetuity. The downside, of course, is that they can be resistant to change. However, their formalized structures offer clear pathways for arriving at new interpretive perspectives. The organizational framework that can sometimes seem constraining can serve as a stable platform for a lasting, successful, and sustainable engagement with food issues, solidly grounded in the organization's culture.

This work begins where all cultivation begins: with careful preparation of the ground to create conditions capable of nurturing new projects and relationships.

We suggest that the following three steps are essential prerequisites to crafting a contemporary, civically engaged interpretation of food and farming.

Find a Seedbed in the Mission

In any mission-driven organization, the mission statement provides the strongest anchor point for interpretive work. The mission offers not only a justification for new initiatives, but also an imperative to further the institution's purpose. Initiatives that align well with principles and ideas in the mission statement—whether those principles are directly stated or implicit—will stand a greater chance of finding permanent expression in institutional culture.

The Missouri History Museum (MHM) offers an excellent example of finding a basis for action in a museum mission. After the widespread civic unrest in response to the 2014 death of Michael Brown, a young, unarmed African-American man who was shot by a white police officer, the MHM turned to the purpose expressed in its mission: "To deepen the understanding of past choices, present circumstances, and future possibilities; strengthen the bonds of the community; and facilitate solutions to common problems." The staff recognized in this mission a mandate to act and put together community programs in response to the event, including a panel discussion on race and policing and a town hall meeting on the recent history of racial tensions and ideas for healing. A program planner told *Museum News*, "I never thought of asking permission to address controversial topics that are clearly present in the community. From the board of trustees to the president, the museum has always been supportive of programs and exhibits that appear controversial, but are really just part of the institution's mission – bringing people together to facilitate solutions to the common problems that history produces."[2] Staying true to their institution's purpose, the staff brings relevant historical content and perspective to current events and then shares inquiry with audiences who, in turn, contribute their own ideas, experiences, and expertise.

That kind of clarity and conviction is a strong argument for grounding food history work in the mission. Before you begin work on new food and farming interpretation efforts revisit and review the mission statement, discussing it in depth with both the core interpretive team and members of the external community. Where does the mission overlap with or suggest a connection to critical food issues your audiences and communities face? You may want to use a facilitated process to generate, test, question, and prioritize those points of connection until they are clear in the minds of all the participants, crafting additional supportive language as needed to document and share your thinking. Identify and highlight key words and phrases when introducing ideas, presenting proposals, or writing reports. Be prepared to let go of initiatives that don't support the mission in a clear way.

Unfortunately, some practitioners find themselves stuck with institutional mission statements that might best be described as flaccid. Dated, vague, and unambitious, these statements offer little more than a list of activities: "to collect, preserve, and display" the artifacts of a place or industry, or to "tell the stories of" an era or group of people. These missions lack a major critical component: a compelling, convincing statement about *why* these activities should be undertaken. Museum gurus Hal and Susan Skramstad have forcefully argued that "a good mission establishes the distinctiveness and importance of what the organization does and its value to the communities it serves," adding that if a museum's mission statement does not supply an answer to the questions "So what?" and "Who cares?" it will be useless as a guide to action and leave room for other, sometimes unspoken, agendas to drive decisions about where to invest resources and what topics to explore.[3] History practitioners facing the challenge of a weak mission statement may need to consider a push to revisit, clarify, rewrite, or otherwise renew it. If that's unlikely to move forward—and few projects are larger or more time-consuming—consider supplementing the existing mission by writing a department or group *statement of purpose* that describes specifically how proposed food history projects will link to, and help fulfill, the institution's fundamental purpose.

Connect to Strategic Goals

At any given moment, most museums and historical institutions are in the midst of implementing one or more strategies to enhance sustainability, improve efficacy, or widen impact. Some have elaborate strategic plans in three-inch-thick binders listing multiple goals, subgoals, objectives, responsible parties, and timelines; others have a more succinct set of key priorities, or a single major one, written or unwritten. No matter which is the case, strategic goals are another place to seek both inspiration for project design and the institutional support necessary for building solid new food and farming projects.

Strategic documents can suggest synergies between potential interpretive goals and activities and the institution's self-described near-term needs and aspirations. Strategic plans often highlight what the institution cares about most at a particular moment, whether increasing attendance, raising funds for capital projects, attracting partnerships, or expanding educational services. Identifying one or more existing strategic goals that could be advanced through a food-related project can strengthen support and attract resources, while easing concerns about whether the moment is right to take on food topics. In project proposals, cite strategic goals specifically, demonstrating how projects align with and further those goals and illustrating exactly how they will accomplish that—with quantification, if possible. The discipline of structuring food-project proposals around tough strategic questions can only make them stronger and more likely to succeed.

Build a Shared Vision

History practitioners often find that their work pulls them in dozens of different directions. Departments struggle over resources and priorities; directors and administrators have their eyes on finances and ten-year plans; trustees focus on long-term institutional sustainability; donors want demonstrations of impact; volunteers want participation and recognition; neighbors have opinions about what the museum ought to be doing for the locals; and various other groups—interest, affinity, cultural—also weigh in. Since not all stakeholders are drawn in for the same reasons, they may not automatically subscribe to the same values or beliefs about what the museum should be doing, and they might not care about how well the project aligns with mission and strategy. That's where the process of building a shared vision comes in.

The good news about having a multiplicity of stakeholders is that it is also a pool of potential advocates. As ideas for food initiatives form, consider approaching stakeholders—as individuals or groups—and broaching ideas. When invited in at an early stage, they may become valuable partners, improving the ideas, identifying resources and new contacts, pointing out hidden obstacles, and serving as evangelists and allies.

As you build the project coalition, look back at the many actors in the food movement listed in Chapter 2. You may be surprised to find that key stakeholders care about one or more of these issues—hunger, gardening, school lunch, or fine dining. That personal interest may act as a means toward enlisting involvement and linking the organization with new networks. Also, consider which of these subgroups are represented in your local community, on your board, in your neighborhood, in local schools and universities, and among your professional partners and vendors. Rather than assuming those groups will be only your target audience, approach them at early stages as planning partners and participants in shared inquiry.

Allies may be found in surprising places. Within the institution, avoid going only to the "usual suspects." Curatorial departments, of course, may be great supporters of new initiatives, digging out objects and documents never before viewed in light of what they have to say about food and farming history. But don't overlook marketing staff, who may rush to promote the strong appeal of food-related efforts and get the attention of local and regional press, or buildings and grounds teams, whose knowledge of land, equipment, seasonality, and the physical possibilities and constraints of museum spaces may lead to more successful, and often more expansive, visions of what might be accomplished. A broad, diverse, and enthusiastic base of support, in which many internal and external stakeholders can see a valuable and appreciated role to play, can advance an idea more rapidly and be helpful in overcoming the kinds of obstacles we discuss in Chapter 8.

Interpretive Planning and the Triple Top Line

Though most museums and historic sites think of themselves as informal, free-choice learning environments, most audience experiences still result from an internally driven planning process that specifies goals for communicating historical information—what we call interpretation. The intentional design of these platforms for experience is the distinguishing feature of museum learning, the quality that makes it different from the similarly enriching experiences found at a farmers market or on a food tour. Even a simple heirloom apple tasting or biscuit-making demonstration should have clearly articulated and documented interpretive goals.

Why is this so important? Without interpretive planning to link detail to larger ideas, experiences in museums can feel like a pleasant but unconnected hodgepodge of facts, events, and sensory impressions, vaguely tied together by some continuity of period or place. As interpretive planner Lisa Brochu puts it, planning allows us to "look at an apple and see the orchard, the processing plant, the grocery store, and tonight's dessert."[4] With that example, Brochu underscores the particular relevance of planning to the interpretation of food, in which so many aspects of production, processing, consumption, and disposal are chronically absent from typical museum experiences.

This kind of planning becomes essential when we aim to go beyond the "butter churn" experience and link to the interlocking contexts of food production in history introduced in Chapter 3—the triple top line of *environment, economy,* and *energy.* A well-thought-out planning process can help public historians keep sight of how localized histories have been influenced by the interactions of economic systems, modes of food production, and different energy sources and how matters of scale influence both food production and consumption—interactions that remain relevant both in explaining and making decisions about the conditions surrounding food systems today. Public history places and projects can become sites of inquiry that use the past to inspire creative problem solving, bringing disparate community sectors together to understand and improve food conditions. Guided by the triple top line, public historians can help their participants retrace past transportation and sourcing links and discover dormant food industries that might have the potential for revival. They can reconstruct historical methods for managing urban livestock or distributing food in the historical equivalent of "food deserts" and evaluate the outcomes of those projects. They can help audiences see how enslaved, immigrant, and child labor have contributed to driving down food prices, both in the past and today, to the point that most people are unaware of the true costs of food.

The Interpretive Planning Process: Key Questions

The field of interpretive planning has been developing for more than half a century, generating a number of commonly used frameworks. These process outlines offer step-by-step methods for working through multiple phases of planning, moving from the macro scale of the institution's purpose to the micro level of decisions about specific interpretive modalities (text, multimedia, display, performance, demonstration, participation, etc.) and ways of implementing them. There's no need to reinvent this particular wheel. But it is time to adapt our process to reflect recent thinking. Here, we will draw on three of the most commonly used works on interpretive process: the thoughtful and highly adaptable visitor-centered planning model developed by Marcella Wells, Barbara Butler, and Judith Koke in their 2014 *Interpretive Planning for Museums: Integrating Visitor Perspectives in Decision Making*, the work of Lisa Brochu in *Interpretive Planning: The 5-M Model*, and Barbara Abramoff Levy's "Interpretive Planning: Why and How," in *Interpreting Historic House Museums*.[5] Below, we summarize the stages most interpretive planning processes move through as a series of simple, reflective questions and note ways in which specific adaptations will help increase the quality and impact of food and farming interpretation.

Question 1: Where Are We?

Most interpretive planning approaches begin with an internal analysis of the current situation and justification of the need for planning, aiming to create connections among mission, strategy, priorities, and interpretive initiatives. But attending only to internal considerations about institutional needs, academic goals, and so on immediately risks disconnection with the wider food community. As Wells et al. note, this starting point is an appropriate time to consider the needs and issues of constituent communities and to think about what kinds of impacts and outcomes the organization could produce in the wider world. Remembering the concern to consider all scales of action, interpretive planners should include a survey of current conditions such as national policies with local impact, such as the Farm Bill; regional master plans; state agricultural, economic development, tourism, and food security plans; local initiatives; and regional and local food media. Planners should also examine challenges faced in local communities. For instance, is there concern about the impact of climate change on local food industries? Are shifting demographics bringing new food traditions to the area or transforming earlier ones? What food products help to define the region and place? What food issues threaten public health?

Question 2: Why Are We Doing this?

Planning processes normally ask institutions to list their purposes, goals, and intended outcomes, articulating the differences they are trying to make. In our view, these goals should be developed not just for the institution itself but also in collaboration with constituent communities. The interpretive possibilities that emerge with deep consideration of community goals may lead in surprising new directions. Andrea Jones of the Accokeek Foundation in Maryland provides an example:

> Last year I had a meeting with two teachers at a high school that has an environmental/agriculture program. We went to the school to drum up business for our new environmental school tour, but one of the needs that we discovered was that their students needed places to do outside projects

and internships related to agriculture. Many of them were involved in the Future Farmers of America. Because we could see funding opportunities for an intensive teen summer internship, we created a program called the Agriculture Conservation Corps just for these students. The program turned out to be a huge win for us. We were able to raise a decent amount of money to pay the interns because funders loved the "story" of the museum helping teens, and the clear impact of this program. It was a hit with the press, board members, and other stakeholders because you could really see what a difference the program made in these nine students' lives. I guess with this program, the community didn't provide the vision, just the need for a space for teens to do projects. We responded while still fulfilling our mission to reconnect the students with nature and the food system.[6]

Jones entered the relationship with the school thinking mainly about promoting her own institution's goals. But through exploration, she made new discoveries about the school's needs, resulting in a completely different program that better served students', teachers', and funders' goals.

Question 3: What Do We Have to Offer? What Don't We Have?

Understanding the assets and resources your project commands—and what it may lack—is a critical step in interpretive planning. Wells et al. also suggest asking who wants the organization's products and why. A key component of the inventory process should be an understanding of your own site's or organization's history of interpreting food and farming topics, as discussed in Chapter 1. It may be that you find that everything old is new again, rediscovering programs and experiences that could have been inspired by a week-old blog post. Or you may find that old interpretive goals point to messages your institution no longer wishes to send—uncritically nationalistic or parochial ones, for instance. In addition, resist considering the history organization as the only "supplier." Remember stakeholders' and audiences' supplies of knowledge and resources, too, and consider at the outset what they might contribute.[7]

Finally, to involve wider audiences, the resource assessment stage should also include research and reflection on potential barriers to participation, considering such factors as cost, language, hours, physical access, child-friendliness, and perceptions of the organization in the wider community. Wherever possible, interpretive planning should aim to reduce barriers to access.

Question 4: What Do We Make of It All?

Most planning processes center on a thoughtful stage in which participants gather and analyze the information and ideas collected in the previous steps. As always, we believe this analytical phase should include participation from constituents outside the museum. Often, museums aren't aware of all the ways in which their assets might be valuable to others, and this is especially true for food interpretation. For example, the northeastern U.S. is home to several Shaker museums, interpreting the history of religious communities that supported themselves through crafts and agriculture. Shakers devoted enormous energy to improving the seed stock of food plants. Many unique varieties are still in cultivation at Shaker sites, accompanied by rich archival records documenting their culinary properties. Over the past decade, people in the food movement began seeking garden and farm plants well adapted to the northeastern climate and gradually found their way to Shaker seeds. Many of these sites, such as Hancock Shaker Village, now conduct workshops in seed saving, while Slow Food USA is currently evaluating several Shaker plant varieties for inclusion on its preservation register, the Ark of Taste. Including stakeholders from outside the museum in the analysis phase can reveal possibilities that staff alone might not discover, such as potential affinity groups interested in the content, or possible uses of historic resources.

Question 5: Which of Our Ideas Are Most Compelling?

After the wide scope has been established, most interpretive planning models move to the development of themes and supporting experiences. This is the place where the triple top line concept will find concrete application, as it helps to inform the ideas and themes with which audiences will enter into dialogue. "Big ideas" that reveal how site food history is connected to issues of environment, economy, and energy can relate a site's technologies, objects, and stories to more widely resonant personal and civic concerns. Consider food and farm interpretation in light of the "counter-history" of agriculture, the narrative that navigates a middle way between the simplistic progress narrative of industrial success and the nostalgic and romantic narrative of the "olden days." A more questioning and critical history of food will include unintended consequences, damaging effects, and unpredicted problems raised by large-scale industrial production as the foundation of the food system. Audiences are eager to understand contemporary issues in light of past struggles to secure a continuous and safe food supply—a side of the narrative that has often been unavailable through public history experiences. At the same time, interpretation should acknowledge that there is no *perfect* way of farming or eating. Food production, even of the most ecologically sensitive variety, remains a human project that shapes and changes both the human and non-human worlds in a multitude of ways.

Interpretive themes might poke at the concept of "localness"—what were families in the period of interpretation producing on their own, and where was the production prompted, supported, or complemented by larger forces? Trade networks—shipping, overland transport, canals, and rail—often linked households to much larger systems of food production, whether in the form of seeds and tools to establish a new homestead, expensive European and tropical imports to grace a New England planter's table, valued customary foods like sugar and coffee that could not be locally produced, or the shipping infrastructure that allowed farms access to new and more distant markets. Unearthing local relationships with regional, national, and international markets and investigating the reverberation of events at the national and international scale in individual lives create a strikingly relevant picture of the ongoing, open-ended, and fundamental interconnectedness of food systems, today and in the past.

Question 6: How Do We Communicate About these Ideas?

Once themes and key ideas are developed, planning moves to the concrete and practical: the selection of specific interpretive events, exhibitions, projects, programs, or media to produce. This stage calls for a considered approach to design. As with any museum or public history project, passive, static displays are unlikely to produce new insights, profound feelings of connection, or commitment to improving the food system. Participatory, multi-sensory, and open-ended approaches, the integration of visitor storytelling and information sharing, and unconventional installations are likely to be more effective. Challenge yourself to create initiatives that enable participants not just to take in information, but to teach, to create, to influence outcomes (Figure 6.1).

When making interpretive choices for a historic site or re-created environment, give careful consideration to the pros and cons of choosing "moment-in-time" interpretive tactics. As we discussed in Chapter 1, living history, period room installations, and historic villages are a two-edged sword: they can create vivid representations of the past and develop contextual thinking, but in their apparent settled coherence, they can also obscure the uncertainties, anxieties, and deep differences of opinion inherent in any historical moment. In his critique of living history, Scott Magelssen points out the constraints of the technique, implying as it does that events proceeded along an inevitable path to the present: given the confined nature of living history performance, "only a single, agreed-upon ending is ever possible, and thus, the possibilities for discourse are limited before the reenactment is even performed."[8] Observers come into the process only after these presentations receive official sanction, leaving the audience locked out of the moments of design and debate in which the "creative potential" to explore other viewpoints and alternate paths remains present.

But Magelssen also suggests that second-person interpretation and participatory museum theater offer some ways to both present coherent historical settings and explore multiple possible outcomes. Methods that "break the frame" of living history through creative interjection, "bracketing" experience with interpretive conversations before and after, and debriefing about these experiences with guided facilitation, can offer audiences a chance to learn from depictions of the past while maintaining a strong connection to the present. Sites committed to using this modality at least part of the time may want to consider creative interventions that remind visitors of the array of potential choices available at any time in the past and the multiplicity of perspectives on these events.

FIGURE 6.1 At Plimoth Plantation, an interpreter at the Wampanoag Homesite cooks a fowl. Unlike the site's Pilgrim Village, where most interpreters interpret in first-person character, Wampanoag Homesite interpreters have chosen to present in their modern identities. This allows them to escape the limitations of maintaining the illusion of a specific time period and to bring present-day issues into the discussion, including the ways oral histories, language recovery, and archaeological research are contributing to clearer understandings of pre-Contact Wampanoag agriculture and foodways. Image: Massachusetts Office of Travel and Tourism.

Question 7: Great! Now What?

Our last question is about continuing the work. We notice that most interpretive planning approaches to date have overlooked a key component of the design process: the feedback loop of continuing reflection and iteration. To make something new of the ideas and knowledge being shared and explored by institutions and participants together, interpretive planning must be cyclical, building in a final step that sends planners back to the starting point to work with new ideas and make continuous improvements in content and method. As organizations accumulate perspectives and contributions and generate new social outcomes, interpretive achievements become new assets that can inform new themes and experiences. Our practice should build formal structures for documenting and responding to interpretive experiments, reflecting as a staff and community, and sharing findings widely to expand the impact of public history on the food system.

Creativity, Imagination, and Experimentation: Stylistic Approaches

Food and farming issues can move to interpretive front and center without straying far from the classic vocabulary of museum programming. But as Lisa Junkin Lopez demonstrates in the interview at the end of this chapter, they can—and, we think, should—be a basis for bolder experimentation, inventing remixed, hybrid, and collaborative projects. Working with food in critical, poetic, and imaginative ways offers opportunities to expand on traditional formats. Engagement approaches that match contemporary styles of social and recreational interaction may help audiences see museums in a new light.

What really distinguishes the kinds of programs we believe audiences respond to best is a sensibility that unites shared authority with a spirit of inquiry. To be true participants in the contemporary conversation, we need to work in new ways, many of them less familiar in our practice. These approaches need to be intentional, inclusive, and intellectually honest. They should help to empower people to make a range of changes: to question narratives that no longer seem adequate or complete, to demand responsibly sourced and in-depth information, and to make more knowledgeable choices about improving the food system in ways that make sense to them—not just in the grocery store, but at the voting booth and city council meeting. Changing the way public history projects connect to popular understandings of food means changing not just the topics we talk about, but also the very tactics we use to conceive, design, and implement programs. Below, we offer some examples of trends and ideas from our survey of activities advancing the field.

Privilege All the Senses

Museums tend to privilege sight and hearing above other senses, partly because humans can glean information through those senses without risking direct harm to objects. But especially when the topic is food, the omission of touch, taste, and smell becomes glaring. Some of the most promising learning opportunities include new ways of integrating taste and smell. For example, Conner Prairie's "Prairie Plates" series integrates museum content and settings with the farm-to-table trend, inviting local growers, chefs, and other food producers to teach skills ranging from craft brewing to whole-hog butchering. Participants and instructors then sit down at an outdoor table to enjoy a meal crafted during the teaching session, as conversation ranges around topics like the rise of microbrews or the ethics of meat eating and humane husbandry. Such programs captivate all the senses while generating new interpersonal connections, creating platforms for raising questions, and building practical skills that participants might integrate into their daily lives.

Be Responsive to Identified Needs

Some museums who identified a community need during the interpretive planning process have elected to meet it directly. Wyck House in Philadelphia, PA, began as a historic house shrine to a family's participation in the American War of Independence. In 2011, a new strategic plan re-oriented the house and its 2.5-acre garden landscape toward deeper involvement with its urban neighborhood, promoting "values of innovation, social responsibility, and environmental sustainability."[9] In Wyck's substantial garden, staff, invited experts, volunteers and neighbors practice and teach urban agriculture. In the process, the museum has become a clearinghouse on urban beekeeping; their annual Honey Festival brings more than 2,000 people to study and celebrate bees' role in food production, a topic that spans the gamut from entry-level learning about food systems to engagement with questions about colony collapse disorder and its increasingly well-documented connections with pesticides.

Find Hooks in the Headlines

A simple place to begin iterating on existing interpretive methods is to conduct a review of current (or past) presentations, asking "What does the problem, issue, or activity this presentation highlights look like today?" Interpreters seeking "hooks" have always used analogies to present-day life to create bridges to better understandings of the past. This strategy turns that practice around, instead allowing the historical presentation to become a shared text for conversations about how the past led to issues in the present that audiences encounter in news headlines, on television and in social media.

For example, at Strawbery Banke Museum interpreters in a historic kitchen have long listed "food sourcing" among their interpretive points. But recently, by asking what issues are connected to food sourcing *today*, interpreters developed a conversational platform using eighteenth-century confections to explore the contemporary issue of "food miles," or the use of energy to transport food products across great distances. This ripped-from-the-headlines discussion unfolds as interpreters juice lemons and grate sugar, while sharing the source points of these then-exotic treats and the resources required to get them to New England. Through conversation, audiences are invited to re-visit common preconceptions ("back then, everyone ate locally produced food") and to complicate that understanding, discussing the resource investment needed to enjoy certain foods out of season and the mechanisms by which this luxury, once largely confined to elite dining rooms, has become basic to what we consider the good life for everyone. Drawing on the commitment to constant iteration, museums might build in a regular occasion to brainstorm for this kind of nimbleness, allowing a quick-turnaround response to timely but relatively predictable recurring food events—safety scares, blights and shortages, trends and fads.

Share Skills and Resources

Interpreters in history organizations have often mastered a wide range of food management skills. Which of those can be productively shared with audiences as practical additions to their own skills for living? For audiences interested in gardening, seed saving, food preservation and other skills, history organizations can be excellent places to learn not only *how* to, but *why* to learn new skills and how and where they might be applied—or are already being applied—to improving today's food systems.

Also at Strawbery Banke, a re-created 1940s Victory Garden testifies to a short period in which, at the program's peak in 1944, Victory Gardeners produced up to 40 percent of the nation's fresh produce in small plots, community gardens, and containers. Daily garden tours (featuring the occasional chomp into a freshly picked peapod) create an extended opportunity to talk with participants about their personal gardening histories (or lack of access to that experience), illuminating many of the conditions responsible for ebbs and flows in home gardening. How on earth did the United States' federal government get thoroughly urbanized populations—few of them with any personal farming or gardening experience—to learn to grow food in only a few short years? What kinds of people found it easiest to follow the patriotic mandate to garden and put up produce, and who found it physically challenging, insulting (because, out of necessity, they had never *stopped* doing it), or just too expensive?[10] Going one step beyond the red, white, and blue narrative to explore Victory Gardening as it was lived can provoke thinking about the remarkable spike in home gardening over the past decade and perhaps also in previous eras of "back to the land" enthusiasm, exploring questions about whether more people today could grow their own food and what degree of awareness, inclusion, and resource investment would be needed to make that happen.[11] Using a contemporary lens, museum staff can help interested audiences connect with gardening resources or outfit them with seeds, garden plans, and other practical tools, along with the encouragement to begin growing some of their own food or expand beyond their current base of knowledge.

Practice Free-Range Public History

Historical learning doesn't necessarily have to take place at a historic site or in a museum or classroom. Why not look at retail outlets and restaurants as potential sites of food learning? Why shouldn't a museum have a presence at regional food festivals and agricultural fairs? Museums might find interpretive communication is possible by maintaining an educational plot in a city park or community garden, contributing to the food sourcing of schools or senior centers, sharing historical perspectives through op-eds and other local media, co-hosting conferences or training programs, authoring publications or developing web and video projects. The Smithsonian National Museum of American History made friends across the food world with a series of "potluck" posts, in which staff made, photographed, and taste-tested recipes from period cookbooks, decade by decade, tracing technological changes, flavor trends, and social history through Jell-O salads and cheese balls. Taking food preservation into an enthusiastic affinity community, brewing historian and preservation expert Tanya Brock began a series of Picklecraft workshops in Ohio craft breweries. Brock leads a class making pickles using locally grown cucumbers and locally brewed beer; participants learn a simple pickling technique and highlights from the history of food preservation and fermentation.

Create a Hybrid Project or Program

Partly driven by recessionary expediency and partly by a more informal, collaborative zeitgeist, museums are generating exciting, innovative, and promising hybrid models for reducing resource demand while maximizing access. In its 2014 *TrendsWatch* report, the American Alliance of Museums' Center for the Future of Museums called out two related trends: "for profit, for good," or social entrepreneurship, and "collaborative consumption," also known as the sharing economy.[12] These trends are linked by a recognition that conventional organizational models and revenue structures, developed to fit tax codes originating in the 1890s, can limit flexibility, create waste, and impose collaboration-killing legal and bureaucratic barriers.

In response, many kinds of organization are blending activities previously considered separate spheres. Public libraries are lending garden tools and canning equipment. Markets host how-to classes and issue forums. Food tours are taking people into the field to harvest scallops and milk goats. As Darwin Kelsey's interview following Chapter 1 shows, some national parks and other cultural and conservation sites are partnering with farmers to provide access to hard-to-find farmland. Hybridity itself is nothing new—the coffeehouse-slash-art gallery, for instance, has been around a long time—but museums and other similar sites are newly exploring hybrid models to meet their own goals for education and financial sustainability. Some of the most powerful new approaches in food interpretation are questioning basic assumptions of what a museum is and does. Could a museum—on its own or through partners—engage in for-profit food production, making and selling things like cider, honey, farm produce, cured meats, or food service, like running a food truck or a themed destination restaurant?

The Lower East Side Tenement Museum took a hybrid approach in developing its "Foods of the Lower East Side" tour. Urban walking tours featuring restaurant tastings are usually the province of private, for-profit tour operators, but education specialist Adam Steinberg saw an opportunity to link both venerable and recently opened neighborhood food businesses to narratives of immigration, appreciation for diversity, and emotional connection with the past articulated in the museum's mission. On the two-hour tour, a museum guide takes small groups to local storefronts, offering tastings and stories along the way. Snacking on sopressata, pickles, and fried plantains, tour-goers trace demographic changes in the neighborhood's population over time as reflected in the food Steinberg calls "central to the immigrant experience."[13] The tour challenges notions of "authenticity," which guides re define as not a specific correct preparation, but rather a relationship to food as experienced in culture and memory. The ongoing gentrification of the Lower East Side adds a layer of complexity to the tour, one that the Tenement Museum has also sought to engage with in its dialogic encounters with visitors and neighbors.

A hybrid project can be as atomized as a tour or as ambitious as a farming venture. The 2014 *TrendsWatch* highlights the CSA at Gore Place, a historic site in Massachusetts related to Christopher Gore, an early state governor and founder of an agricultural improvement society. On its 10-acre farm, museum staff took a past-focused, illustrative small livestock and farming operation and turned it into a working commercial farm, growing produce and flowers and raising pigs and chickens for meat. The museum is currently engaged in a three-year plan to make the farm financially self-sustaining, running a CSA and selling produce through farmstands, in hopes that it can continue without drawing on the museum's operational budget. As Elizabeth Merritt, TrendsWatch author, observes, though, like many farms in the "real world," Gore Place has found it challenging to break even by growing food alone, and "earns more by selling tickets to farm-related activities"—an "agritainment" strategy that contributes to many other small-scale farms' survival.[14]

This dilemma of course has a long history of its own, one very familiar to generations of back-to-the-land homesteaders, food cooperatives, and farm women supplementing the family income by selling value-added products or taking in summer boarders. Sharing and *interpreting* the dilemma rather than simply struggling with it behind the scenes can be a way to invite visitors and community partners into conversations about what it might take to escape the very long-standing cycle of small-scale farms attempting to become or remain viable within large-scale food systems. As Brian Donahue notes in the interview following Chapter 3, there are enormous and telling challenges in the attempt to combine "real" food production and historic sites: "If you're going to put these things together then you've got to support it and subsidize it and that's *not a bad thing.* We haven't made it fake when we do that." The question of what could keep small-scale food production really real is a complex and important one, and projects like that at Gore Place can help practitioners to ask it in provocative and timely ways.

Hybrid projects excite the imagination and spark attention. At the same time, as new forms, they're inherently unpredictable and come with their own kinds of challenges. Educational and commercial outcomes can vie for dominance. Partnerships, if poorly managed or ill-starred, can turn prickly. Ambitious plans can hit the rocks due to inexperience as institutions stretch into operational zones outside their areas of expertise. Defining outcomes and roles clearly is essential to the success of a hybrid venture, as Rolf Diamant shows in the interview that follows Chapter 8. But these boundary-breaking projects also have immense potential to communicate refreshed messages about history, food, and farming.

Using the resources in this chapter, public historians can plan to deeply embed the triple top line into institutional culture, mission and strategy, and interpretive planning, perhaps experimenting with some of the strategies suggested above, or moving beyond them into entirely new imaginative territory. The next chapters discuss two important components of a healthy culture of planning and iteration: creating and maintaining positive working relationships and overcoming logistical hurdles to new forms of food interpretation.

WORK IN PROGRESS—AN INTERVIEW WITH LISA JUNKIN LOPEZ: VALUING WHAT MUSEUMS DO BEST

FIGURE 6.2   Lisa Junkin Lopez.

Lisa Junkin Lopez is currently exploring the empowerment of women and girls as director of the Juliette Gordon Low birthplace in Savannah, Georgia but she is also well known for her former role in the leadership of the Jane Addams Hull-House Museum in Chicago. Widely admired as a model for reimagining a historic site museum as a socially responsive organization, Hull-House's programs transcend the typical scope of historic house museums. Built in 1889 as part of the Settlement House movement of the period, in which mostly affluent, educated, native-born women moved into poor urban neighborhoods to help ameliorate problems caused by dense urbanization, mass immigration, and industrialization, Hull-House was home to leading social reformer Jane Addams and a group of residents

(Continued)

and participants engaged in projects ranging from art, music, and cooking classes to daycare and kindergarten, English classes, employment services, and medical and mental health services. Today, the Jane Addams Hull-House Museum remembers this legacy by serving as what its website terms a "dynamic memorial," offering community shared meals, an heirloom seed library, and food preservation classes. In an interview conducted while she was still with the institution, Junkin Lopez highlights the interpretive planning approaches behind Hull-House's high-impact programs, emphasizing that the work done by the staff and partners of Hull-House today is rooted in the specifics of the site's history and the mandate provided by its mission and strategic goals (Figure 6.2).

What's the relationship of Hull-House's historic past, its institutional mission, and its core content?

Through all our work at Hull-House, we do our best to make connections from history to the present really clear to our audiences. For us, that's the best way to ensure that people see the value of our site, and the value of history, period. Hull-House has always been a place for education, social change, innovative and creative thinking about social issues, so we really do feel we're working in the legacy of those who came before us.

But we're in no way trying to replicate the programs and activities that took place at Hull-House when it was a settlement house in the early twentieth century. It's important to understand our work at a more symbolic level. At the original Hull-House, in all of their programs, whether related to food or immigrants' rights or children's rights or arts education, Jane Addams and the other reformers were doing their best to address the issues of their time in a way that made sense for their communities. From a community organizing standpoint, it wouldn't make sense to use those same methods today, because we're in a different time and community. For us it's about taking those broader strategies and thinking about how they relate to our times.

How is that historical legacy expressed in your programs about food and farming?

Our flagship program for the last seven years was Rethinking Soup, a really lovely community gathering where people from all over the city of Chicago would join together for a meal of a fresh bowl of soup and bread created by chefs at Hull-House, using local organic ingredients whenever possible. In addition to enjoying the meal, we would address issues of food justice in Chicago. Over the seven years, we explored a huge number of issues—the rights of workers in Immokalee, Florida [a farmworkers' movement organized as the Coalition of Immokalee Workers] and other places harvesting our food, environmentalism, access to fresh water. We talked about what the "local" food movement means in a city like Chicago, which is cold for six to nine months a year, and different cultural values around food, such as eating meat, and how that trickles down to food education programs, especially in urban communities.

We launched our program in 2008, right when the food movement was about to hit the mainstream, and that allowed us to grow with the movement. Early on we were asking questions at a basic level: "I understand what it means to eat local, but how can I eat seasonally in a place like a Chicago?" "Can I never eat a pineapple again?" We grew with the program. Recently, we were able to address more intersections, to run alongside of what's happening nationally and watch audiences grow in their knowledge and enthusiasm for what the food movement can be and can do.

We concluded the program in May of 2015, but we are working to evolve it, and but will continue to do work around food and food justice. What has always been important to us and, again, speaks to our symbolic strategy we use when addressing the content of our site is to look at how folks in the past were understanding these social issues, and look at how people today are understanding and addressing them. We look at how they can be in conversation together, look for the gaps that historical voices can fill in a contemporary conversation.

Can you give an example of one of those gaps, and how you identified that intersection between your institution's history and contemporary conversations about food issues?

We find that activists do great work organizing their communities today, but they're not always aware of the history of their own organizing. We've had a lot of great experiences going to activists and saying, "Hey, let me tell you how food justice activities were working in this community a hundred years ago."

One of the big questions in the food movement is that of elitism in this movement for local food and organic food. Does that come from a really exclusive or privileged place, or is it something we can make possible for everyone? What does it mean to bring those values outside your own community? That's why it's so exciting to work from Hull-House, where middle-class American-born women were providing programs for diverse immigrants. They 2 had a public kitchen. What we learned from doing research was that it was, in some ways, one of Hull-House's biggest failures. The residents of Hull-House learned from the public kitchens in Boston.[15] These kitchens were being run by home economists—women, really feminists, using this domestic sphere as a way of doing social work, using the kitchen to address social issues. Because that was the legacy of the Hull-House Public Kitchen, all the recipes came from Boston's New England Kitchen. The thing about New England is that it's not really known for having delicious foods. All these meals that Hull-House was very thoughtfully preparing—gruels, porridges, beef tea—just did not interest the immigrant community that largely came from Italy, Greece, and Poland. Middle-class Protestant reformers thought garlic, peppers, and tomatoes were bad for your digestion, so they didn't serve them. This is a moment where you see what we might call a

(Continued)

patronizing attempt at offering something that residents needed. They were hungry, they didn't have time to prepare food because they were working ten to fourteen hours a day, six days a week, in factories—but [the settlement workers] didn't get it right. Jane Addams talks about a story where a man [rejecting reformers' food] says "I'd rather eat what I'd ruther." Nobody liked it!

I think that's such an important story for Chicago today, when we think about food-insecure neighborhoods, when we think about educational and service-based programs. Where are the voices of the community coming in? Where are *their* preferences coming in? Is it right to bring kale (to pick on kale a little bit) into a community that doesn't care for it? As we move forward with Rethinking Soup, we're interested in having those conversations not just on a community level, but also a policy level. Not just around food, but all social issues.

Hull-House stands out for its embrace of partnership as a working practice. How do you identify potential partners and build mutually beneficial relationships? How do you ensure that you're operating from a place of strength and authenticity, while offering something valuable to your partners?

We have learned a lot from the community organizers that we partner with. A number of people we've hired to do programs at Hull-House come from a community organizing background, not from a history background. They have a networking ability, an ability to work with communities that values their expertise. I would call our work a form of cultural organizing and cultural activism. We are not able to do the kind of [direct service] work people do on the ground, but we are able to support that work through educating people, winning hearts and minds, connecting to this history. That's how we frame our work. We've learned from the ways community organizers are collaborative, how they share authority with their communities. There are more than 100 community partners on our list of organizations. We don't do anything in a vacuum. Every single program and exhibition is done with partners here in Chicago and beyond. They include scholars, artists, activists, community organizers, other cultural partners, and all ranges of skills.

Any organization working with contemporary issues of food, farming, and policy begins to get into the civic and political sphere. In your institution, how do you navigate the zones where education and activism can overlap?

We are a state institution [the museum is part of the College of Architecture, Design, and the Arts at the University of Illinois at Chicago]. There are real boundaries. Those boundaries are pretty specific: we cannot advocate for specific candidates or policies. But that's only one way of being political, and there are ways that every organization, including non-profits, is political or politicized, in the sense that they have issues they are advocating for in different ways. This is a site about people making social change, but I don't think we are telling anyone *how* to do that—we see ours as an expansive role, and not one that shuts down conversation.

I think we need to shift the conversation around what it means to do our jobs well. Our organizations should play the role in society that they need to play. One reason we're able to do this work is that we're part of the university, and that brings a value of academic freedom, and a value around discussing social issues—we're part of an urban campus that discusses the issues of this time. We take that very seriously. We can speak to the history of Hull-House in a way that truly draws out the political issues people were interested in at that time, but that also highlights possibilities today.

With so many potential issues to embrace, how do you go about making choices, weighing opportunities, and making decisions as to where resources will go?

Weighing opportunities—this is maybe our biggest challenge. We take on a lot. I've been doing work around *slowness*—as cultural institutions, how do we do work that's both responsive to the community, and that's sustainable, so we're not burning ourselves out doing too much? What does it mean to look at slowness from a social justice standpoint? It's not always clear that the two have a relationship.

The museum uses a complex matrix to make decisions. First and foremost, our history is at the forefront of our decisions. Sometimes people assume that because we're addressing contemporary subject matter that we've set the history aside, but we do a *lot* of work behind the scenes to research these topics. We're always going back to our history to see what we can learn about the reformers at Hull-House, where we disagree with them or our partners may disagree, and where there are these productive tensions that may push our work forward.

In Chicago, there's a lot of public programming, a lot of social justice programming. It's just an incredibly rich conversation. We try to pay attention to what's *not* being said, what our history can bring that's unique to these issues, and we don't want to step on their toes. How can we amplify marginalized voices? We take seriously the cultural capital that we have as an institution, and we try hard to leverage those assets to support those who don't have the most funding or the loudest microphone.

What advice would you give to colleagues who are just beginning to find ways for their public history work to be responsive to present-day issues—in food, or in any realm?

I always encourage people to make connections to issues on the ground and in their communities. What I've learned as a museum person and a public historian is how much I have to learn from other historians and from people who are doing the political and social activism on the ground. For me, the sweet spot in doing this work has been finding relationships that are mutually beneficial, when people and organizations value what you have to share in terms of the history of these issues and can incorporate it into their organization, and that you find things that you value about ways they understand these issues that you can learn from. What I see when museums begin to do work around social issues is that the missteps have to do with not finding this mutual benefit. Either the museum is being used for its assets, funding, resources, or name recognition, or, more often, community groups are taken advantage of while the museums use them to claim how relevant they are or how much work they do in the community. Our best partnerships have been really beautiful because

(Continued)

they allow us to do what we do best, which is to be a museum, to do research, to create conversations, to do public programs and exhibitions, and allow our partners to do *their* work as organizers, dealing with policy, drumming up the base, and changing behavior. I recommend that organizations really think about what they bring to the table and what other people bring to the table, and have a lot of conversations about where they can meet in the middle.

Notes

1 Mary Rizzo succinctly summarized 50 years of shifting perspectives on this issue in her post "Finding the roots of civic engagement in the public humanities" on *History@Work* (blog of the National Council on Public History), July 21, 2014.
2 Melanie Adams, "Inside View: From Dred Scott to Michael Brown: Following Tradition and Responding to Ferguson," *Museum Magazine*, a benefit of membership in the American Alliance of Museums, May–June 2015, 27.
3 Hal Skramstad and Susan Skramstad, "Mission and Vision Again? What's the Big Deal?" in *Small Museums Toolkit, Book I: Mission, Vision and Governance*, Cinnamon Catlin-Legutko and Stacey Klingler, eds. (Lanham, MD: Altamira, 2012).
4 Lisa Brochu, *Interpretive Planning: The 5-M Model for Successful Planning Projects* (Fort Collins, CO: National Association for Interpretation, 2003), 43.
5 Full citations can be found in the Bibliographic Note at the end of Chapter 8.
6 Andrea Jones, quoted in Rebecca Herz' post "What is the relationship between 'community need' and museums?" *Museum Questions* (blog), April 18, 2016.
7 The concept of considering the community's assets, not just its needs, comes from public policy concepts of "asset-based community development." Critical of community planning that focused on deficits and challenges, social scientists in the 1990s shifted from a "needs-oriented" approach to a "capacity-oriented" approach aimed at leveraging community strengths. See John L. McKnight and John P. Kretzman, *Mapping Community Capacity. Asset-Based Community Development Institute, Institute for Policy Research* (Evanston, IL: Northwestern University, 1996), accessed via *ABCDInstitute.org*.
8 Scott Magelssen, "Making History in the Second Person: Post-Touristic Considerations for Living Historical Interpretation," *Theatre Journal* 58:2 (May 2006), 304.
9 "About Wyck," *Wyck.org*.
10 Jennifer Jensen Wallach discusses perspectives on Victory gardening in her *How America Eats: A Social History of US Food and Culture* (Lanham, MD: Rowman & Littlefield, 2013), 162–163.
11 In 2014, the National Gardening Association reported that home food gardening had reached a 10-year peak, with more than 35% of all households growing some of their own food in home or community gardens. "Food Gardening in the U.S. at Highest Levels in More Than a Decade," National Gardening Association, April 2, 2014, *Garden.org*.
12 Elizabeth Merrit, *TrendsWatch* 2014, American Alliance of Museums (AAM), 2014, pp 8–40. Past TrendsWatch reports are available at the AAM website, http://www.aam-us.org/resources/center-for-the-future-of-museums/projects-and-reports/trendswatch
13 "Food as Immigrant Experience," *Rutgers Magazine* website, Winter 2015.
14 Merritt, p. 14.
15 Here, Junkin refers to experiments with takeout kitchens serving low-cost food to recent immigrants and low-income workers, especially the prominent New England Kitchen run by domestic science pioneer Ellen Richards. Laura Shapiro describes the operation of the kitchen in her *Perfection Salad: Women and Cooking at the Turn of the Century* (Berkeley, CA: University of California Press, 2008, 38–42 and 139–142).

7

GROWING RELATIONSHIPS

Coalition building, partnership, and collaboration are among the most critical skills required for working on food issues. The reason is obvious: we need help to develop fuller experiences of food interpretation. Most of us are keenly aware of everything we don't know (in fact, that awareness prompted the writing of this book!). As history professionals, we like to feel sure of our footing as we take responsibility for the interpretations we put forward. Many of us have little scholarly background in food history in general and even less on current policy or specific issues within the food movement. It's in our professional DNA to be aware of these knowledge gaps and resist presenting ourselves as authorities on material we don't know well. An important principle for public historians seeking to engage with the contemporary food movement is to bring the strengths and skills of our profession into collaboration with those who have other forms of knowledge about food.

Fortunately, such partners can be found everywhere. Food and farming activists like to observe that, among all of society's thorny issues, food is unique in its universality, encouraging people to cross divides imposed by polarized electoral politics, economic disparities, and geographic and social segregation. In reforming the food system, people who never previously worked or socialized together can find themselves at the same table. But new relationships carry a risk of missteps that can set back progress and frustrate all parties. Common cause exists alongside deep-seated differences of class, race and ethnicity, gender, geography, religion, educational attainment, personal mission, and professional specialty. This chapter acknowledges and investigates ways to navigate some of those divisions and helps practitioners bring into their work an awareness of their own positions and privileges, as professionals and individuals, challenging the social structures that have historically kept potential collaborators separate.

Finding Allies

Food systems stitch society together. Following food through the chains of production, consumption, and disposal can reveal unexpected points of connection. Few products so concretely link suburbanites with fieldworkers, school kids with chicken processors, dairymen with desert dwellers. That means that everyone who has a hand in working with or eating food is a potential partner—that is, everyone. Where to begin?

When most people think about the food and farming resources in their own communities, they go to the obvious: farms and farmers markets. Indeed, many key partners are likely to be found in these busy but self-selecting places. Market organizations themselves are the product of collaborations among different farmers, food producers, other vendors, and sometimes third parties like community development agencies, Main Streets programs, and even museums. Local markets concentrate smaller-scale food producers who are comfortable with connecting with customers and explaining their farming practices. Farmstands and CSA programs create points of interface for publics, farmworkers, and owners and involve communication, marketing, and information exchange. The farmers and food producers active in these zones are the "low-hanging fruit" of collaboration—people who likely share many identities and values with museum audiences and who have an incentive to promote a brand and increase buyership and loyalty.

However, as we discussed in Chapter 2, investigating local and regional food systems more closely reminds us that food producers are only one node—a very important node, but still one point in a complex web that takes in many other forms of involvement with food. The number of involved people and industries may surprise you. In 2008, the Vermont Sustainable Agriculture council asked itself "Who are the actors in the state's food system?" By breaking down activities related to food supply into eight categories, they revealed a complex web uniting dozens of actors in the food system, whose relationships with one another had previously gone largely unnoticed. Taking it one step further, they identified which entities were acting on the local, state, and regional levels and explored the motivating ideas, goals, and values of each one to identify common ground. Finally, they were able to use this for gap analysis, asking which ties were weak or missing and what productive partnerships could emerge from connections never before explored to fill those needs (Figure 7.1).

Public historians may make some of their most valuable contributions by identifying those gaps. Using food systems mapping to draw a clearer picture of the current landscape, historians can identify like-minded partners who can easily see value in working with you, as well as more unexpected "stretch" targets for relationships that may take a bit more groundwork to develop. It makes sense to begin with those actors who can partner easily and enthusiastically, people and groups with whom you already share values and visions. But be sure not to stop there. Rich collaborations await those who seek personally and institutionally

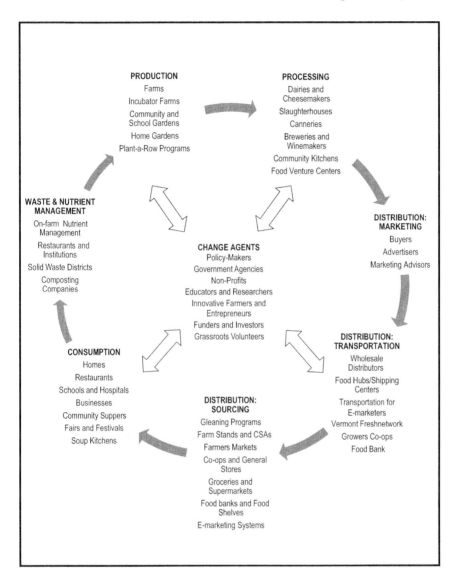

PRODUCTION
Farms
Incubator Farms
Community and
School Gardens
Home Gardens
Plant-a-Row Programs

PROCESSING
Dairies and
Cheesemakers
Slaughterhouses
Canneries
Breweries and
Winemakers
Community Kitchens
Food Venture Centers

**WASTE & NUTRIENT
MANAGEMENT**
On-farm Nutrient
Management
Restaurants and
Institutions
Solid Waste Districts
Composting
Companies

CHANGE AGENTS
Policy-Makers
Government Agencies
Non-Profits
Educators and Researchers
Innovative Farmers and
Entrepreneurs
Funders and Investors
Grassroots Volunteers

**DISTRIBUTION:
MARKETING**
Buyers
Advertisers
Marketing Advisors

CONSUMPTION
Homes
Restaurants
Schools and Hospitals
Businesses
Community Suppers
Fairs and Festivals
Soup Kitchens

**DISTRIBUTION:
SOURCING**
Gleaning Programs
Farm Stands and CSAs
Farmers Markets
Co-ops and General
Stores
Groceries and
Supermarkets
Food banks and Food
Shelves
E-marketing Systems

**DISTRIBUTION:
TRANSPORTATION**
Wholesale
Distributors
Food Hubs/Shipping
Centers
Transportation for
E-marketers
Vermont Freshnetwork
Growers Co-ops
Food Bank

FIGURE 7.1 From "Understanding Vermont's Local Food Landscape: An Inventory and Assessment of Recent Local Food Initiatives" prepared for the Vermont Sustainable Agricultural Council, 2008 by Virginia Nickerson.

transformative partnerships with constituents who have not yet been engaged via public history or food movement activism.

For example, in Chapter 2 we noted the presence of low-wage, often invisible workers throughout all sectors of food production, processing, and marketing, from the most industrialized to the most locally oriented. There are particular challenges to engaging these workers and other marginalized food producers as potential partners or collaborators in public historical projects. However, their importance in the food system—and the work of organizations that advocate for them—is crucially important to remember when framing questions about what keeps that system running and what kinds of inequalities and exploitation have historically played a role in it. As the eat-local movement continues to expand and mature, strange new comparisons are appearing between these food- and farmworkers—often migrants and people of color—and an emerging class of young farmers who are generally white and well-educated, yet whose unpaid or under paid labor as interns and apprentices forms a kind of parallel to that of lower-status workers. Convening conversations where these kinds of topics can be raised and seen within longer historical trajectories can be a step toward understanding these troubling patterns and strengthening discussions about how to achieve greater equity and security for all those who feed us.

Thinking Like a Community Organizer

Over and over again in our research, we were struck by a similarity that linked many of the practitioners we interviewed and studied: even though those people had never spoken to one another, they were speaking the same language. They raised certain common themes: that museums can't do all the work of using history to improve the food system on their own, that partnerships strengthen projects, that it's important not to duplicate the effort of other organizations, that we need to contribute from our own strengths and expertise, that inclusion is non-negotiable, and that lasting and valuable work takes time. Gradually we became aware that, though they may not all have realized it, all these practitioners were drawing on a common body of wisdom about getting things done—one that arises from the history of community organizing.

For more than a hundred years, change-makers have been sharing (and to some extent codifying) what "community organizing" means and entails. Public policy theorist and organizer Marshall Ganz offers a succinct definition: community organizing consists of "practicing democracy by mobilizing people to combine their resources to act strategically on behalf of common interests."[1] Few museums, working alone, can marshal the resources needed to support the common interest in historically informed democratic decision-making about the food system. Museums can contribute historical thinking, research skills, site facilities, collections and archives, curatorial and educational expertise, and more—but it's less likely they can contribute the kinds of knowledge deeply understood by commercial farmers and food producers, processors and retailers, community members at all socioeconomic levels, scientists, policy analysts, activists, or others. Taking on aspects of the role of community organizer, museums must think about how to bring these perspectives together for a more deeply informed understanding of food's past and present, learning as much from the complex interactions of perspectives from many quarters as from the study of the past.

Coalition-building skills fuel the work of community organizers. Outreach, inclusive thinking and practice, careful and patient relationship building, recruiting, networking, and consciousness raising allow project leaders to assemble a diverse group of interested, engaged participants willing to involve themselves in a project. Valuing each new perspective enriches the dialogue and improves the outcome.

Like leading museum thinkers, community organizers also value collaboration. But as Lisa Junkin Lopez emphasized in her interview at the end of Chapter 6, collaborations must be mutually beneficial, not one-sided, and participants must be truly willing to share authority. Organizers are mindful also of avoiding the duplication of effort. Museums and historical sites have unique contributions only they can make to the public discourse: they are not primarily food banks, social work agencies, retail or food production operations, even though they may take on some of those activities some of the time. Respect for one another's work and clarity around boundaries of activity help every partner offer their strongest contributions and avoid waste of effort and resources.

Community organizers also think in terms of campaigns—time-limited projects to create change, with an end goal in mind. Campaigns involve messaging, public relations, communications, and calls to action. Though museums will not usually be willing or able to participate directly in formal political campaigns, they can use many of the tools of campaigning to promote a project or highlight an idea: crafting clear messages, developing communications plans, using viral networks to share information, deploying the power of exhibition and visual design and program planning.

In general, community organizers launch their work with open minds and outstretched hands, ready to engage in imagination and fluid thinking. Sometimes, the endpoint isn't fully visible at the outset, something that can feel uncomfortable to those of us used to identifying specific, measurable outcomes for grantors or writing lesson plans to meet state standards. But to make their work more relevant and help our audiences think more productively about the real-world issues in which we are immersed, museum planners may want to consider becoming more comfortable in the mushy and sometimes maddeningly vast middle ground of building coalitions, identifying mutually generative possibilities, and sharing the work of projects where there is a strong overlap of interest but little duplication of skills.

Apart from the Jane Addams Hull-House, where the community organizing model of museum programming emerged from the site's own history of social reform, few museums so far have adopted this model for food and farm programming. One exception—though notably not a history museum—has been the Queens Museum of Art. In 2006, its newly developed Community Engagement Team created a full-time community organizer position to advance the museum's "Heart of Corona/El Corazon de Corona" initiative, which aimed to "improve the health of residents, and to activate and beautify Corona's public spaces, thereby creating a better climate for residents and businesses alike." Among other projects, Heart of Corona formed a coalition of insurance companies, the American Heart Association and American Diabetes Association, the Hispanic Chamber of Commerce, and the Corona Action Network to produce a bilingual community-authored cookbook featuring healthy versions of culturally specific dishes. This kind of organizing to create a meaningful product draws on oral history, cultural memory, storytelling, cultural geography, and foodways and might fit as naturally in a history museum setting as an art museum setting—or even more so.

A second example—a historic site that does engage with farming history—is the Oliver Kelley Farm in rural Minnesota, once home to a New England businessman and politician best known for founding the Patrons of Husbandry, or the Grange, as a form of mutual support for farmers in the mid-nineteenth century. Funded by a substantial state appropriation, the site is in the process of shifting its interpretation from a "moment in time" living history approach to a much longer timeline encompassing everything from pre-European landscapes and agriculture (as represented by a restored section of prairie) to twenty-first century industrialized farm methods.

When it comes to community organizing, this project may be the exception that proves the rule. As a state-affiliated, largely state-funded agency seeking substantial public funding for a farm-related project in a heavily agricultural state, the Minnesota Historical Society, which runs the Kelley Farm, could hardly ignore the perspectives of the mainstream agricultural sector, including the kind of heavily industrialized farming that is anathema to many food-movement activists. Although those interests were part of the support that MHS built for its funding request, advocates for smaller-scale, lower-input farming were apparently also at the table when the new interpretive approach was being developed, showing that "community organizing" can involve gathering both mainstream and alternative constituencies together. Furthermore, participants in the planning process were able to agree on a core set of issues that they believed the public needed to consider about agriculture—for example, that most people are too disconnected from knowledge about how their food is produced. The agreed-upon issues leave room for divergent opinions and strategies while creating a common basis for ongoing participation in the interpretation at the site—no mean feat within a politicized and often polarizing set of questions.

Reflexivity in Action

To work well with others, we must know ourselves. As discussed in Chapter 1, this means being aware of how we, as both individuals and professional practitioners, fit into the matrix in which we are trying to work. What are your personal qualities, work patterns, and habitual modes of interaction? What privileges have you benefited from or been denied? What skills have your training and work history given you and kept from you? How might people whose life and work have been very different perceive you? Understanding some of the social dynamics around our individual persona and affiliations can help public historians become more sensitive to the ways in which we present ourselves and how we are received by others. We may need to think about use of language, the way we seek introductions, dress, and even seemingly irrelevant details like work hours, the locations of sites and offices, and communication preferences (phone, e-mail, in person). Especially when building collaborations with food producers, thinking about seasonality and work schedules is key—scheduling planning meetings in the middle of planting or harvesting season is not likely to endear you to your prospective new partners! Working across social and occupational boundaries makes it clear that we don't all follow the same routines. Some degree of self-awareness and respectful adaptation is often needed to form strong and productive bonds.

One of the persistent criticisms of food systems reform is that it's a preoccupation of white, affluent, suburban people. While a visual survey of many suburban Whole Foods checkout lines may seem to confirm this, it's an assumption worth prodding. Food activism is more diverse and more complicated than it may appear at first glance. First, ethnicity is not solely responsible for variations in personal food consumption; income and education play a large role. Studies of organic food purchases find that though non-Hispanic white households purchase organic food more often than African-American, Latino, or Asian households, organic purchasing across all ethnicities increases in tandem with education and income levels.[2] Conversely, people of all ethnicities at lower income levels are more likely to lack awareness of and/or access to organic produce.[3] This income disparity disproportionately limits the food choices available to African-Americans and Latinos, who are statistically more likely to occupy the lower income levels. The higher cost of locally raised and organic food—a cost that advocates argue represents the true cost of raising good-quality food without support from subsidies and industrial economies of scale—does limit the ability of lower- and middle-income eaters to shift their food-purchasing patterns. However, we should be careful not to conflate limits to individual purchasing power with lack of concern about negative effects of food industrialization or interest in food reform. Many people who desire a healthier food system simply cannot afford to support its nascent forms at present pricing and income levels.

Since the face of poverty is often rural, and farming produces generally marginal (if any) profits, farmers themselves are paradoxically among those less able to purchase highly priced organic and artisanal foods or buy tickets to locavore dinners and foodie events—a fact sometimes forgotten by well-meaning collaborators and customers. Farmers of color are also rendered largely invisible in the popular food press and in food movement rhetoric, as are the legions of farmworkers who are not in the landowning class but who provide the immense amount of labor required to cultivate and harvest food. Organic, small-scale farming operations also often depend on uncompensated labor, whether the workers are members of the owners' families or unpaid farm apprentices, or on seasonal laborers paid minimum required wages.

The more celebratory, magazine-friendly projects within the food movement—localism, heirloom seed saving, artisanal skills revivals, food preservation—are not always the same issues that galvanize lower-income people and people of color. With lower rates of insurance coverage and higher rates of diet-related disease (such as heart disease, diabetes, and high blood pressure), Native Americans, African-Americans, and Hispanics may be more commonly found engaging in food activism around these critical issues affecting basic health outcomes or working in health professions that treat these illnesses directly. Hunger, food security, food sovereignty, fair labor and wage activism, and food access may also be of more immediate concern to food activists of color, whose communities are disproportionately affected by these issues. The organizers of the Detroit Black Community Food Security Network observe on their website that "many of the key players in the local urban agriculture movement were young whites, who while well-intentioned, never the less, exerted a degree of control inordinate to their numbers in Detroit's population.... It was and is our view that the most effective movements grow organically from the people whom they are designed to serve. Representatives of Detroit's majority African-American population must be in the leadership of efforts to foster food justice and food security in Detroit."[4] In Seattle, the organization Clean Greens is "owned and operated by long-standing African American residents of Seattle's Central District," who work to bring locally and sustainably raised produce to local low-income families.[5] The group formed in response to the lack of access to healthy food and its impact on the health of poor African-Americans.

These and many other similar organizations have grown around the country in step with other food movement activities. It is hard to say whether their relative invisibility in the mainstream discourse results more from lower participation (as is often theorized), a focus on trendier issues by the media and more affluent participants, or a generalized bias against the concerns of people of color and people living with poverty. What is certain is that the food movement is not as white and middle-class as it initially may seem. In a blog post titled "Concerning the Unbearable Whiteness of Urban Farming," food justice activist Antonio Roman-Alcala shares lessons learned from his work. His first point is important for public historians seeking to build broader coalitions: "Go to where people are at, not where you want them to be."[6]

It's good advice; museum staff, who on the whole are disproportionately white, highly educated, and economically secure (among other widely shared characteristics) sometimes develop programs in total isolation from communities they hope to involve, then bemoan the fact that the same old (mostly similar to themselves) audiences turn out to participate. Their fundamental error (in the words of the baseball movie *Field of Dreams*) lies in assuming that "if you build it, they will come"—and that if "they" don't show up, the fault is theirs rather than the lack of time and attention paid to outreach, shared visioning, and project design. If people are not "where you want them to be," where are they? It's likely they are participating in organizations in their own communities, toward ends they've identified as vital next steps for the health of the food system as they experience it. For any community you wish to newly engage, whether defined by culture, ethnicity, economics, gender, age, or geography, begin by seeking out the change-makers, movers, and shakers who are already working on the ground. Get to know and understand their efforts and interests before seeking the common ground on which to build new initiatives.

It's not only individual practitioners who need to be aware of their relative privilege and position. Institutions have profiles, as well. Perceptions about the value and trustworthiness of any public history organization may differ between the in-group that already uses the resource and outside groups that presently don't. In a *New York Times* editorial titled "Why Are Our National Parks So White?," Glenn Nelson, founder of The Trail Posse, an online community promoting diversity in outdoor activities, described perceptions of national parks among people of color. Many expressed a pronounced wariness: "They are worried about unfriendly white people, hungry critters and insects, and unforgiving landscapes… There was always nervous banter as we cruised through small rural towns on our way to a park. And there were jokes about finding a 'Whites Only' sign at the entrance to our destination or the perils of being lynched or attacked while collecting firewood after the sun went down. Our cultural history taught us what to expect." Public history institutions can occupy a similarly unknown ground for many current non-participants—and not without good reason. Recent projects like the video series "Ask a Slave," based on the experience of historical re-enactor Azie Mira Dungey's experiences interpreting an enslaved character at a living history site, and @AfAmHistoryFail, an anonymous historic site interpreter whose Twitter account shares visitors' negative or uninformed reactions to representations of slavery, show that many people of color are rightly uncertain about what kinds of microaggressions and misconceptions they may face when interacting with a historic site's staff and visitors. Many Native American people, in particular, bring a reasonably cautious stance to engaging with museum projects. The use of museums as a tool of colonial power imposed legacies that still reverberate today; skepticism about museum motives and trustworthiness is well placed when considered against histories of the inappropriate seizure and display of indigenous cultural objects and the exclusion of Native voices from museum narratives.

Though many in the majority culture find museums highly trustworthy, when disparities of class, culture, and race exist among staff, planners, visitors, and partners, the trust gap widens. It's possible, as a staff member, to be largely unaware of the negative associations and impacts an institution has had in its community or to its cultural stakeholders. Listen and learn. Using your historians' skills, analyze the power dynamics, inequalities of access, economic constraints, and political agendas around your partnership projects and community issues. As you begin developing partnerships, ask about how community members see and think about your work and your institution and consider how you can grow strong relationships that last beyond a single project. It's likely you'll find partners in quarters you have never before explored.

Productive Partnerships

To begin broadening relationships, museums can start looking for their fellow travelers concerned with the regional food system—people and organizations with shared interests in food. A diabetes education group, an industrial composter, an organic brewery, a new mothers' association, an immigrant aid organization, a tourism board—all are potential partners who have some reason to care about the food system and get involved in exploration of its history. Yet it's likely many of them have never been approached by a public historian or given any thought to how museum projects might dovetail with their own goals and enrich their thinking. To forge bonds where none previously existed, public historians must apply their skills at relationship cultivation to develop connections with activists across various sectors of the food movement. Below, we've listed some steps you can take to build mutually beneficial, respectful, and productive partnerships.

Mapping Your Foodshed

One of the most useful tactics we have encountered for identifying partnerships is the food systems mapping process as developed by the Vermont Sustainable Agriculture Council (see Figure 7.1). This approach breaks a local or regional food system into eight sectors of activity: Production, Processing, Distribution/ Marketing, Distribution/Transportation, Distribution/Sourcing, Consumption, Waste and Nutrient Management, and Change Agents. This mapping process helps planners surface the many links that bind a foodshed together and reflect the entire cyclical journey of food from source to plate and beyond, into waste disposal, composting, and soil and water maintenance. Many of us would not immediately think of reaching out to soil scientists, solid waste management districts, or marketers and wholesalers, for example. Yet when we see the "big picture," we can see places where stronger connections are needed and where the processes of history can help interpret systemic changes past, present, and future.

We suggest that museum historians sit down with the eight (or more!) categories and a stack of sticky notes and begin identifying—with specific names and titles wherever possible—the players involved in each of the eight sectors in their own local and regional settings. In addition to clarifying the food system landscape, this exercise can help define the most feasible scale for specific food history projects. Where is "the local" on your area's map? A multi-generation dairy farm, for example, might be both highly local and fully regional, if it sells in regional markets. National, global, and other scales are similarly likely to overlap in complex ways, and seeing their interrelationships more clearly can help interpreters move beyond a too-simple expectation that participating in "the local food system" only means working with small-scale, hyper-local producers.

Resisting Stereotypes

Pop-culture and mass-media images of "farmer," "migrant worker," "restaurant dishwasher," or "college professor" are rarely adequate to reflect the full complexity

FIGURE 7.2   In an early experiment with collaboration, Strawbery Banke Museum developed a Harvest Supper outdoor event by working with local meat growers and trainee chefs from a nearby culinary academy. Using produce harvested from historic gardens onsite and meats purchased from small-scale local producers, trainees under the instruction of faculty chefs learned to work with vegetables of non-standard size and shape and to bring out the flavor in heirloom produce and heritage meats. Because the trainee chefs donated their labor as part of their educational program, members of the community were invited to attend and celebrate local food production at a low-cost $10 ticket price. Image: Michelle Moon.

of real-life individuals. As Brian Donahue discusses in his interview in Chapter 3, farmers, in particular, seem to suffer from shallow stereotypes—"simple rural folk"— though many are highly educated, skilled in a variety of disciplines from genetics to mechanics to law to chemistry, and experienced at outreach, marketing, customer service, and public education. In a discussion on collaboration, Vermont farmer and Slow Food leader Mara Welton, who participates frequently in collaborative projects, emphasizes the need for farmers to communicate the sophisticated skills and irreplaceable worth they contribute: "I approach all collaborations with the mindset that I am working with colleagues—not that I am donating a lesser service because I am a farmer, but that I am providing an equally valuable component to the partnership as other contributors. I have worked hard to remind myself that I need to assert my value in collaborations so that I get something out of it, fundamentally, and don't end up feeling taken for granted."[7] Farmers and other partners must be approached as equals who are expert in their own knowledge areas (Figure 7.2).

Negotiating Conflict

Partnerships are challenging. There will be times you, your institution, and your partners see things differently. Relationships built on listening, respect, and doing what you say you will do establish a foundation of trust that can withstand minor disagreement and tension. (And as Rolf Diamant suggests in the interview following Chapter 8, mutually revisiting those expectations periodically can be important for keeping a relationship healthy.) For a public historian, the essential skills to call on are those you would use with any community member who entrusts you with personal stories and knowledge. Be reliable and honest. Protect sensitive information and shared confidence. Show up on time, but be patient if partners are delayed. Keep everyone in the loop. Pay attention to fairness in representation and equity of access. Admit to being uncertain, confused, or vulnerable; ask for help, respectfully, when there's something you don't understand. These communication strategies help to cement mutually respectful relationships; they aren't afterthoughts, but core components of collaborative work. As Welton says "I spend a lot of time reinforcing relationships, with lots of touching base to make sure everyone is happy with the arrangement."[8]

Sometimes, when conflict seems impossible to resolve, the right decision is to end a partnership (as organizer Niaz Dorry acknowledges in the interview at the end of this chapter). In rare cases, obstinate individuals can become toxic to a project, alienating other allies and sabotaging outcomes, or groups can mutually determine they no longer share a vision for collaboration or that their productive work together is concluded. In those situations, it's best to call an amicable end to the connection before it consumes the valuable and limited resources of time, money, goodwill, and reputation.

Sharing the Burden

Any project involves work. Sharing authority includes sharing the responsibility for getting that work done—the big, shiny tasks like putting on exciting events and speaking to the press, and the small, dull, but necessary chores like setting meetings, taking minutes, arranging for rides and rentals, and taking out the trash. A veteran of many event partnerships through her CSA and local Slow Food chapter, Welton advises that "true collaborative partnerships happen when the best of both parties are clearly utilized in the partnership, and it's an equal load on both sides—and that the responsibilities of both are clearly outlined. A collaboration killer is when there is a clear unbalance in the partnership. It should be equally matched in what both parties bring to the table, or resentment can settle in and future collaborations will likely not occur."[9] Make sure the logistical and procedural arrangements of any project are crystal clear and agreed on by all, from monetary compensation (Who gets an honorarium? Who pays for gas to get to the site? Will food be donated, or is it more appropriate to support providers by purchasing from them at market rate?), to task assignments, to who will be presented as having authored the project.

Planning for Mutual Benefit

Public historians should be wary not just to be "takers" who absorb and represent information gleaned from others. Look for opportunities to benefit partners and meet individual and community goals. That might mean offering access to precious or interesting collection items, providing speaking or program services to others' audiences, or granting access to special kinds of museum participation, such as private events, consultations on new exhibitions or programs, or backstage tours.

Public historians often undervalue some of their most elemental skills. A short laundry list includes knowing how to generate an interested audience; boiling complex and confusing bodies of information down to clearly communicated interpretive messages; organizing raw ideas into thematic strands; facilitating discussions; locating sources and accessing and using them; working with historical and contemporary documents from deed surveys and almanacs to digital county GIS maps; writing narratives and exhibit texts; securing funds; recording oral histories; creating documentation (writing, making films, and building websites and online archives); analyzing and contextualizing sources and arguments; questioning dominant narratives; making effective use of visual and audio materials; researching and mounting exhibitions; getting public relations attention; and mobilizing other museum and history specialists through institutional and academic networks. A mutual partnership might involve deploying these personal and institutional skills to the benefit of your partners as well as within your shared projects. As Welton advises, "Both parties should be able to shine brightly in the partnership—both skill sets should merge to form a new, unique creation."

Beyond all the practical reasons to collaborate lies a higher-order purpose: to find ways for history practice to benefit public audiences. As museums and other history organizations increasingly take the long view, asking how they are contributing to the broad project of enhancing human thriving and improving well-being, it is hard to imagine a practice of public history that does not begin with an openness to the rich possibilities of collaboration.

WORK IN PROGRESS—AN INTERVIEW WITH NIAZ DORRY: THE SLOW WORK OF BUILDING TRUST

FIGURE 7.3 Niaz Dorry.

(Continued)

Building long-term, mutually beneficial, and trusting relationships is a slow and painstaking process but a deeply rewarding one. Niaz Dorry, coordinating director of the Gloucester, Massachusetts, based Northwest Atlantic Marine Alliance (NAMA), has reason to know. Following a career in environmental justice issues as a Greenpeace toxics campaigner, Dorry began working with small-scale, traditional, and indigenous fishing communities in the U.S. and around the globe as a Greenpeace oceans and fisheries campaigner. She then moved on to independent work advancing the rights and ecological benefits of small-scale fishing communities as a means of protecting global marine biodiversity. In 2008, she took the helm at NAMA, which describes itself as "a fishermen-led organization working at the intersection of marine conservation and social, economic, and environmental justice. We're working to build a movement toward a healthy ocean, a just seafood system, and community-based fisheries that are diverse, fair, and equitable for all" (Figure 7.3).

Dorry began working at the tension-filled intersection of fisheries and the environmental movement in 1994, a time fraught with anger and fear over ever-tightening regulations on fishing activity—regulations that threaten to consolidate fishing licenses into a marketable commodity, removing community-based access to seafood resources, destabilizing the local culture of centuries-old fishing ports, and pushing multi-generational fishing families out of business in favor of multi-national corporations. Dorry's deliberate work building trust, growing understanding of fisheries issues, and communicating with people who care about both environmental and community health is a remarkable example of community organizing and partnership principles at work. In her work with the Northwest Atlantic Marine Alliance, Dorry challenges herself to reconcile goals mainstream markets often see as competing: "to bring local fresh seafood to consumers while providing a fair price for fishermen, and build a movement of eaters advocating for policies that allow community-based fishermen to sustain themselves and continue bringing local fish to market. We believe changing how and where the seafood that ends up on dinner tables comes from is key to fisheries conservation." NAMA's spirited outreach program features fun events like the Seafood Throwdown, an Iron Chef-style competition in which fishermen supply locally caught, sustainable seafood and compete in teams with prominent local chefs to prepare the tastiest dish.

Your work with fishermen sought to rebuild a set of relationships that had not existed within living memory: personal connections between fishermen and the people who buy and eat seafood. As transportation networks expanded and fresh fish became a profitable export commodity, middlemen and long shipping lines separated these two communities. As a result, the general public knew very little about the work of fishing, the health of the oceans, and the regulatory environment in which fishermen operate, while the fishermen knew very little about marketing their product, telling a story, and communicating the value of their work. How did you go about rebuilding the relationships that allowed that to happen again?

Creating relationships that really weren't there yet was almost the easy part. I come at this work from a community organizing perspective. All my adult life has been learning how to make connections and build relationships, which is the essence of organizing. But particularly with seafood, there's a current paradigm to get beyond. There's the narrative that we see, from the fishing community perspective, and then there is the narrative embedded in the policy solutions being offered to fix the program. Our differences are rooted in these two narratives. To get the average consumer to talk with fishermen and make those brand new connections was the easy part in some ways. The hard part was to try to convince those who are rooted in the current paradigm to think differently. It takes time; I don't want to convince people we can go from zero to 60. I have to avoid getting frustrated when I work with people who see things differently, who have been rooted in these old narratives, and I have to really go into those conversations with the goal of changing minds and hearts. It's hard not to get mad and frustrated and say "Don't you see what I see?" But you don't want to leave the room having people think you think they're stupid. Those conversations are hard, and require a lot more care.

What strategies did you use to bridge the disconnect between fishermen and consumers?

When it came to connecting fishermen with consumers, people who care about their food sources were thinking "I'm already buying stuff on the 'green' list, so why do I need to get to know fishermen? I don't understand why this element is important." We actually had to tap into the work that was happening on land. After the farm crisis and consolidation of our land-based food system, we were told to move to a corporate food system with the promise of efficiency and cheap food. The land-based local agricultural movement that reacted to that really laid the groundwork for us. Great! We learned from the things they were doing. But over the years we found we needed to go deeper—to think harder, to do more, because fisheries issues are complex in their own way. But what connecting it to land-based systems meant was that we had a common language, and we could easily talk to these audiences that were becoming comfortable with this language and acclimated to it from their agricultural activism.

And it takes a long time. At the beginning I heard a lot of "No one's going to care about this. Nobody's going to buy that. How will I get a fair price?" Almost like the "Nobody loves me, everybody hates me, I'm gonna eat some mud" kind of thing. No one could see their way to understanding how we're going to get people out of that place. That's one of the reasons we started doing Seafood Throwdowns at farmers markets and festivals, places where people were already thinking about their landfood. They already understand that the land matters, that animals matter, and who takes care of both matters. The Seafood Throwdown was built on the strategy

(Continued)

of starting a rapid conversation by tapping into a model they were already familiar with—local landfood—and it expressed a lot of the values we wanted them to connect with through having known that model, and let us build from there. Our farmers market manager here in Gloucester was asking "How do we get this idea out? How do we show the fishermen there's support for them, show the audience that the fishermen are there and need them as supporters?" I did not want to be running another literature table, did not want to have a passive activity. I wanted to deal with all of these ideas at the same time in a two-hour period. We were trying to come up with something that makes people come to you, that they find they *have* to come to you, that it's not a choice—it's the smell, the activity, the conversation, the loudness that makes them wonder "What's going on over there? I wonder what's happening!"

We spent time on all the conversations around the purpose and the methods and finding the right partners and creating an atmosphere where fishermen are seeing the positive environment around them and people are expressing their appreciation, they're enjoying the food, and they're asking "what can I do?" instead of getting beat over the head with data and demands. I know so many fishermen who came to the Throwdowns in the early days in 2008 who had no idea people wanted to hear from them and wanted to support them. The same year, we were doing surveys around Community Supported Fisheries (CSFs),[10] and had the public at the Throwdowns give feedback about what they wanted to see in a CSF. And we got that to happen, and a lot of those farmers markets now have a seafood vendor—and this was the start of getting it going. We needed to show fishermen that there's hope, and not because I'm telling you, but because all these people are telling you. We wanted people in coastal communities to connect to seafood as part of their local food movement.

Many people see the fishing community as independent and slow to trust due to the long history of changing policies and resistance to those changes; some even see fishermen as "bad guys" because of the reporting they hear about over-fishing and the depletion of the oceans. The industry is also one built on generations of family tradition and rooted in close-knit communities and may be one of the hardest kinds of communities to become accepted into. Coming to this as an outsider, how did you go about building trust?

The process of building trust and relationships in fishing communities is where I began in this work 20-some-odd years ago. It's been a long road. Going back to community organizing values, once you are transparent about why you are there, what's less relevant are the specifics of why you're working with someone than about how you're going about getting to know them. What's important is trust building and connectivity and aligning basic values, maybe even foregoing some of the near-term campaign objectives you may have in the process, to create those relationships that might end up lasting a long time. Then you can come back and connect on something that resonates with both of you. That initial care in the relationship has come back to reward me and the work over and over and over again, because people get to know what you're coming from, the level of integrity you're bringing to the community and the relationships. You have to be clear on fundamental values that you stand for, so that when individual campaigns come up they're rooted in the values you share. So when a new idea comes up, I can go back to those fishermen I had long relationships with to say "What do you think about this?"

Sometimes your support is going to be in places you don't expect. Be willing to turn over rocks and have a deep conversation about finding those places. The tendency is to gravitate toward those you think are likely allies but are going to take longer to get to. By building relationships with the unlikely ones, we managed to broaden our base and power enough that some of those likely allies who were not talking to us before were now approaching us. That was really important.

We understand that doing good work with organizations working in food systems is absolutely dependent on building those sorts of mutually beneficial coalitions. But relationship building and maintenance is tough. What advice do you have from your work connecting these disparate communities?

One of the keys is patience, first of all. Relationships end up blooming at their own time. It's not always a sign of success or failure if everybody doesn't arrive where you want them to arrive at the same time. Sometimes there is backtracking, and there's a loss of trust for some reason and you have to go back and have the patience to not get defensive and angry and work it out.

If there's any division in the communities, there may be some deep-rooted stuff that's working against you. Sometimes these issues pop up among allies that you think are on the same page, but their alliances are really far apart. When Anwar Sadat was doing peacekeeping work, one of the criticisms of his work was that he spent a lot of time in Israel and not enough time in Egypt. I think about that a lot—how to not take any relationship for granted, and how to make sure you spend enough time and care with those who should be your natural allies, as well as making new ones. It's always a learning process.

Being prepared for breakups is also a part of this work, and it happens often. It happens often enough that I have to think about it as part of my process, and be okay with that, because as with all relationships, breakups happen. How do you manage it? How do you temper yourself in the process without being disingenuous or untruthful? How do you get out of it whole? My experience has been that the breakup with toxic members doesn't happen often enough. In a lot of coalitions, they are the ones who are trying to grab power, or have dissenting views but who represent a powerful organization, and no one wants them to leave because they have money and power, and they become toxic. Often, all others fall off and that entity becomes dominant. How do you end the relationship early enough so others can keep growing? One of the things I focus on is knowing when it's time to say "We're

(Continued)

just not friends anymore" or "We are actually completely on opposite ends." It's not unlike necessary pruning to keep a whole tree healthy.

Something that I've been learning how to do better over the years dawned on me 25 years ago or so, when I started to hear people using the word "indispensable"—as in, "as a member of this coalition you're indispensable." I feel this word does not belong in an advocate's vocabulary. It puts too much pressure on organizations and individuals and makes us feel we need to do more and more and more, but that doesn't necessarily make us more and more effective. I've really tried to practice being dispensable, and building an organization that should be able to exist without me, and a movement that should be able to exist without a leader. If anybody, any organization, any source of funding suddenly falls off the face of the earth, you can still succeed in the work. We end up getting so deep in this work, we want to own it, but there are things we can let go of. That takes some confidence, some risk. We tend to not want to take the risks, but I'm learning how important it is to distribute power. To distribute resources, knowledge, leadership, just makes the work so much lighter and easier, and you end up surrounding yourself with amazing like-minded people, and suddenly see the work going in 50 directions that there is no way you alone could have done.

Fishing is one of the most complex food industries imaginable. You have dozens of commercial species, migration patterns, seasonality, and then add to that licensing, economics, constantly changing regulations, a number of governmental oversight agencies, and a policy-making process that's pretty obscure. How did you learn what you needed to know to make sense of fishing and translate it into messages the general public can understand?

My personal strategy is to immerse myself. When I started to do the fisheries work (just like when I started other environmental and economic justice work before that), I was coming into the work completely ignorant— and as someone who worked for Greenpeace, I had a double whammy, which I wasn't ignorant about. I knew nothing about fisheries, nothing about bio-accumulative pollutants. I moved to Gloucester because it seemed like the place to be biologically, culturally, historically. Then I learned as much as I could, and that depended on who was willing to take me out fishing. I spent a couple years on various kinds of boats where I was given any opportunity, because I couldn't get anywhere if I was accused of not knowing what I was talking about.

In the policy side, I immersed myself in learning about policy—going to meetings, reading all the news. I started to mobilize what I learned on the boats and in the communities to leverage toward policy. At that point, it really boils down to how to plan a really good political campaign. That's what it turns into at that point—it's just access and strategy and information, and you build on that. The connection I made early on was that it started to seem very similar to related issues, like a fight against an incinerator. The language, the strategies, the global movement of capital behind it, all the moving pieces, some of them invisible, some public—all of this became really clear to me. I knew from twenty years of work that all these fights are similar (and sometimes you're even fighting the same companies, which you discover when you start peeling back the layers).

In my fifties, it's the last issue I'm going to immerse myself in. But it felt right. When it feels right, it connects to your own sense of mission, your own sense of knowing what you want to do with your life—you may ignore it, but once you enter this work, something in you is telling whether this work will be what you dive into or not. The language becomes natural, my understanding is intuitive.

You mentioned that after you've learned the information and accumulated the experience, it comes down to developing a campaign. In museums, we more often structure our work as projects or events, but there is a lot of overlap. Can you describe what you think makes for a successful campaign?

Not trying to overwhelm people is key. I've been really focusing NAMA's work on making people do one thing different: look at their seafood the same way they are looking at the rest of their food. It's a pretty simple ask.

You also have to divide people into buckets, prioritize which broad sectors of people you're going to talk with first. Some people say "I don't look at my food, I just eat." They require special care. So they're in one bucket, and they may be at the bottom of your priority list. You have to weigh those buckets, think about the sectors and their variations. And if you think a certain bucket is most important, that doesn't mean the language has to be more complicated. You want to create language that crosses these sectors as much as you can. Ideas are going to be shared, they are going to become your meme and part of your campaign, so that language needs to become your campaign. As you meet with people, you go deeper, based on your priority and where they're coming from, and you ask where you can go from there.

You also spend some time getting creative, possibly over bottles of whiskey, gathering in circles with others and doing some creative brainstorming ways of getting across those sectors. Fooling around with things you think others might react to, but not judging things based on your own reaction. One of the fishing communities we've worked with has told us a number of times that there is language they wish people would use, but they can't put it out there because of how it would reflect on them, in their position in their own community. So we can use it, and be bold with it, to represent those who are unable to say it themselves. Eventually, the least-priority bucket may be standing up and paying attention to something they've never heard before.

How do you know you're making progress? How do you define success?

I'm a visual thinker, and I mean that literally—my brain literally comes up with that final picture that I'd like to see. I can experience that moment when we've reached that point of where we want to be, some sort of paradigm shift

(Continued)

that I've visualized. You know those old flipbooks? My brain literally creates those pictures along the way, and it becomes a little flipbook for me. How do you create each one of those images? Eventually, you get to that final picture. That's how I measure my success—are those images manifesting themselves? Are you seeing those things happen?

You'll know when you hit your own feeling of success. There are metrics, assistants, worksheets, very fact-oriented elements of the work. We need to have some measures of success: we want to do these things at this time. But it's the big picture that really has that emotional impact. People sometimes reverse how they talk about the what and the why—I encourage people to start with the why, and the whats will become much more practical, much more doable, and have much more clarity around them.

Notes

1 Marshall Ganz, "PAL-177: People, Power and Change," course syllabus, Harvard Divinity School, Fall 2006. For more on the history of community organizing and an expansive collection of literature, Internet links, and training resources, visit the website COMM-ORG: The Online Conference on Community Organizing, edited by sociologist Randy Stoecker, at http://comm-org.wisc.edu/.
2 Travis A. Smith, Chung L. Huang, and Biing-Hwan Lin, "Does Price or Income Affect Organic Choice? Analysis of U.S. Produce Users," *Journal of Agricultural and Applied Economics* 41:3 (December 2009), 731–744.
3 Rachael L. Dettman, "Organic Produce: Who's Eating It?" (United States Department of Agriculture Economic Research Service; presentation at the American Agricultural Economics Association Annual Meeting, Orlando, FL, July 27–29, 2008). http://ageconsearch.umn.edu/bitstream/6446/2/467595.pdf.
4 "Detroit Black Community Food Security Network" on https://sites.google.com/site/urbanag16unai/.
5 "About Us" on www.cleangreensfarm.com/page/about-us-1.
6 On the blog of "Planting Justice," a San Francisco, California-based food justice organization.
7 Mara Welton, farmer, personal interview with Michelle Moon, July 23, 2015.
8 Welton, personal interview, 2015.
9 Welton, personal interview, 2015.
10 Adapting the CSA (Community Supported Agriculture) model, in which food consumers pledge to support a farm operation by contributing funds in advance of the harvest and collecting food disbursements throughout the season, CSFs originated in a 2007 collaboration of North Carolina Sea Grant staff, university researchers, and Port Clyde, Maine, fishermen. The CSF model they developed, known as Port Clyde Fresh Catch, has been adapted widely. LocalCatch.org maintains a list of CSF programs across North America. For more CSF history, see Benjamin Young Landis, "Community Supported Ingenuity," *Coastwatch*: A North Carolina SeaGrant magazine, Winter 2010, https://ncseagrant.ncsu.edu/coastwatch/previous-issues/2010-2/winter-2010/community-supported-ingenuity/.

8

LEAPING THE BARRIERS

Even with the best preparation in place, well-intentioned practitioners can encounter obstacles that cause us to talk ourselves out of new ideas. Perhaps because food is politicized in many ways—through issues of identity and economics as well as public policy—it can feel like a tricky subject to engage, as we've discussed in earlier chapters. It can also be plain old messy, smelly, heavy, and expensive, among other challenges. In this chapter, we identify some of the roadblocks that can prevent practitioners from moving into action, offering recommendations for ways to overcome, work around, or dismantle those obstacles. We step back to encourage analysis of the historical processes by which these challenges arose and call for creative thinking to enable new interpretations.

Negotiating Regulations

Over the past century, a legal net has been woven in, around, and under all places of public accommodation (museums and historic sites included), doing a great deal of good to protect workers and public safety and prevent discrimination. At the same time, food itself has become very highly regulated in response to concerns about public safety and health. Taken as a whole, this regulatory environment presents some predictable barriers to easily implementing certain food interpretation strategies. Among the most commonly cited as frustrating are the restrictions that health codes place on the preparation and service of food, which prevents many sites from sharing the products of farm fields and kitchen demonstrations.

Rather than throw up our hands and give up entirely, though, we urge people to delve into these regulatory relationships to discover what *is* possible. First, historicize the problem and look for interpretive opportunities that link to site specifics: who regulates our food supply, and why and when did that organization get started? It may be that the very regulations we experience as a restraint are great fodder for interpretive presentations. An 1890s role-playing character ranting about the dangerous and poor quality of food might lead right into the passage of the 1906 Pure Food & Drug Act and wider discussions of the continuing need for food safety monitoring in an economic environment that rewards shortcuts and price cuts.

Second, don't assume that regulations are utterly insurmountable. At Old Sturbridge Village in Massachusetts, for instance, staff members arrange to use an inspected commercial kitchen to prepare dozens of historic confections in a single blitz. These legally made foods go into the freezer and are thawed to serve as tastings throughout the year, offered with the regulation sanitary toothpicks and napkins. At the Peabody Essex Museum in Salem, Massachusetts, audiences on a tour of the cooking and dining facilities in historic houses leave with a sugar cookie made from a historic recipe, prepared and pre-packaged by a local catering business. Thanks to these creative work-arounds, visitors get to enjoy a taste of the past and staff members are comfortable in the knowledge that they're operating safely within the law.

To begin discovering what's possible, do some searching online or pick up the phone to figure out what regulatory agencies govern your site. Federal agencies tend to have the least direct involvement, though they do license food facilities, manage food safety recalls, and regulate interstate sales. The critical relationships for museums and historic sites will be with state departments of health and local boards of health. Municipal health officers are often the best first point of contact, as they are familiar with the entire chain of requirements up to and including the federal government. In many cases, they can also offer solutions once they understand your goals—solutions that may include installing a certified commercial kitchen for programs of very large scope but may also involve linking you with kitchen incubators or commercial kitchens that can be rented, training staff to be Certified Food Managers, and other approaches that can increase your site's ability to work with and share food as an educational experience. Boards of health and their agents are required to follow their own legal mandates, and these can sometimes be in tension with the practices and plans of historical institutions—and sometimes with those of food producers and local food advocates as well. Approach health officers as potential partners to be cultivated rather than as merely bothersome hurdles along the road to your own projects. And as with any potential partner, as Niaz Dorry articulates in the preceding "Work in Progress" interview, be prepared to devote time to both educating others about your own goals and learning about the constraints and conventions under which others are operating.

Institutional Constraints

Sometimes the toughest barriers are internal. Most museums are working with strictly controlled budgets and long-range calendars, posing challenges to those seeking to retrain staff, change interpretive directions, or hire additional labor.

Some of the solutions to these constraints lie in revisiting the mission, strategy, and strategic plan, as outlined in Chapter 6. Below, we call out a few common challenges and suggest some avenues for making progress.

Talent and Training

Where staff and time shortages hobble new efforts, work with the support of Human Resources officers to determine whether launching a new volunteer corps or a dedicated (and, ideally, paid) internship in food programs or sustainable agriculture might be possible. Look outside the institution for sources of knowledge and labor—corporate volunteer crews, school and university community service programs, or local "day of service" coalitions that can provide many hands at once to build garden beds, prepare ground, or put up gallons of produce in one-day events.

When it's time for volunteer and staff training, the world of food media is a great friend. Structure low-cost, high-yield training programs around shared explorations of books in the popular food press or online media, such as the short film winners of the Real Food Media competition, the growing library of TED Talks on food-related topics, or podcasts like *Gastropod* or National Public Radio's *The Salt*. Using media as a catalyst, even informal discussion groups can begin to develop the information store of interpreters and volunteers and undergird new interpretive structures.

As for professional development experiences, look to your partners for assistance in planning low-cost field trips or on-site tutorials—perhaps in exchange for museum passes or programs. Armed with prepared questions that relate to their own information needs, museum staff can visit a farming operation, a dairy, a restaurant kitchen, or a fish auction and come back with new insights and ideas to integrate into their interpretation work. Make use of the resources of local Cooperative Extension and SeaGrant programs, funded through state and federal budgets and often low or no cost.

Collections Care Standards

The use of real food can run up against entrenched curatorial, conservation, and maintenance protocols, challenging assumptions about museum objects that have traditionally treated all spaces and furnishings with the same level of care as fine art. These conventional standards are sometimes a tough barrier. Possibilities are limited in historic kitchens where open flame is not permitted, or exhibition spaces that prohibit any crumb of food. Brainstorming solutions with those empowered to make decisions about space use and collections care can help open things up. You might work together to review and discuss some of the ideas of the "Active Collections" movement (listed in the Bibliographic Note at the end of this chapter) such as organizing objects into tiers with different treatment standards to allow low-risk objects to be used in certain defined ways.

Sometimes a chimney repair, metal fireplace surround, or other simple fix can bring a static display back to life. Non-heat cooking methods, like preserving, salting, pressing, or drying might take the place of stoves and hearths while still delivering powerful sensory experiences. Temporary protective barriers and flooring, stanchions, portable ventilators, and other interventions can help make gallery spaces usable for short, focused events. Explore the use of adjacent spaces and "pop-up" stations, in or out of doors, to present the desired programming, or go "free-range," as discussed in Chapter 6, to bring programming to another, more flexible site through a partnership or event.

Finding a Voice

Sometimes institutional resistance centers around a discomfort with the contemporary focus of the kind of new food interpretations we are advocating for here. Turning the lens of historical inquiry onto present-day policy discussions and consumer choices can come uncomfortably close, for some, to seeming like political activism. Different institutions will have different levels of tolerance for putting forward provocative questions and providing pointed perspectives—but it's likely that it's precisely by doing that that the institution will find its greatest opportunity to provide an educational and civic service.

Sometimes an institution serves best as convener. In a *Museum News* interview, Museum of Food and Drink (MOFAD) director Peter Kim describes one example, the MOFAD Roundtable program. As Kim says, the discussion panel is

> our way of demonstrating the role that MOFAD can play as a forum for differing opinions on controversial food issues… We bring together four people who fundamentally disagree on an issue and leave them to talk with very light moderation… This has been spectacular. We did the first one on the New York soda ban. We brought together a libertarian who represented the soda industry's perspective on the soda ban, a nutritionist who had advised the city on the drafting of the regulation, an economist and an anti-hunger advocate who opposed the ban just like the libertarian—on totally different grounds because he viewed it as being paternalistic toward poor communities. All four people had different perspectives, and it made for a lively discussion. A common response we've been getting from people who walk away from these roundtables is that they've been prompted to reevaluate their positions on an issue.[1]

Another museum might find it more appropriate to expand beyond historical issues in a lecture series, as the Concord Museum in Massachusetts did during the run of its 2012–2013 exhibition *The Greatest Source of Wealth: Agriculture in Concord*. Recognizing that Concord's agrarian past struck chords with agricultural reform efforts in the community today, the exhibition connected "the innovations of the 19th century, when Concord was at the forefront of agricultural reform, and the challenges of the 21st century" by presenting big-name food speakers involved in transforming agricultural business: Gary Hirshberg, chairman and former CEO of organic giant Stonyfield Yogurt; Joel Salatin, "grass farmer" and sustainability guru; and Brian Donahue, environmental studies scholar (also interviewed in Chapter 3).[2]

Some museums might historicize issues by serving as journalistic contacts, writing newspaper op-eds on relevant issues or offering a speakers' bureau, while others might find their most powerful voice in teaching and contextualizing skills useful in contemporary food systems reform.

Other Challenges

Related institutional concerns include finding appropriate provisioning sources, especially for specialty ingredients; developing protocols for staff and visitor safety or pest control; securing the funding to purchase a supply of consumables; and thinking about coherence between the event's messages and its staging (for example, making sure there's a plan in place for any uneaten food so that attendees don't leave with a memory of good food being dumped into a trash can). Logistical hurdles like these are so commonly experienced that the best solution is to take part in professional communities that exchange concrete information about potential solutions to specific problems. The robust and growing network of people involved in food and farming interpretation is often generous with practical ideas. Conferences such as those offered by the Association for Living History, Farm, and Agricultural Museums (ALHFAM), American Association for State and Local History (AASLH), National Council on Public History (NCPH), and the American Alliance of Museums (AAM) as well as the Agricultural History Society, state and local historical societies, and those more directly related to food and farming, such as the meetings of the Association for the Study of Food and Society (ASFS), the Agriculture, Food, and Human Values Society (AFHVS), and the Farm-Based Education Network are good places to begin building a personal network on food and farming interpretation. Most of these organizations also maintain websites, Facebook pages, and sometimes Twitter accounts or e-mail lists that can be used to share queries. The website for this book, themissingingredient.net, also includes links, news, and suggestions for building your own network of knowledge and support.

Whatever tactics they ultimately choose, public historians should continually be paying attention to how they can assert the value of bringing history to the table. Understanding and prizing their strengths as historians and drawing on the expanded toolkit offered here in addition to the professional skills of public history will help them competently and confidently enter into complex topical areas, delivering on the purpose and promise of bringing richer educational experiences to our constituent communities. In the final interview of the book, Rolf Diamant discusses how those professional skills come to the forefront in careful negotiations of the complicated relationships that can arise between museums and historians and the organizations and individuals they seek as partners.

Bibliographic Note for Chapters in Section III

Helpful resources for museum mission and strategic planning can be found through the American Alliance of Museums (AAM), whose members have access to an online resource library containing whitepapers on mission and institutional planning, interpretive planning, and more. Small museums will find an invaluable resource in the *Small Museums Toolkit* (Rowman & Littlefield, 2011), a six-volume set by Cinnamon Catlin Legutko and Stacy Klingler covering the basics of museum practice in smaller-scale settings. Book One focuses on *Leadership, Mission and Governance* while Book Five discusses *Interpretation, Education, Programs and Exhibits.* Many of the considerations needed for planning new museum food interpretations are covered thoroughly in the literature about museum planning and management. Freeman Tilden's venerable but still relevant *Interpreting Our Heritage* (4th edition, ed. by R. Bruce Craig, University of North Carolina, 2007) is the precedent-setter for all contemporary museum interpretation, but for practical purposes it's wise to consult more recent considerations of history museum interpretation. Two especially strong works are *Interpretive Planning for Museums: Integrating Visitor Perspectives in Decision Making* by Marcella Wells, Barbara H. Butler, and Judith Koke (Left Coast Press, 2013) and Lisa Brochu's *The 5-M Model for Successful Planning Projects* (National Association for Interpretation, 2003). We have also drawn on Barbara Abramoff Levy's outline in *Interpreting Historic House Museums*, ed. by Jessica Foy Donnelly (AltaMira, 2002).

Historic house museums invite particular kinds of interpretive explorations; planning frameworks specific to those settings can be found in the provocative recent game-changer *Anarchist's Guide to Historic House Museums* by Franklin D. Vagnone and Debra E. Ryan (Left Coast Press, 2013), Donnelly's classic *Interpreting Historic House Museums*, and *Voices from the Backstairs: Interpreting Servants' Lives at Historic House Museums*, by Jennifer Pustz (Northern Illinois University Press, 2010). Several volumes in the *Interpreting American History* series published by Rowman & Littlefield may provide helpful guides to specific topics in food history interpretation, for example *Interpreting Slavery at Museums and Historic Sites* by Kristin L. Gallas and James DeWolf Perry (2014), *Interpreting Native American History at Museums and Historic Sites* by Raney Bench (2014), *Interpreting Food at Museums and Historic Sites* by Michelle Moon (2015), and *Interpreting African American History and Culture at Museums and Historic Sites*, Max van Balgooy, ed. (2015).

A growing literature also deals with the development of educational experiences and programs. Philosophies of shared inquiry in museums are explored in *Letting Go? Sharing Historical Authority in a User-Generated World* edited by Bill Adair, Benjamin Filene, and Laura Koloski (Pew Center for Arts and Heritage, 2011). Nuts and bolts of interpretive communication and program and facilitation are offered in *The Museum Educator's Manual: Educators Share Successful Techniques*, by Anna Johnson, Kimberly A. Huber, Nancy Cutler, Melissa Bingmann, and Tim Grove (Rowman & Littlefield, 2009). Detailed discussion of, and inspiration for, the crafting of powerful museum experiences can be found in *Creativity in*

Museum Practice by Linda Norris and Rainey Tisdale (Left Coast Press, 2014), *The Participatory Museum* by Nina Simon, (Museum 2.0, 2010), *The Engaging Museum* by Graham Black (Routledge, 2005), *The Convivial Museum* by Kathleen McLean and Wendy Pollock (Association of Science-Technology Centers, 2010), and *Creating Great Visitor Experiences: A Guide for Museums, Parks, Zoos, Gardens and Libraries* by Stephanie Weaver (Left Coast Press, 2006).

The need for change in conventions of collecting and object care has occasioned much recent discussion. Of particular interest to food interpreters are James Vaughan's "Rethinking the Rembrandt Rule" in *Museum*, Mar-Apr 2008; Rainey Tisdale's "Do History Museums Still Need Objects?" in *AASLH History News* 66:3 (Summer 2011), 19–24; Ron Potvin's "Chasing the White Whale? Flexible Use of Museum Collections," *AASLH History News* 69:4 (Autumn 2014), 11–16; and Trevor Jones' "Active Collections: Rethinking the Role of Collections in Your Museum," October 23, 2015, available on the web home of the Active Collections initiative, *ActiveCollections.org.*

Finally, much of the bleeding-edge criticism of and conversation about new programs and experiences in history museums happens online. Check the blogs of the National Council on Public History, the American Association for State and Local History, and the American Alliance for Museums' Center for the Future of Museums, as well as the blogs and social media feeds of individual historic sites and museums, influential independently edited museum blogs such as *Museum 2.0* and *ExhibiTricks*, and the website for this book at *themissingingredient.net*.

WORK IN PROGRESS—AN INTERVIEW WITH ROLF DIAMANT: KEEPING FOOD ON THE INSTITUTIONAL AGENDA

FIGURE 8.1   Rolf Diamant.

What does a landscape architect have to tell public historians about interpreting food? Plenty, when the landscape architect in question has been envisioning and developing new, more holistic approaches to conservation and interpretation for over four decades. Rolf Diamant, recently retired after a long career

(Continued)

with the U.S. National Park Service, was at the center of a number of innovative projects within that agency, including the creation of the Frederick Law Olmsted National Historic Site in Brookline, Massachusetts, and the Olmsted Center for Landscape Preservation, the NPS technical center for stewardship of historic landscapes. Most notably for the discussions in this book, he was the founding superintendent of Marsh-Billings-Rockefeller National Historical Park in Woodstock, Vermont, established in 1992. This unique park puts a reflexive spin on the history of the conservation movement itself by preserving a preserved landscape—which also happens to be a working forested and farmed landscape (Figure 8.1).

As he discusses in this interview, the task of combining active forestry and farming with education and stewardship requires many of the skills that are already in the public historian's skill set, but also a keen awareness of how to keep this aspect of the mission fresh and vital over time—how, as he explains it, even at a site where food is not the main interpretive focus, it can become part of an institution's "heart and soul."

What skills and knowledge do you think public historians need to be able to function as advocates or within these sorts of settings where there are multiple agendas, some of which have to do with making a living out of a living landscape?

There are basic skills, number one, being able to understand your operating environment, being able to work effectively in an organization. And then the sort of flip side is also being empathetic and open to new information and working in a community setting and working with getting to know people. Being able to approach the problem not just with a large measure of scholarship but also a large measure of emotional intelligence and a certain amount of political acumen.

And that applies both within a bureaucratic context of whatever organization you're working with, but always keeping in mind that there's a larger audience. And that could be the community, it could be a much larger group of interests. So there's no magic formula, but you have to be aware that you're working in the public realm, it's very visible, your work has political implications and impact and so you need attributes that prepare you for that environment.

Do you think there's anything particular to that realm that just a good generalist public historian wouldn't be able to do?

I really do believe that historians can take on subjects and they learn about them. I'll just give you an example. I came to my last posting with the National Park Service in Vermont with largely a forested landscape and with a challenge of maintaining an active managed forest. I don't have a degree in forestry, I've not worked as a forest manager or in the forestry profession. But of course I came into this as a manager, not necessarily just as a historian, but the point is that you *find* people who know about the subject matter. You get to know people who are doing the work and it's a little bit research, it's a little bit a political campaign. You have to build the relationships and the trust. And you get to know the subject matter, nowhere ever quite as good as the practitioner, the farmer in the field or the forester, but well enough that you can say something of value, add something of value to the conversation.

When I talk about a political campaign, and I use a very small "p" here, I'm talking about being able to make sure that you don't lose sight of any of the component parts. You're constantly making sure that people in your own organization are on the same page. And if they're not, you've got work to do. And you're constantly making sure that your neighbors are always aware of what you're doing and why you're doing it. When we would do harvesting we would post a ranger at the site just to meet and greet people and discuss what was going on, because we didn't want that one person to walk up there and say what the hell is this about? And the next minute we've got a real problem. That could always happen, but find ways to the greatest extent possible to mitigate it.

With food, it also is so much easier. You know, you can have community dinners, you can have some pick-your-own. There are so many ways in to this where the community can get involved.

Forestry's a little trickier.

It's a little trickier, but we made bowls, we had bowl-turning demonstrations. We tried to actually put things in people's hands and they could buy them and take them home. You find ways to appeal to what they're interested in, whether it's furniture or utensils or whatever. With food, it's so much easier. Every citizen, every person who is tied into the larger community—it's in their interests to have some understanding of where their food comes from. This is not just for the public historian. This is an aspect of living, of being part of a society. So I would expect everyone to have an interest and build on that.

Let's talk about politics and what considerations come into play there, other than diplomacy and a certain sense of political savvy. Can you just deepen that a little bit?

Well, I'll speak from my experience. To some extent you approach it as almost a political campaign. As much as you can, you lay out a strategy, you kind of take the pulse of your communities, interested parties. You do some kind of analysis of how you're going to navigate your own organization and how you will be responsive to a larger authorizing environment as you go along. And these were components of what we did with the forest at Marsh-Billings-Rockefeller.

We also had in this case the enormous benefit of some time. And we laid out a very methodical process. We were aware from the very beginning that whatever we were going to do had to be codified by both statute and policy, that we couldn't operate outside of that realm. So it was really a question of how do you interpret policy and how do you explain this in the language that people within your own organization understand and at the same time you had to build a level of trust outside the organization, in the public, who were very skeptical that you had, number one, any credentials or number two, that the track record of the organization gave them any confidence whatsoever

(Continued)

that you weren't just blowing smoke. So when I speak of a political campaign it was a complicated one that had both internal and external aspects to it.

And even with documentation like that, which was really good, institutional memory is short. People forget. It gets lost. There's a break in the chain and then it's forgotten. So it needs constant oxygen, constant daylight, sunlight, to remind them that they've already crossed that bridge, they don't have to re-cross it a second time. That bridge has been crossed already. So every step of the way, with every new document, we went from a General Management Plan to a Cultural Landscape Plan for the forest and to eventually a Forest Treatment Plan, we drilled down to greater and greater amounts of detail, but constantly referring back to each previous layer of planning so that by the time we started the actual forest work, we hoped our position was unimpeachable.

It's really interesting to hear you say that even with that there was I'm assuming a kind of tendency to default to the older patterns, to the more static sense of how you preserve land.

It has to really become part of the DNA of the organization. In other words, it's not just a responsibility of resource management or the forester, or it's not a departmentalized initiative. It becomes the *raison d'etre* for the organization, it becomes their heart and soul. I am emphasizing the attention that was given to the forestry program at Marsh-Billings, but it was by no means the centerpiece of the park, nor did the donor ever assume it was going to be the centerpiece of the park. However, we made sure that when we were building a narrative, an overall narrative of the place, that it was in the narrative.

You understand what I mean by a narrative—it's whenever we're asked about what are you doing, what are you doing that's important, why is this place here, what does it do, it's part of that story. It's not the whole story, but it's part of that story. It's being conscious that you have to find a way to make sure it's not compartmentalized, because you can always have a sympathetic person in the organization who has an interest in this, but they're not always going to be there. And so I guess what I'm saying is that it's just important to find ways to reinforce the message that not only do we do this, do we have this relationship with agricultural and forest lands, but in fact they add value to the park and its mission and it's part of its narrative. To the greatest extent possible, we try to prepare people to understand that these activities are normal, it's what we do, it's part of our DNA, it's part of the narrative, it's not an aberration. And to do that, you have to make it interesting for them. It has to be part of the interpretation, the story, they have to be engaged in it to the extent possible. They have to be taken on tours, they have to meet the people who are doing the work.

Can you say something about the choice of partners or who was there, how you negotiated that? How did you decide what was an appropriate partner for Marsh-Billings-Rockefeller?

We always chose partners very carefully and we had different kinds of partners. There were organizations and individuals we would work with, and then there would be organizations and individuals [where] we'd actually be in some kind of agreement. And that was usually a legal relationship with either a non-profit organization or another agency. We also made extensive use of third-party arrangements. We were a little bit of a square peg in a round hole in terms of the way the federal government does this kind of work. In the world of forestry, which is what we were dealing with, the model was really established by the U.S. Forest Service. And there's one kind of template that they work with, and they basically lease the land to foresters who then harvest it and pay a fee. We really didn't want any of that. We wanted to do the work ourselves in effect and then find ways to sell some of the product, use it or sell it. So we worked through a third party. You need to have another organization. You can't use the Park Service or Forest Service or an NGO or an organization that doesn't do this sort of thing regularly. You need a cut-out. We didn't have to create a new organization—in that case we had the Woodstock Foundation that was prepared for that function.

You're talking about settings where the National Park Service or whatever the agency might be has a high degree of control and can frame this as interpretation or a kind of living interpretation of a living practice. Do you think a historic site should be trying to control as much as possible so that there can be that cohesive vision?

You're always striving for the best outcome, but it's not going to be a perfect outcome. This is a moving target. Yes, you need some control. No one wanted to see an industrial forestry operation [at Marsh-Billings-Rockefeller]. On the other hand, we're not farmers [or foresters] and these people need to make a living. And so there's going to be a lot of give and take.

Most agreements, when they start out, the parties have shared expectations but over time, people change, they come in and out of jobs, organizations undergo transitions. And the agreements may still be on paper in place, but the expectations start to shift and you're not on the same page as your partner. So every so often it's just probably good management to go back and renegotiate, to make sure you still share the same expectations. Now you may not be renegotiating the agreement, but you find a venue and a reason for having a conversation.

That makes a lot of sense, and it helps me in thinking that the historic sites need to really become much more knowledgeable about farming—maybe not! They are knowledgeable about interpretation, they need to be knowledgeable enough to know what questions to ask or who shares their values or—

They need to have an advisor. They need to have a third party in their court, either a friend or a consultant or somebody who speaks the language. It's sometimes just fortuitous, it'll be on your staff. If not, find a friend or someone who cares about the place and who can function in that role.

Notes

1   Reprinted from *Museum* magazine, a benefit of membership in the American Alliance of Museums, May–June 2015, 47.
2   "Past Exhibitions: The Greatest Source of Wealth," *Concord Museum.org* http://www.concordmuseum.org/past-special-exhibitions.php#2012

EPILOGUE

How Do We Measure Success?

In early spring, a gardener tucks a seedling into the soil. Before long, pairs of tender leaves reach outward from leggy stalks. As the weather warms, bushy leaves spread in all directions, and yellow flowers pop out here and there. By the time summer arrives, heavy green fruits droop from the plant, and at harvest time, the gardener is eating tomatoes at every meal and giving away the extras to anyone within reach. It's easy to tell when it's been a great season.

Museum and public history projects aren't always as easy to evaluate. As we discussed what this book should say about the outcomes of a new, engaged form of food interpretation, we found ourselves wrestling once again with the same productive tension we noted at the outset of the book: food issues are urgent and concrete, but historical institutions are typically not direct action organizations. Unlike some of our partners, we can't measure our successes in terms of meals served, legislation passed, or acres transitioned to organic production. At the same time, we're adamant about the need to steer clear of do-nothing interpretive projects—the kind in which practitioners "talk about" topics with participants but can't demonstrate any ultimate effects flowing from the experience. We found that we needed to ask not just *how* we should measure success, but what success *is*. What kinds of differences should public historians aim to make in the food system?

Setting Goals That Matter

The once-controversial idea that museums should be providing an educational service to a diverse, democratic public is now mainstream. There's no doubt in our minds that public history institutions can and should be engaging with the food questions that communities are wrestling with. But what kind of difference should we be making? Based on our interviews and our observations, we believe that the wisest path in setting goals for our food work is to remain authentic to the unique contributions only historians and museums can offer.

How abstract and open-ended should those goals be? Defining goals loosely lets us remain open to infinite possibilities, but unless we specify the hoped-for impact, the result may be vague speculation about whether our ideas are working and an inability to demonstrate real-world outcomes worthy of the museum or historic site's commitment of limited resources. On the other hand, overly structured and narrow goals could blind museums to opportunities to contribute usefully to a debate that pops up suddenly, shift resources to a more promising area of inquiry, or include emerging audience sectors. Calibrating a workable response to the question of specificity versus abstraction is a project each site must undertake uniquely. The answers depend in part on site mission and resources, as well as tolerance for ambiguity and current conditions in the community being served. In addition, we believe that working in new ways and in relation to dynamic questions and partnerships demands that even sharply defined goals leave room for iteration, revision, and the occasional dash of serendipity.

Another meaty question concerns what kinds of changes museums should seek to make through their food work. Practitioners need to consider whether they are interested in changing audience *behaviors* (shifting purchasing patterns, planting home gardens), audience *attitudes* and *ideas* (revising an opinion on extra-legal immigration because of a better understanding of how undocumented labor affects the cost of produce), or *social structures and institutions* (passing local land-use policies more favorable to tenant farmers, contributing historical knowledge about wild food sites to a regional master plan). Productive goal-setting processes will consider how the museum thinks about engagement at all scales: individual, community, local, institutional, regional, and governmental.

Defining Impact Areas

We've come to believe that public historians doing food work are most effective when they are operating from their core strengths. Practitioners should be deliberative in selecting project areas with strong links to historical narratives and to their specific site content, considering the ways in which historical approaches might helpfully affect understanding and/or action on issues critical to the community. By locating work within these areas of strength, museums can prevent "initiative fatigue," avoid creating shallow interpretations, and work from their most deeply grounded intellectual and physical positions.

The chosen impact areas will necessarily be ones unique to and valued by the communities served by each individual museum, but some potential realms of activity include:

*   *Strengthening the debate.* Changing the nature of local and regional conversations around food issues by building historical consciousness and supporting the development of skills like questioning, critical inquiry, and historical thinking.

- *Relocating history.* Inserting historical perspectives into spaces where they are currently absent. This might be as simple as writing seasonal-food columns or op-eds in local papers or community blogs, presenting at meetings of community groups, or bringing historical content into festivals, fairs, or outdoor markets.

- *Creating common ground.* Our institutions and projects can serve as platforms for forthright but civil conversation inclusive of a range of opinion. By organizing conversations around solid ground rules and selecting informed and interesting presenters and moderators, museums and historic sites can raise the level of discourse even on food issues that generally incite passionate reactions.

- *Adding to the picture.* Rendering visible histories of individuals, landscapes, plant and animal beings, and communities that have often been omitted from or unconnected to public discussions of food and farming.

- *Connecting the dots.* Discovering ways in which land use and preservation, tourism and recreation, justice, economic development, employment, immigration, and other complex issues intersect through—and affect—food issues.

- *Enabling relationships.* When they aim to function as culturally "safe spaces," museums and historic sites can offer alternatives to the now-normalized experience of social segregation. As we've noted above, these institutions sometimes wrestle with perceptions that they are only for particular kinds of visitors or that the materials inside them aren't relevant to most people's lives. But the flip side is that they may be able to provide a common ground that is removed from familiar contentions in everyday experience, offering diverse audiences a premise for introductions and shared experiences. This kind of social bridging strengthens community resilience, adding another dimension to the impact museums may have on food systems reform.

- *Developing and reforming systems.* Fulfilling their democratic mandate, museums can assist people in building the understanding to better navigate public systems. A more informed sense of history can support audiences in becoming more effectively involved in issues of local government (such as planning and zoning, food policy councils, and purchasing), shaping food programs in local and community institutions (schools, hospitals, prisons, senior centers), and enhancing community infrastructure (improving systems for food waste recovery, developing food hubs).

Measuring Outcomes

Successful projects can't be called "successful" unless they include the measurement and evaluation of outcomes. In a 2002 speech, Stephen Weil emphasized externality in his definition of outcomes as "what happens outside an organization as a consequence of distributing the goods and/or services that the organization produces. In the for-profit organization, that consequence is an economic outcome. For the not-for-profit, it must—of necessity—be a social one."[1] Weil's words hold two important messages: first, that internal museum conversations, no matter how relevant to food and farm issues, produce zero outcomes for the community; second, that outcomes by their nature can't be read through what happens on museum grounds—only in changes to the society in which museums operate. Some of these outcomes may occur on a long timeline and be tricky to measure—but they must be real, observable, and reportable. Institutions may need to embrace creative thinking and become sensitive bellwethers of community change in order to quantify and qualify the impact they are having. For example, in his interview in Chapter 1, Darwin Kelsey counts the expansion of farmers markets and organic land in Cuyahoga County as one of the indirect results of his organization's work. In some cases, evidence for success might be found in considering how social outcomes would look different—and perhaps more impoverished and less sustained—if they did not include the kinds of insights that historical research and interpretation can offer.

Staying Reflexive

Finally, we urge public historians to maintain the reflexive stance we have advocated for throughout this book, thoughtfully observing and responding to their own practice even as it evolves. Like the work of food systems themselves, the work of food and farming interpretation is ongoing, changing shape as new horizons and challenges emerge. As we step forward, we need to welcome opportunities to adapt, changing our own systems of asking and learning, our own perceptions, and our own behaviors. Rather than a fixed set of standards for engaging with food issues, we hope this book encourages you to preserve dynamism and responsiveness, to share and reflect with peers both inside and outside of your profession. To continue engaging usefully with contemporary happenings, we need to watch for the bleeding edge of public conversation, always asking ourselves where history plugs in.

Exciting times lie ahead. We'd like to hear about how you have applied and experimented with ideas in this book and beyond, how you are discovering creative new ways to further the project of adding historical dimensions to public conversations about food. We invite you to continue the conversation, online and in person, connecting our efforts in a growing network for continuing progress across the field, learning and being inspired by one another's efforts to break new ground. This is not an ending—it's a start. We'll see you in the field.

Note

1 Stephen Weil, *Are You Really Worth What You Cost, or Just Merely Worthwhile?* (San Francisco: Getty Leadership Institute, 2002), 5.

APPENDIX

"TRIPLE TOP LINE" TIMELINE OF U.S. FOOD AND FARMING HISTORY

This selection of key moments and events in U.S. food and farming history is intended to support interpretations built on the "triple top line" framework set out in Chapter 3 and used throughout the book. Most of the entries that follow are general factual information drawn from a variety of readily available sources. One invaluable and clearly presented resource is the "Growing a Nation: The Story of American Agriculture" set of timelines produced by the U.S. Department of Agriculture, available online. Comparative information about corn production and fertilizer use comes from those timelines. Data on the numbers of farms and farmers come from the U.S. Census Bureau. Douglas Hurt's *American Agriculture* supplied much of the other factual information. On supermarkets, see Tracey Deutsch, *Building a Housewife's Paradise: Gender, Politics, and American Grocery Stores in the Twentieth Century* (University of North Carolina Press, 2010). On the rise of car culture, see Tom McCarthy, *Auto Mania: Cars, Consumers, and the Environment* (Yale University Press, 2007). Other information about specific topics can be found in the bibliographic essays following most of the chapters in this book.

c. 12,000–7,000 years ago

- Emergence of agriculture in many parts of the world

c. 1300–1400 CE

- Mixed-crop cultivation and animal husbandry in male-centered, generally feudal system of land ownership dominant system of agriculture in Europe

c. 1600–1900

- European model of agriculture diffused around the world in era of colonial expansion

1776–1783

- Revolutionary War economic boom for farmers

1786–1787

- Farmer-led Shays' Rebellion in response to post-Revolutionary-War deflation and taxation

1790s–1820s

- Emergence of industrial manufacturing in the American northeast, especially New England
- Expansion of commercial markets for food and other products, new competitive pressures and limited control over prices for farmers
- Creation of many agricultural fairs and societies for agricultural improvement in U.S.

1807–1809

- Economic depression during embargo before War of 1812

1810–1814

- War of 1812 brings uneven prosperity

1819

- First significant economic panic in the new United States, brought on by renewed international competition after the end of the Napoleonic Wars

1820

- Farmers make up 72% of American workforce

1822–1823

- Slow recovery from 1819 panic

1820s–1850s

- Establishment of railroads in much of eastern U.S. creates new competitive pressures for older, smaller farms as well as opportunities for Americans to tour more of their nation

1837

- Another major economic crisis in the U.S., sparked by the Andrew Jackson administration's insistence that land speculation on the western frontier be backed by gold currency, not paper; depression lasts until 1843

1844–1856

- Economic recovery and expansion of U.S. businesses

1849

- Chemical fertilizers first sold commercially

1850

- 75–90 hours of labor required to produce 100 bushels of corn

Mid-nineteenth century

- Growth of agricultural journals and other publications, often linked with farm reform movements
- Expansion of farming into American Midwest and west
- Emergence of a conservation movement and Romantic ethos about pastoral and natural landscapes

1847

- George Perkins Marsh's "Address to the Agricultural Society of Rutland County" warns of limits to expansion and productivity, based on limits of natural lands

1850

- U.S. Census shows 4.9 million farmers, 64% of the American population

1858

- Mount Vernon saved from demolition and reopened as a historic site, signaling the emergence of an American historic preservation movement

1859

- Edwin Drake drills first commercial oil well in the U.S. in western Pennsylvania

1861–1865

- American Civil War brings inflation of prices and economic prosperity for many farmers
- Early "period kitchen" displays developed for fundraising events for the U.S. Sanitary Commission

1862

- Huge expansion of federal involvement in U.S. agriculture, with resistant Southern bloc temporarily out of government
- U.S. Department of Agriculture created

- Land-grant colleges established by Morrill Land-Grant College Act and charged with keeping agriculture up to date and productive
- First Homestead Act encourages new settlement of western territories

1864

- Chicago Board of Trade established as world's first agricultural futures and options exchange, trading wheat, corn, cattle, and pigs

1866–1867

- Postwar recession

1867

- The Order of the Patrons of Husbandry ("the Grange") founded as national farmers' organization; "Granger laws" regulating railroad and grain elevator prices passed in the following decade

1868–1873

- New boom in railroads

1869

- Start of industrial food-processing and vertical integration in agriculture with ventures like Henry J. Heinz's food-packing company in Pennsylvania and Louis McMurray's combined farming and canning business in Maryland

1870

- U.S. Census shows that for the first time farmers are a minority of the American population (47.7%)

1873–1878

- Depression and deflation

1874–1880

- Start of Farmers' Alliance movement, a coalition that became the Populist Party in the 1890s, advocating for debt relief for farmers and limitations on forms of speculation that drove up land prices

1875

- Margarine (known as "oleomargarine") first produced in the U.S., sparking a long-running controversy and first battle over the safety and labeling of food produced in laboratories

1876

- Philadelphia Centennial International Exhibition featured prototypical food displays and interpretations linked with regional and cultural histories

1879–1893

- Expansive period for businesses, including farmers

1886

- Colored Farmers National Alliance and Cooperative Union founded in Texas in response to segregated Farmers Alliance

1887

- Hatch Act creates a system of agricultural experiment stations at land grant colleges, designed to help farmers keep up to date with latest scientific methods

1888

- First transcontinental shipment of refrigerated foods from California to New York

1889

- USDA elevated to cabinet level

1890s

- Nearly 2 million tons of commercial fertilizers used in U.S. annually
- Labor required to produce 100 bushels of corn drops to 30–45 hours

1891

- Cotton-pickers strike by Colored Farmers National Alliance and Cooperative Union fails to gain traction and leads to demise of organization, reflecting deep racial divisions between better-off white farmers/landowners and poorer black farmworkers and sharecroppers in the South

1893

- World's Columbian Exposition in Chicago brings together cultural and culinary displays from around the world, exemplifying many of the qualities of the great industrial expositions of the era

1893–1894

- Panic of 1893, followed by many bankruptcies and multi-year economic depression

- Detroit Mayor Hazen Pingree's plan to use vacant urban lots as food gardens for the poor ("Pingree's Potato Patches") becomes model for urban work relief programs in several U.S. cities

Late nineteenth century

- First significant American "back to the land" movement, prompted by economic uncertainty and concerns about the social and civic effects of urbanization and modernization
- Many farmers, especially in older farming areas, turn to offering "value-added" products, farmstands, and farm vacations as another source of income

1895–1906

- Economic boom period

1902

- Farmers' Union founded in Texas, aiming to give farmers more control over setting prices through collective and cooperative efforts

1906

- Publication of Upton Sinclair's muckraking novel *The Jungle* draws attention to labor and health problems in Chicago's meatpacking industry
- Pure Food and Drug Act gives federal government power to regulate food additives and labeling

1907–1908

- Panic of 1907 spurs renewed "back to the land" impulse

1908

- Ford Motor Company begins mass-producing the Model T, a key moment in both the rise of American car-centered culture and the shift into much larger-scale, vertically integrated industrial models of production, including in agriculture and food processing

1900–1910

- Nearly 4 million tons of commercial fertilizers used in U.S. annually

c. 1900–1920

- "Golden age" for farmers in many parts of the U.S.: relatively high agricultural prices intersect with new technologies and methods that make production more efficient; requirements for new capital investment not yet as burdensome as they become in later decades

- Overall number of farms in U.S. grows from 5.7 million in 1900 to 6.5 million in 1920

1909

- Expanded Homestead Act spurs massive migration to the Great Plains and use of farming techniques that contribute to later Dust Bowl problems

1910

- Over 6 million tons of commercial fertilizers used annually in the U.S.

1912

- Great Atlantic & Pacific Tea Company (A&P) introduces the "economy" grocery store; has 650 stores two years later, launching an era of chain store expansion in the food sector

1914

- Smith-Lever Act creates extension system at land grant colleges, linked with USDA

1914–1918

- World War I in Europe expands markets for American foods; U.S. entry into war in 1917 helps farmers by creating new demand in supplying the military, as in previous wars

1916

- Original Piggly Wiggly store opens in Memphis as first successful self-serve grocery store
- American farm population reaches its peak size, at 32.5 million (32% of U.S. population)

1917

- Mass production of Fordson tractor, the first affordable machine for agricultural draft work, which was quickly superseded by International Harvester's lighter and cheaper Farmall; key moment in shift toward fossil-fuel dependence in U.S. agriculture

1918

- 4H Clubs founded in USDA extension programs; become widespread in rural America by 1924, part of effort to train future farmers as well as educating non-farmers about the importance of agriculture

- For the first time, federal government requests wartime civilian participation in food conservation with "Wheatless Wednesdays," "Meatless Mondays," and a "Liberty Garden" movement

1919

- Farm Bureau founded in Chicago as business- and efficiency-oriented organization
- A&P has 4,224 stores

1919–1932

- Chain groceries' share of the food market goes from 4.2% to 28.8%

1920–1921

- Sharp postwar recession; prices for agricultural products driven quickly downward because of surplus production enabled by increased efficiency (in large part because of application of products developed and improved during World War I, particularly nitrogen used in explosives and fossil-fuel-powered vehicles and machinery)
- For the first time, more Americans live in urban than rural places
- Farmers make up 30% of the overall population

1922

- Capper-Volstead Act gives legal status to cooperatives, sparking the formation of many farmers' coops in response to falling prices

1923

- A&P is operating about 8,000 stores

1921–1940

- Agricultural depression, starting well before the 1929 crash and culminating in the Dust Bowl years when over-exposed, over-exploited soils literally blow away in many parts of the country

1922–1929

- Speculative boom, ending with October 1929 stock market crash

1920s

- Self-service grocery stores begin adding perishable items, which were formerly sold more directly by farmers

1927

- Food and Drug Administration created to regulate food safety, content, and labeling

1929

- 23 million passenger vehicles registered in U.S.
- Henry Ford opens Greenfield Village in Dearborn, Michigan, as a nostalgic monument to older ways of American life

1930

- First King Kullen opened in Queens, New York, arguably the first true supermarket in gathering all the facets of food shopping together under one roof

1930s

- Great Depression sparks new homesteading/back-to-the-land movement
- Farm population grows to 31.2 million in 1933
- Some backlash against the rise of national chain groceries
- Extensive New Deal agricultural policies and reform put in place
- Over 6½ million tons of commercial fertilizers used in U.S. annually
- 100 bushels of corn can now be produced in 15–20 hours

1932

- Farmers' Holiday movement organized to protest farmers' inability to make back their costs of production, a key cause of bankruptcies and foreclosures

1933

- Agricultural Adjustment Act (the first Farm Bill) aimed to bring agricultural supply and demand into balance, in part through a controversial program of destroying surplus food

1934

- Eli Lilly opens Conner Prairie pioneer village in Fishers, Indiana, part of continued nostalgic turn to older ways of life (increasingly facilitated by automobile tourism)

1936

- Commodity Exchange Act brings commodity and futures trading under federal oversight

- Robinson-Patman Act requires wholesalers to charge the same price to all retailers, temporarily curtailing the competitive advantage of supermarkets

1938

- Agricultural Adjustment Act of 1938 establishes a five-year cycle for Farm Bills

1939

- Food Stamp Program established as a way to feed urban poor while making use of surplus farm production

1940

- "An Agricultural Testament" published as organic farming manifesto by Sir Albert Howard
- J.I. Rodale buys a farm in Emmaus, Pennsylvania, to experiment with organic methods; Rodale later founds *Organic Farming and Gardening* magazine, a key publication in the American resurgence of small-scale, low-input modes of farming

1939–1945

- World War II Victory Garden movement in U.S. reconnects many Americans with the experience of growing their own food
- Food Stamp Program ends in 1943 with higher employment levels
- 10–14 hours of labor required to produce 100 bushels of corn

1944

- Farmers' Museum opens in Cooperstown, New York, reflecting repurposing of some older "model" farms as historic sites

1946–1970

- Postwar economic and industrial boom

1940s

- 13½ million tons of commercial fertilizer used in U.S. annually

1948

- General Agreement on Tariffs and Trade (GATT) establishes the shape of international trade in the postwar decades

1952

- Car culture continues to expand, with 52 million passenger vehicles registered in the U.S. in 1952

1950s

- More than 22 million tons of commercial fertilizers used in U.S. annually

1954

- Publication of "Living the Good Life" by Helen and Scott Nearing, a widely read statement about "simple living"

1956

- For the first time in the U.S., number of passenger vehicles exceeds number of households

1957–1958

- Economic recession

1958–1970

- Extended business expansion

1960s

- United Farm Workers begins unionizing California farmworkers
- Commodity producers gains new political influence in Congress
- "Living history farms" grow in popularity, with Association of Living Historical Farms and Agricultural Museums (ALHFAM) founded in 1970 and many existing historic sites (e.g., Conner Prairie and Old Sturbridge Village) adopting experiential and "first-person" interpretation

1962

- Rachel Carson's "Silent Spring" published as a warning about the environmental effects of pesticides

1964

- Food Stamp Act revives food stamps as a way to get food to (mostly) urban poor people while supporting farmers by finding a use for surplus agricultural commodities; by 21st century, 80% of total Farm Bill funding goes to Food Stamp program

1968

- Biologist Norman Borlaug coins the term "Green Revolution" to describe the widespread development and technology transfer projects that expanded industrial agriculture worldwide

1970s

- Inflation rates increase while economic growth slows
- More than 43 million tons of commercial fertilizers used in U.S. annually
- 100 bushels of corn can now be produced in 3.3 hours

1970

- *Mother Earth News* founded, reflecting the addition of environmentalism to the mix of motivations for going "back to the land"

1971–1976

- Earl K. Butz serves as U.S. Secretary of Agriculture; changes many New Deal policies and encourages farmers to increase surplus production rather than curtail it
- Inflation and rising food prices early in the 1970s spark consumer fears and create political will to keep prices low
- Policies move the U.S. back toward a more fully market-driven agricultural economy that make it harder for small producers to remain competitive in mainstream markets

1972

- First recombinant DNA molecules produced by Paul Berg, opening the way to production of genetically modified organisms (GMOs), seen by many as the next wave of scientific and industrial agriculture

1977

- American Agriculture Movement formed in Colorado to demand government guarantees that food prices keep pace with farmers' costs of production; in 1978 and 1979 thousands of farmers drive their tractors to Washington, DC, as part of protest

1981–1982

- Economic recession

1980s

- "Farm crisis" continues for farmers carrying heavy debt loads
- More than 47 million tons of commercial fertilizers used in U.S. annually
- 100 bushels of corn can now be produced in 2.75 hours
- Advent of computerized inventorying helps spur more globalized delivery of food to grocery stores

1983–1990

- Expansive period for U.S. business in general

1985

- Farm Aid concerts/organization founded to support farmers facing foreclosure

1986

- Robyn Van En of Massachusetts begins selling shares of her farm's produce in advance, helping launch the CSA (Community Supported Agriculture) movement
- In Italy, Carlo Petrini joins anti-McDonald's protest and founds Slow Food movement to support traditional and regional cuisines and food systems

1987

- Number of farmers in U.S. has dropped to 5 million, just 2% of the total population; half are in the Midwest, a third in the South; overall numbers have fallen for decades, with occasional upticks

1990–1991

- Economic recession

1991–2000

- Renewed business expansion

1994

- The Marrakech Agreement, successor to GATT, creates the World Trade Organization (WTO) to facilitate a more fully globalized system of exchange
- USDA counts 1,755 farmers markets in U.S.

1995

- At least 500 CSA farms operating in U.S.

2005

- Chicago Board of Trade becomes a publicly traded company, part of trend toward global market speculation in commodity foods and futures

2006

- Film *An Inconvenient Truth* raised awareness (and political controversy) about humans' role in climate change

- Michael Pollan's *The Omnivore's Dilemma* added to recurring debate about the merits of industrial and alternative food systems

2007

- USDA reports over 12,000 CSA farms in U.S.

2008

- Debates over "food vs. fuel" as biofuel production expands
- 4,685 farmers markets in U.S.
- Economic crash

2010

- 6,132 farmers markets in U.S.

2014

- 8,321 farmers markets in U.S.

BIBLIOGRAPHY

Ackerman-Leist, Philip. *Rebuilding the Foodshed: How to Create Local, Sustainable, and Secure Food Systems.* White River Junction, VT: Chelsea Green, 2011.

Adair, Bill, Benjamin Filene, and Laura Koloski, ed. *Letting Go? Sharing Historical Authority in a User-Generated World.* Philadelphia: Pew Center for Arts and Heritage, 2011.

Agricultural Research Service, "Glossary of Agricultural Terms," 2017 edition. U.S. Department of Agriculture. https://agclass.nal.usda.gov/glossary.shtml

Albala, Ken. "History on the Plate: The Current State of Food History." *Historically Speaking* 10:5 (2009): 6–8.

American Farmland Trust, Conservation Law Foundation, and the Northeast Sustainable Agriculture Working Group. *New England Food Policy: Building a Sustainable Food System.* American Farmland Trust, Conservation Law Foundation, and the Northeast Sustainable Agriculture Working Group, 2014. www.clf.org/wp-content/uploads/2014/03/1.New_England_Food_Policy_FULL.pdf.

Anderson, Gail. *Reinventing the Museum: The Evolving Conversation on the Paradigm Shift.* Lanham, MD: AltaMira, 2012.

Anderson, Jay. *Time Machines: The World of Living History.* Nashville, TN: American Association for State and Local History, 1984.

———. *A Living History Reader.* Nashville, TN: American Association for State and Local History, 1991.

Association for the Preservation of Virginia Antiquities. *Yearbook of the Association for Virginia Antiquities.* Richmond, VA: George M. West, 1896.

Bager, Simon, Bruce Campbell, and Lucy Holt Sonja Vermeulen. "Food Emissions: Direct Agricultural Emissions." Research Program on Climate Change, Agriculture and Food Security, Consultative Group on International Agricultural Research (CGIAR). No date. http://ccafs.cgiar.org/bigfacts/.

Ball, Richard A. and J. Robert Lilly. "The Menace of Margarine: The Rise and Fall of a Social Problem." *Social Problems* 29:5 (June 1982): 488–498.

Barkan, Ilyse D. "History Invites Regulation: The Passage of the Pure Food and Drug Act of 1906." *American Journal of Public Health* 75:1 (1985): 18–26.

Barron, Hal. *Those Who Stayed Behind: Rural Society in Nineteenth-Century New England.* Cambridge and New York: Cambridge University Press, 1984.

Bell, David and Gill Valentine. *Consuming Geographies: We Are Where We Eat*. London: Routledge, 1997.

Bell, Michael M. "Did New England Go Downhill?" *Geographical Review*, 79:4 (October 1989): 450–466.

———. "Stone Age New England: A Geology of Morals." In *Creating the Countryside: The Politics of Rural and Environmental Discourse*, 29–64. E. Melanie DuPuis and Peter Vandergeest, eds. Philadelphia: Temple University Press, 1996.

Bench, Raney. *Interpreting Native American History at Museums and Historic Sites*. Lanham, MD: Rowman & Littlefield, 2014.

Bennett, Drake. "The Localvore's Dilemma." *Boston Globe*, July 22, 2007.

Berlow, Ali. *The Food Activist's Handbook*. North Adams, MA: Storey Publishing, 2015.

Berry, Wendell. "Energy in Agriculture." In *Bringing It to the Table: On Farming and Food*, 57–65. Berkeley, CA: Counterpoint, 2009 (1979).

Black, Graham. *The Engaging Museum*. London: Routledge, 2005.

Brochu, Lisa. *Interpretive Planning: The 5-M Model for Successful Planning Projects*. Fort Collins, CO: National Association for Interpretation, 2003.

Brown, A. et al. itallithographer, and Henry McCloskey. "Brooklyn Sanitary Fair, 1864." *Henry McCloskey's Manual of 1864*, 1864. Library of Congress. https://www.loc.gov/item/2013650035/.

Brown, Dona. *Inventing New England: Regional Tourism in the Nineteenth Century*. Washington, DC: Smithsonian Institution Press, 1995.

Bruegel, Martin. *Farm, Shop, Landing: The Rise of a Market Society in the Hudson Valley, 1780–1860*. Durham and London: Duke University Press, 2002.

Buzby, Jean C., Hodan Farah Wells, and Jeffrey Hyman. *The Estimated Amount, Value, and Calories of Postharvest Food Losses at the Retail and Consumer Levels in the United States*. Washington, DC: USDA Economic Research Service, Economic Information Bulletin No. EIB-121, February 2014.

Carson, Jane. *Colonial Virginia Cookery*. Williamsburg, VA: Colonial Williamsburg, 1968.

Caswell, Julie A. and Ann L. Yaktine, eds. "Supplemental Nutrition Assistance Program: Examining the Evidence to Define Benefit Adequacy." Washington, DC: Institute of Medicine and National Research Council of the National Academies, 2013. https://fns-prod.azureedge.net/sites/default/files/ops/IOMSNAPAllotments.pdf.

Choices. "Local Food—Perceptions, Prospects, and Policies" (special issue). Agricultural and Applied Economics Association, 2010. www.choicesmagazine.org/magazine/article.php?article=107.

Christensen, Jonathan. "Four Stages of Social Movements." *EBSCO Research Starters*, *EBSCOhost*. Ipswich, MA: EBSCO Publishing Service, 2009.

Clancy, Kate and Kathryn Ruhf. "Is Local Enough? Some Arguments for Regional Food Systems." *Choices: The Magazine of Food, Farm and Resource Issues*, First Quarter 2010.

Clark, Christopher. *The Roots of Rural Capitalism: Western Massachusetts, 1780–1860*. Ithaca, NY: Cornell University Press, 1990.

Conklin, Paul. *A Revolution Down on the Farm: The Transformation of American Agriculture since 1929*. Lexington: University Press of Kentucky, 2009.

Dettman, Rachael L. "Organic Produce: Who's Eating It?" United States Department of Agriculture Economic Research Service; presentation at the American Agricultural Economics Association Annual Meeting, Orlando, FL, July 27–29, 2008.

Deutsch, Tracey. *Building a Housewife's Paradise: Gender, Politics, and American Grocery Stores in the Twentieth Century*. Chapel Hill: University of North Carolina Press, 2010.

Donahue, Brian. *The Great Meadow: Farmers and the Land in Colonial Concord*. New Haven and London: Yale University Press, 2004.

———. "Another Look from Sanderson's Farm: A Perspective on New England Environmental History and Conservation." *Environmental History* 12:1 (January 2007): 9–34.

Donnelly, Jessica Foy, ed. *Interpreting Historic House Museums.* Walnut Creek, CA: AltaMira, 2002.

Effland, Anne B.W. "U.S. Farm Policy: The First 200 Years." *Agricultural Outlook.* Economic Research Service of the U.S. Department of Agriculture, March 2000. www.farmlandinfo.org/sites/default/files/US_Farm_Policy_March_2000_1.pdf.

Elias, Megan. "Summoning the Food Ghosts: Food History as Public History." *The Public Historian* 34:2 (2012): 20–27.

Farrell, Betty and Maria Medvedeva. "Demographic Transformation and the Future of Museums." Washington, DC: American Alliance of Museums Press, 2010.

Fitzgerald, Deborah. *Every Farm a Factory: The Industrial Ideal in American Agriculture.* New Haven and London: Yale University Press, 2010.

Food Solutions New England. *A New England Food Vision.* Durham, NH: Food Solutions New England, 2014.

Gallas, Kristin L., and James DeWolf Perry. *Interpreting Slavery at Museums and Historic Sites.* Lanham, MD: Rowman & Littlefield, 2014.

Gardner, James. "Contested Terrain: History, Museums and the Public." *The Public Historian* 26:4 (Fall 2004): 11–21.

Garrison, J. Ritchie. *Landscape and Material Life in Franklin County, Massachusetts, 1770–1860.* Knoxville: University of Tennessee Press, 1991.

Gill, Corrington. *Wasted Manpower.* New York: W.W. Norton, 1939.

Goodland, Robert and Jeff Anhang. "Livestock and climate change: What if the key actors in climate change are…cows, pigs, and chickens?" *World Watch*, November/December 2009, worldwatch.org/node/6294.

Gray, Margaret. *Labor and the Locavore: The Making of a Comprehensive Food Ethic.* Berkeley, CA: University of California Press, 2014.

Guthman, Julie. *Agrarian Dreams: The Paradox of Organic Farming in California.* Berkeley, CA: University of California Press, 2004.

Haley, Andrew F. "The Nation before Taste: The Challenges of American Culinary History." *The Public Historian* 34:2 (May 2012): 53–78.

Handler, Richard and Eric Gable. *The New History in an Old Museum.* Durham, NC: Duke University Press, 1997.

Harris, Marvin. "Mother Cow." In *Cows, Pigs, Wars and Witches: The Riddles of Culture,* 11–32. New York: Random House, 1974.

Haydu, Jeffrey. "Cultural Modeling in Two Eras of U.S. Food Protest: Grahamites (1830s) and Organic Advocates (1960s–70s)." *Social Problems* 58:3 (August 2011): 461–487.

Hedrick, Ulysses Prentiss. *A History of Agriculture in the State of New York.* New York: Hill and Wang, 1969 (1933).

Hetzel, Susan Riviere. "The Mary Washington Monument." *The American Monthly Magazine* 15 (July–December 1899).

Hewitt, Ben. *The Town that Food Saved: How One Community Found Vitality in Local Food.* Emmaus, PA: Rodale Books, 2001.

Hurt, R. Douglas. *American Agriculture: A Brief History.* Iowa City: Iowa State University Press, 1994.

———. *Problems of Plenty: The American Farmer in the Twentieth Century.* Chicago: Ivan R. Dee, 2002.

Huston, Reeve. "The 'Little Magician' after the Show: Martin Van Buren, Country Gentleman and Progressive Farmer, 1841–1862." *New York History* 85 (Spring 2004): 93–121.

Johnson, Anna, et al. *The Museum Educator's Manual: Educators Share Successful Techniques.* Lanham, MD: Rowman & Littlefield, 2009.

Kenin, Richard, ed. "Gloucester Fisheries, Agricultural Hall." *Frank Leslie's Illustrated Historical Register of the Centennial Exposition 1876.* New York: Paddington Press, 1974.

———. "Kansas and Colorado Building." *Frank Leslie's Illustrated Historical Register of the Centennial Exposition 1876.* New York: Paddington Press, 1974.

Kingsolver, Barbara. *Animal, Vegetable, Miracle: A Year of Food Life.* New York: Harper Collins, 2007.

Laudan, Rachel. "A Plea for Culinary Modernism." *Jacobin*, May 22, 2015. www.jacobinmag.com/2015/05/slow-food-artisanal-natural-preservatives/.

Legutko, Cinnamon Catlin and Stacy Klingler. *Small Museums Toolkit* (Vols 1–6). Lanham, MD: Rowman & Littlefield, 2011.

Leon, Warren and Roy Rosenzweig. *History Museums in the United States: A Critical Assessment.* Urbana and Chicago: University of Illinois Press, 1989.

Levenstein, Harvey. *Revolution at the Table: The Transformation of the American Diet.* Berkeley, CA: University of California Press, 2003 (1988).

———. *Paradox of Plenty: A Social History of Eating in Modern America.* Berkeley, CA: University of California Press, 2003 (1993).

Magelssen, Scott. *Living History Museums: Undoing History through Performance.* Lanham, MD: Scarecrow Press, 2007.

———. "Making History in the Second Person: Post-touristic Considerations for Living Historical Interpretation." *Theatre Journal* 58:2 (May 2006): 291–312.

Manning, Richard. *Against the Grain: How Agriculture Has Hijacked Civilization.* New York: North Point Press, 2005.

Mattie, Erik. *World's Fairs.* New York: Princeton Architectural Press, 1998.

McCarthy, Tom. *Auto Mania: Cars, Consumers, and the Environment.* New Haven: Yale University Press, 2007.

McGranahan, Devan A., et al. "A Historical Primer on the US Farm Bill: Supply Management and Conservation Policy." *Journal of Soil and Water Conservation* 68:3 (May–June 2013): 67A–73A. www.jswconline.org/content/68/3/67A.extract.

McKnight, John L. and John P. Kretzman. *Mapping Community Capacity. Asset-Based Community Development Institute, Institute for Policy Research.* Evanston, IL: Northwestern University, 1996. https://mn.gov/mnddc/parallels2/pdf/90s/90/90-MCC-McKnight_Kretzmann.pdf.

McLean, Kathleen and Wendy Pollock. *The Convivial Museum.* Washington, DC: Association of Science-Technology Centers, 2010.

McWilliams, James. *A Revolution in Eating: How the Quest for Food Shaped America.* New York: Columbia University Press, 2007.

Merrit, Elizabeth. *TrendsWatch 2014.* Washington, DC: American Alliance of Museums (AAM), 2014.

Moon, Michelle. *Interpreting Food at Museums and Historic Sites.* Lanham, MD: Rowman & Littlefield, 2015.

Mushkin, Scott et al. "Trouble in Aisle 5." Jefferies and Co., Inc. Industry Update, June 2012. http://www.jefferies.com/CMSFiles/Jefferies.com/files/PressReleases/2012/TroubleinAisle5_062712.pdf.

National Resources Defense Council. "Left-Out: An Investigation of the Causes and Quantities of Crop Shrink." National Resources Defense Council, 2012. www.nrdc.org/resources/left-out-investigation-causes-quantities-crop-shrink.

National Restaurant Association. "Positive Outlook for 2015." January 27, 2015. www.restaurant.org/News-Research/News/Restaurant-Industry-Forecast-Positive-outlook-for.

Nestle, Marion. *Food Politics: How the Food Industry Influences Nutrition and Health.* Berkeley, CA: University of California Press, 2013 (2002).

Norris, Linda and Rainey Tisdale. *Creativity in Museum Practice.* Walnut Creek, CA: Left Coast Press, 2014.

Norwood, F. Bailey, et al. *Agricultural and Food Controversies: What Everyone Should Know.* New York: Oxford University Press, 2014.

Oliver, Sandra Louise. *Saltwater Foodways.* Mystic, CT: Mystic Seaport Museum, 1995.

Patel, Raj. *Stuffed and Starved: The Hidden Battle for the World Food System.* Brooklyn, NY: Melville House, 2012.

Perez, Inez and ClimateWire. "Climate Change and Rising Food Prices Heightened Arab Spring." *Scientific American,* March 4, 2013. www.scientificamerican.com/article/climate-change-and-rising-food-prices-heightened-arab-spring/.

Plumber, Brad. "The $956 Billion Farm Bill, in One Graph." *Washington Post,* January 28, 2014.

Pollan, Michael. *The Omnivore's Dilemma: A Natural History of Four Meals.* New York: Penguin Press, 2006.

————. "The Food Movement, Rising." *New York Review of Books,* June 20, 2010.

Poddendieck, Janet. *Breadlines Knee-Deep in Wheat: Food Assistance in the Great Depression.* Berkeley, CA: University of California Press, 2014 (1986).

Potvin, Ron. "Chasing the White Whale? Flexible Use of Museum Collections." *AASLH History News* 69:4 (Autumn 2014): 11–16.

Preservation Virginia. "Mary Washington House," Preservation Virginia website, http://preservationvirginia.org/visit/historic-properties/mary-washington-house.

Price, T. Douglas and Ofer Bar-Yosef, eds. "The Origins of Agriculture: New Data, New Ideas." *Current Anthropology* 52:4 (October 2011).

Pustz, Jennifer. *Voices from the Backstairs: Interpreting Servants' Lives at Historic House Museums.* DeKalb, IL: Northern Illinois University Press, 2010.

Rand McNally. *Rand McNally and Co.'s A Week at the Fair.* Chicago: Rand McNally and Co., 1893.

Rydell, Robert. *World of Fairs: The Century-of-Progress Expositions.* Chicago: University of Chicago Press, 1993.

————. *All the World's a Fair: Visions of Empire at American International Expositions, 1876–1916.* Chicago: University of Chicago Press, 2013.

Schlosser, Eric. *Fast Food Nation: The Dark Side of the American Meal.* New York: Houghton Mifflin, 2001.

Shapiro, Laura. *Perfection Salad: Women and Cooking at the Turn of the Century.* Berkeley, CA: University of California Press, 1986.

Simmons, Amelia. *The First American Cookbook: A Facsimile of "American Cookery" 1796, by Amelia Simmons.* New York: Dover, 1985.

Simon, Nina. *The Participatory Museum.* Santa Cruz, CA: Museum 2.0, 2010.

Skramstad, Hal, and Susan Skramstad. "Mission and Vision Again? What's the Big Deal?", in *Small Museum Toolkit, Book I: Leadership, Mission, and Governance,* Cinnamon Catlin-Legutko and Stacy Klingler, eds. Lanham, MD: Altamira, 2012, 66–75.

Slow Food USA. "Our Philosophy." SlowFoodUSA.org/frequently-asked-questions.

Smith, Travis A., Chung L. Huang, and Biing-Hwan Lin. "Does Price or Income Affect Organic Choice? Analysis of U.S. Produce Users." *Journal of Agricultural and Applied Economics* 41:3 (December 2009): 731–744.

Stanton, Cathy. "Between Pastness and Presentism: Public History and Local Food Activism." In *Oxford Handbook of Public History.* James Gardner and Paula Hamilton, eds. Oxford University Press, 2017.

Steinberg, Adam. "What We Talk about When We Talk about Food: Using Food to Teach History at the Tenement Museum." *The Public Historian* 34:2 (May 2012): 79–89.

Stoll, Steven. *Larding the Lean Earth: Soil and Society in Nineteenth Century America.* New York: Hill and Wang, 2002.

Strasser, Susan. *Never Done: A History of American Housework.* New York: Pantheon Books, 1982.

Thornton, Tamara P. *Cultivating Gentlemen: The Meaning of Country Life among the Boston Elite, 1795–1860.* New Haven and London: Yale University Press, 1989.

Tilden, Freeman. *Interpreting Our Heritage,* 4th edition. R. Bruce Craig, ed. Chapel Hill: University of North Carolina, 2007.

Tisdale, Rainey. "Do History Museums Still Need Objects?" *AASLH History News* 66:3 (Summer 2011): 19–24.

Tsing, Anna. "Unruly Edges: Mushrooms as Companion Species." *Environmental Humanities* 1:1 (2012): 141–154.

Turow, Eve. *A Taste of Generation Yum: How the Millennial Generation's Love for Organic Fare, Celebrity Chefs, and Microbrews Will Make or Break the Future of Food.* New York: Pronoun, 2015.

Tyson, Amy. *The Wages of History: Emotional Labor on Public History's Front Lines.* Boston and Amherst, MA: University of Massachusetts Press, 2013.

United Nations Food and Agriculture Organization (FAO). "Major cuts of greenhouse gas emissions from livestock within reach." September 26, 2013. www.fao.org/news/story/en/item/197608/icode/.

U.S. Environental Protection Agency (EPA). "Sources of Greenhouse Gas Emissions." www.epa.gov/ghgemissions/sources-greenhouse-gas-emissions.

Vagnone, Franklin and Deborah Ryan. *Anarchist's Guide to Historic House Museums* Walnut Creek, CA: Left Coast Press, 2015.

van Balgooy, Max, ed. *Interpreting African American History and Culture at Museums and Historic Sites.* Lanham, MD: Rowman & Littlefield, 2015.

Vaughan, James. "Rethinking the Rembrandt Rule." *Museum,* March–April 2008.

Wallace, Mike. "Visiting the Past." In *Presenting the Past: Essays on History and the Public,* 4–32. Philadelphia: Temple University Press, 1986.

Wallach, Jennifer Jensen. *How America Eats: A Social History of U.S. Food and Culture.* Lanham, MD: Rowman & Littlefield, 2013.

Weaver, Stephanie. *Creating Great Visitor Experiences: A Guide for Museums, Parks, Zoos, Gardens and Libraries.* Walnut Creek, CA: Left Coast Press, 2006.

Weil, Stephen. *Rethinking the Museum and Other Meditations.* Washington, DC: Smithsonian Institution, 1990.

———. "From Being about Someone to Being for Somebody: The Ongoing Transformation of the American Museum." *Daedalus* 128.3 (1999): 229–258.

———. *Making Museums Matter.* Washington, DC: Smithsonian Books, 2002.

———. *Are You Really Worth What You Cost, or Just Merely Worthwhile?* San Francisco: Getty Leadership Institute, 2002.

Wells, Marcella, Barbara H. Butler, and Judith Koke. *Interpretive Planning for Museums: Integrating Visitor Perspectives in Decision Making.* Walnut Creek, CA: Left Coast Press, 2013.

Wilde, Parke. *Food Policy in the United States: An Introduction.* New York: Routledge, 2013.

Wiley, Laura. "Farm to Fable." *Tampa Bay Times,* April 13, 2016.

Wilkenning, Susie. "Do Museums Need to Care about Foodies?" *Center for the Future of Museums* blog. Washington, DC: American Alliance of Museums, September 22, 2011. http://futureofmuseums.blogspot.com/2011/09/do-museums-need-to-care-about-foodies.html

Zeigelman, Jane. *97 Orchard: An Edible History of Five Immigrant Families in One New York Tenement.* New York: Harper, 2011.

INDEX

Accokeek Foundation 131–2
agrarianism 58, 67, 73
Agricultural Adjustment Act of 1938 91
agricultural census 102–3
agriculture: environmental impact of 38;
    history of 64–71, 77–8, 88–92, 133
agritourism 28, 51–2, 131, 140
audience 5–7, 30–1, 47, 87, 110–11, 124,
    126, 129, 132–4, 136–8, 155–6, 178

campaigns 151, 164–5, 174–5
civic engagement 5–7, 31, 87, 97–8, 105,
    125–6, 136, 144, 170–1, 175, 178–81
Clean Greens 154
climate change 1–2, 51, 68, 71, 76, 109, 131
collaboration 37, 47, 131–2, 147–50, 153,
    157–9; see also community organizing;
    cultural organizing
collections 105, 108–9, 169–70, 173
Colonial Williamsburg 29
colonialism 57–8, 65, 155
community organizing 37, 114–16, 118,
    142–4, 145–6, 150–2, 161–6; history of
    143
community partnerships 45–53, 129, 131–2,
    140, 144, 145–6, 147–66, 169, 176–7
Conner Prairie 28, 136, 191, 193
cookbooks 29, 104–5, 111, 139, 152
cultural organizing 56–7, 144–5, 161–2
Cuyahoga Valley Countryside Conservancy
    37–9

Detroit Black Community Food Security
    Network 154
diversity see inclusivity; indigenous peoples;
    intersectionality; race and ethnicity

domestic science see home economics
Diamant, Rolf 173–7
dialogic museums 31, 111, 125, 140
Donahue, Brian 79–83, 140, 171
Dorry, Niaz 159–66

economic disparity 48, 50, 117, 150, 153–5;
    see also food justice; labor; race and
    ethnicity
Effland, Anne 92–3, 94–8
energy see fossil fuels
environmentalism 51, 67, 81, 91, 103,
    118–19 note 5, 160, 185; in food
    movement 51, 194; in policy 105
expositions 23–5, 33

Farm Bill 91–2, 93, 119 note 5, 130; see also
    Agricultural Adjustment Act of 1938
farmers markets 37, 148, 161–2, 181, 195, 196
Farmers' Museum (Cooperstown) 28, 192
fisheries 16 note 5, 69, 103, 115, 118,
    160–6
food aid 93–4, 99 note 5, 103
Food and Drug Administration (FDA) 90,
    93, 99 note 4, 103, 115, 191
food deserts see food insecurity
food insecurity 50, 76–7, 91–2, 103,
    117, 144
food interpretation, history of 3, 19–40,
    32–3, 124
food justice 50, 113–18, 142–3, 153–4
food movement 41–55, 143, 161; sources
    on 54; see also food reform, history of
food reform, history of 42–3, 67; see also
    home economics; settlement house
    movement

food safety 43, 87, 89–91, 103, 138, 167–8
food sovereignty *see* food justice
food systems approach 43–53, 148–9, 150, 156
fossil fuels 1, 3, 14–15, 51, 67–9, 70–1, 72, 77–8, 185, 189

gardening 43, 52, 106–8, 133, 137, 138, 139, 192; wartime gardens 138, 190, 192
gender 65, 104, 108, 143–4; in historic preservation movement 20–1; in home economics movement 25–6, 143–4; in agritourism 28
General Agreement on Tariffs and Trade (GATT) 92, 192, 195
genetically modified organisms (GMOs) 43, 69, 92, 115, 194
Gore Place 140
Grange (National Grange of the Order of Patrons of Husbandry) 26, 89, 152, 186
Green Revolution 67, 91–2, 193
Greenhorns, the 55–6

health 26, 36–7, 41, 43, 49–51, 53–4, 76, 93, 103, 114, 131, 154, 167–8; *see also* nutrition, policy
historic house museums 20–2, 172
historic preservation 20–5, 28
historical thinking 6, 42, 53–4, 64, 74–5, 94–8, 109, 143, 159, 179
home economics 25–6, 33, 104–5
Homestead Act 89, 186, 189
Hull-House *see* Jane Addams Hull-House Museum
hunger *see* food insecurity

inclusivity 31–2, 132, 136, 143, 180
indigenous peoples 65, 67, 113–18, 155
interpretation 63–4, 124; *see also* food interpretation, history of; methods
interpretive planning 124, 129–41, 172–3
intersectionality 5, 14–15, 25–6, 37, 44, 54, 59, 71, 80, 143–4, 147–8, 160, 180

Jane Addams Hull-House Museum 141–6
Junkin Lopez, Lisa 141–6, 151

Kelsey, Darwin 34–9, 139, 181

labor 5, 21, 30–1, 45–6, 48, 58, 73, 79, 96, 142, 150, 153–4, 187, 193; in cultural sector 145, 169
living history 24, 28, 33, 34–6, 134

localness 78–9, 133–4, 142–3, 156; definition of 72–3; and "glocalness" 78
Lower East Side Tenement Museum 15 note 2, 29–30, 31, 139–40

Magelssen, Scott 33, 134
Malabar Farm 27
market logic 69–70, 75, 76–7, 81–3, 88–9, 91–2
Mary Washington House 21–2
Marsh-Billings Rockefeller National Historical Park 28, 173–7
media 23, 51–2, 54, 131, 154, 169
methods 29–30, 33, 131–41, 159, 169–71; *see also* campaigns; collections; living history; shared inquiry; tours
Minute Man National Historical Park 80
mission 127–8, 165, 176
Missouri History Museum 127
model farms 26–8, 33
Morrill Act 25, 89
Mount Vernon 19, 21, 27, 185
Muckleshoot Food Sovereignty Project (MFSP) 113–18
museum practice: *see* dialogic museums; interpretation; interpretive planning; methods; mission; participatory museums; planning; shared inquiry
Museum of Food and Drink (MOFAD) 170

National Park Service 37, 118 note 5, 155, 174
New Deal 19, 70, 91, 99 note 4, 118 note 5
New England 66, 74–5, 80, 81, 143–4
non-profit organizations: relationship to for-profit companies 37–8, 82, 139–41, 176–7; relationship to government 89–90
Northwest Atlantic Marine Alliance (NAMA) 160–6
nostalgia 4, 23–4, 28, 33, 66–7, 104, 109
nutrition 25–6, 43, 114–15, 118; nutrient cycle 69; *see also* health

Old Sturbridge Village 34, 35, 168, 193
Oliver Kelley Farm 152
organic food 8, 42–3, 49, 55, 67, 72, 93, 153, 192; "big organic" 50, 73, 79
outcomes 131–2, 135–6, 165–6, 171–81

participatory museums 30, 33, 134, 172–3
planning: organizational 126–9, 145, 172, 175–7; public 80, 131; *see also* mission, strategic planning

Plimoth Plantation 135
policy 70, 81, 86–99, 175, 181; history
    of 88–92, 167–8; *see also* Agricultural
    Adjustment Act of 1938; Farm Bill;
    fisheries; Food and Drug Administration;
    General Agreement on Tariffs and Trade
    (GATT); Homestead Act; Morrill Act;
    Pure Food and Drug Act; World Trade
    Organization (WTO)
Pollan, Michael 25, 36, 47, 54, 78, 196
Pure Food and Drug Act 43, 90

Queens Museum of Art 151–2

race and ethnicity 112–18, 125, 153–5;
    see also food justice; labor; indigenous
    peoples
reflexivity 19, 32, 42, 132, 152–5, 181
region 12–13, 73, 131, 156
regulation 43, 91, 101, 103, 160, 167–8; *see
    also* health; policy
relevance 5, 6, 31, 111, 116, 125, 127, 130,
    137–8, 151
resilience 14, 180; *see also* community
    organizing
restaurants 46–8, 112
rural life movement 25, 28

scale 27, 44, 46, 65–7, 70, 72–7, 78–9, 108,
    140, 156, 179
seasonality 47, 73–4, 114, 153

seeds 51, 106–8, 133
Segrest, Valerie 113–18
settlement house movement 25, 141–4;
    see also Jane Addams Hull-House Museum
Shakers 28, 133
shared inquiry 64, 125–6, 136, 140
Shelburne Farms 28
Simon, Nina 30, 33, 173
Slow Food 14, 16 note 6, 41–2, 47, 133,
    158, 195
soil 38, 66, 67, 69, 76, 103–4
Stone Barns 47
strategic planning 128
Strawbery Banke Museum 13, 102, 137,
    138, 157
subsidy 82–3, 91; *see also* policy

tourism *see* agritourism
tours 138–40

U.S. Department of Agriculture (USDA)
    89–90, 93, 94–5, 97, 103, 186,
    187, 189

Von Tscharner Fleming, Severine 55–9

wasted food 71, 76–7, 91, 191
Weil, Stephen 31, 32, 55, 180–1
Welton, Mara 157–9
World Trade Organization (WTO) 92
Wyck 137

Printed in Great Britain
by Amazon